REDEFINING STALINISM

Cass Series: Totalitarian Movements and Political Religions
Series Editors: Michael Burleigh and Robert Mallett
ISSN 1477-058X

This innovative new book series will scrutinise all attempts to totally refashion mankind and society, whether these hailed from the Left or the Right, which, unusually, will receive equal consideration. Although its primary focus will be on the authoritarian and totalitarian politics of the twentieth century, the series will also provide a forum for the wider discussion of the politics of faith and salvation in general, together with an examination of their inexorably catastrophic consequences. There are no chronological or geographical limitations to the books that may be included, and the series will include reprints of classic works and translations, as well as monographs and collections of essays.

International Fascism, 1919–45
Gert Sørensen and Robert Mallett (eds.)

Faith, Politics and Nazism: Selected Essays by Uriel Tal
With a Foreword by Saul Friedlander

Totalitarian Democracy and After: International Colloquium in Memory of Jakob L. Talmon
Yehoshua Arieli and Nathan Rotenstreich (eds.)

The French and Italian Communist Parties: Comrades and Culture
Cyrille Guiat

The Lesser Evil: Moral Approaches to Genocide Practices
Helmut Dubiel and Gabriel Motzkin (eds.)

The Italian Road to Totalitarianism
Emilio Gentile, translated by Robert Mallett

The Seizure of Power: Fascism in Italy, 1919–1929
Adrian Lyttelton

Redefining Stalinism

Editor

Harold Shukman

WITHDRAWN

FRANK CASS
LONDON • PORTLAND, OR

First published in 2003 in Great Britain by
FRANK CASS PUBLISHERS
Crown House, 47 Chase Side
London N14 5BP, England

and in the United States of America by
FRANK CASS PUBLISHERS
c/o ISBS, 920 NE 58th Avenue, Suite 300
Portland, Oregon 97213-3786

Website: www.frankcass.com

British Library Cataloguing in Publication Data

Redefining Stalinism. – (Cass series. Totalitarian movements
and political religions)
1. Stalin, I. (Iosif), 1879–1953 2. Communism – Soviet Union
– History 3. Soviet Union – Politics and government –
1936–1953 4. Soviet Union – Politics and government –
1917–1936 5. Soviet Union – History – 1925–1953
I. Shukman, Harold, 1931–
947′.0842

ISBN 0-7146-5415-9 (cloth)
ISBN 0-7146-8342-6 (paper)
ISSN 1477-058X

Library of Congress Cataloging-in-Publication Data

Redefining Stalinism / editor, Harold Shukman.
    p. cm. – (Cass series – totalitarian movements and political
religions)
Includes bibliographical references and index.
    ISBN 0-7146-5415-9 (cloth) – ISBN 0-7146-8342-6 (pbk.)
1. Soviet Union – Politics and government – 1936–1953. 2. Soviet
Union – Politics and government – 1917–1936. 3. Stalin, Joseph,
1879–1953 – Influence. 4. Communism – Soviet Union – History
– 20th century. I. Shukman, Harold. II. Series.
    DK268.4.R43 2003
    947.084′2–dc21
                                            2003011125

This group of studies first appeared as a Special Issue on
'Redefining Stalinism'
of *Totalitarian Movements and Political Religions*
(ISSN 1469-0764) 4/1 (Summer 2003) published by Frank Cass.

Printed in Great Britain by Antony Rowe Ltd, Chippenham, Wilts

Contents

1

Introduction

HAROLD SHUKMAN

Is there a Western world leader whose reputation has not been re-analysed and reassessed, usually to his or her detriment? How many societies have their histories carved immutably in stone? The strenuous efforts Stalin made to create an appropriate life story for himself, and the histories of the CPSU and the USSR that were written under his direct supervision to serve the aims of the Stalinist Communist Party and State, were all doomed to an ephemeral existence. However great the political persona of a leader or monumental the trappings of his regime, they are both intrinsically subject to interpretation and reinterpretation. Indeed, the greater the dimensions of the exertion involved in achieving greatness of either, the more certain the reassessment. And this applies fully to Stalin and his regime. Valuable writings on different aspects of Soviet life and politics emerged in the West almost as soon as Soviet Russia came into being, but it was the Second World War, the emergence of the USSR as a major international force after it, and above all the Cold War, that boosted Soviet studies in the West from their once marginal status to a more central position in area studies, political science and international history. Whatever differences of interpretation may have divided Sovietologists in the West, their analyses were continuous, dynamic and broadly well informed. Such freedom of intellectual activity had long ago been wrested from Soviet scholars by a state which gave them in exchange a conditional and precarious right to work and survive. An unhindered approach to the study of their own past had to wait until the last years of the old regime and the first of the new.

In the years after 1917 and before Lenin's death, Stalin managed, actively and passively, to acquire positions in the administration that gave him a wider and firmer grasp on authority than any other Bolshevik. His claim to be Lenin's heir, therefore, was already likely to succeed, despite Lenin's own misgivings, as expressed in his famous – and in the end futile – 'Testament'. But to be accepted by the Party and the population as Lenin's heir, Stalin felt he must secure an acceptable version of his life story. As a former Caucasian bandit who had taken part in bank robberies to enrich Bolshevik funds; as an underground revolutionary organiser who had escaped from prison and Siberian exile too many times not to arouse the suspicion that he might have been favoured by the secret police for some unknown reason; but above all as a provincial from what today would be termed a disadvantaged background who had parachuted into the upper ranks of the pre-revolutionary Bolshevik milieu thanks only to Lenin's calculating patronage, and who had felt uncomfortable in the presence of more brilliant writers and speakers, Stalin was especially determined to be accepted as a Marxist-Leninist theorist.

Soon after Lenin's death Stalin gave a series of lectures on the late leader's ideas which were published as *Foundations of Leninism*, in practice setting himself up as an authoritative source of Party ideology. From this he would go on to consolidate his position as the Party's ideologist-in-chief. Inexorably, as the government – itself managed by the Party – wrestled both to administer the vast country and to carry out the fundamental changes that would justify and fructify the seizure of power in 1917, Stalin's word emerged as paramount.

Cautious by nature, Stalin launched his life story as a revolutionary in the mid-1920s, before his cult took off and with what would soon emerge as unaccustomed modesty. To a gathering of Georgian workers, he described his early role in the movement as an apprentice in Georgia, going on to journeyman status in the cosmopolitan oil city of Baku, then being sent by the Party to the revolutionary engine-room of Petrograd as a master-worker. The imagery was well chosen for an audience of workers, and it was not exaggerated, especially when compared to the fawning accounts by the Party hacks who were already portraying him as a hero second only to Lenin. The account he authorised both for Party members and the wider public appeared, also in the mid-1920s, in the biographical supplement of the *Granat Encyclopedic Dictionary*, entitled 'Activists of the USSR and the October Revolution' (in Russian). Beginning with his activities as a local committee organiser in the Caucasus, through the years of his work as an organiser at the centre and, crucially, a writer in the Party press, a major figure in the planning and execution of the seizure of power in October 1917 and the successful conduct of the Civil War, this was an important opportunity to portray Stalin as Lenin's most diligent lieutenant, and Stalin took it.

Alongside the growth of his power as General Secretary, official doctrine was transformed from Leninism into Leninism-Stalinism; instead of just Lenin, a Siamese-twin figure emerged called Lenin-Stalin; the theoretically separate Party and State would be elided into an entity called Party-State; and the General Secretary of the Party would come into single focus as the Father of the Soviet Peoples. These sleights of hand to a great extent reflected the reality that Stalin created: there would be no Leninism without its Stalinist interpretation, no Lenin-in-history without the attached Stalin, no State without the controlling Party function, and no nation without its omnipotent Leader.

In 1938, having just liquidated some half-a-million Communist Party functionaries and arrested 44,000 Red Army officers (15,000 of them were shot), got rid of huge swathes of the secret service, and launched a bloody assault on virtually every sector of economic and cultural life, Stalin published his *History of the Communist Party (Bolsheviks), Short Course*. With almost every one of the 1917 and Civil War generation of leaders liquidated (and impatiently awaiting news – still two years away – that his order for the assassination of Trotsky, his arch-enemy, had been carried out), he felt no need to mention any other individuals as creators of the revolution and builders of socialism, other than Lenin and Stalin: the Orwellian era of 'unpeopled history' had arrived. Printed in 43 million copies and broadcast to the whole population, the *Short Course* became an essential teaching aid, written as it was in Stalin's simple style and easily understood arguments – a precursor of Mao's *Little Red Book*. Along with the many other rituals promoting and consolidating his personal cult, the catalogue of dogma, typified by the *Short Course*, paradoxically exercised a degree of stabilisation and unification in a country where purge and terror wrought widespread distrust and fragmentation. Hitler, among many others, believed that the USSR had been so weakened by the purges that all that was required to conquer the country was 'to kick down the front door'. Faith in the Leader, in his omnipotence and infallibility, however, proved to be a serviceable substitute for civil society, let alone socialist democracy, and the country remained in one piece.

It may be argued – and often was by internal and external critics alike – that the country's economic and social achievements were accomplished *in spite* and not because of the system. Another way of putting this might be to suggest that, while the regime's central aim was resolutely to pursue the totalitarian principle of state control, all instrumental agencies manifested a degree of autonomous behaviour, usually in the form of evasion or local initiative, that demonstrated native creativity and in effect the failure of the state's own goals. A graphic example of this phenomenon were the 'fixers' who lubricated the economic machinery of the post-Stalin era by illicit if tacitly acknowledged methods. Of even greater significance, once Khrushchev had undone the Stalin myth, those who had borne responsibility under Stalin, and with it the constant threat of sanction, were able to function as officials and managers with authority uncompromised by fear. The universal application of these new arrangements became the hallmark of the Brezhnev era. The 'great stagnation' might well be seen as the introduction of a kind of Stalin-inspired 'civil society', complete with the rule of law (albeit in distorted form), a high degree of stability, relative plenty, a more or less predictable political environment, and more responsible organs of power/rule. This is at least arguable.

The all-pervasive nature of Stalin's cult and the ideological rigidity of the Stalinist state prohibited any unsanctioned reinterpretations. Before the Second World War the justification for such control was found in the need to prepare the USSR for war with the capitalist powers, usually personified by Hitlerite Germany, imperialist Britain and expansionist Japan. After the Second World War, when the Soviet Union itself emerged as a world power with satellites in Eastern Europe, the ideological and military confrontation that was the Cold War provided more than enough reason for inoculating the Soviet people against any West-inspired notions of intellectual or academic independence, and with it the inevitable corollary of political and economic pluralism. The deepening sclerosis of the closed regime, whose political and social pathology had manifested itself at its inception, seemed like a symptom of Stalin's own advancing mental and physical decrepitude.

And yet Stalin had presided over – and, it should not be forgotten, to a great extent personally inspired – the development of the Soviet Union from a basically peasant society into an industrialised, urbanised society, in which the population enjoyed the benefits – however minimal – of social services that many in the West, during the years of the Great Depression, could envy. That Stalin achieved such progress at an enormous cost in human life, widespread terror, and a police regime of unprecedented scale and scope, is not denied, even by those who still cherish his memory. When he died the entire population – outside the Gulag – wept, feeling that their lives and everything that happened in the country were connected to Stalin, and that the future had now become uncertain. (Journalists in Moscow in March 2003 reported that on the fiftieth anniversary of his death, old Muscovites loudly proclaimed that Stalin had given them jobs and food and clothing: 'Who cares about the purges? We were never hungry'.) Nor should it be forgotten that the very harshness of a system whose hallmark could be said to boil down to coercion, was seen by wide sections of the Soviet population at the time as both necessary and good. Above all, for all Russian generations during and since the war, Stalin stands virtually alone as the man who defeated Hitler's armies and won the war for the Allies. And it is Stalin who is credited with turning the USSR into a nuclear superpower strong enough to challenge the United States and keep his country safe throughout the Cold War.

Nevertheless, it is difficult to find a case of more extreme re-evaluation of a leader and his society's political history than that of Stalin and the Stalinist system. Within a very short time of his death, the 'cult of personality' was largely dismantled by his successors and his criminal abuse of the Party exposed, though the task of reassessing the system as a whole was left to a later generation. And as the regime lost the will to survive in the late 1980s, Russian historians, with unprecedented access to State and Party archives, began examining almost every aspect of Soviet history, unblinkered by political correctness and (for the most part) unhindered by official sanction.

Sovietology in the West has long been characterised by a dichotomy between those, on the one hand, who interpret the Stalinist system in terms of totalitarianism, meaning the ambition of the Party/State to control every aspect of human endeavour, and, on the other, 'revisionists' who point instead to the many signs of autonomous or unsupervised behaviour – throughout all of Soviet history – as evidence that the totalitarian model is inaccurate and inappropriate. With the opening of Soviet archives to an unprecedented degree since the demise of the USSR, the totalitarian argument has been strengthened by the research of Russian historians. But at the same time, the 'revisionists' can now display with growing authority widespread examples of the autonomy and resistance that belie the idea of total control. The dichotomy therefore can now be seen as both valid and an exaggeration.

2

Stalinism and the Soviet State Order

ROBERT SERVICE

Stalinism is a vague term. When not being employed as a pejorative description of all things Soviet, it is used as a short-hand way of designating official ideas, policies and practices in the Soviet Union in the long period of Joseph Stalin's rule. This usage conventionally emphasises the peculiarities of those years. Countless books have appeared on the malignant personality of Stalin; indeed some authors have suggested that the peculiarities of governance between the late 1920s and 1953 can be traced predominantly to the paranoid, vengeful and conspiratorial mentality of the Party General Secretary. This has not been the opinion of all writers. Yet most works on the 1930s and 1940s concur in stressing that the Soviet state order under Stalin was importantly different from the forms it took both before and after his despotism. Examples abound. Under Stalin it was normal procedure to arrest, torture and kill millions of persons who had not broken the law or spoken against the state order. Under Stalin, too, central political life lacked broad consultation. Under Stalin, institutions were locked in perpetual rivalry with each other and his individual will shaped the outcome of most supreme affairs of state.

According to such an analysis, these phenomena contrasted with what came before and what came afterwards. Vladimir Lenin was never a personal despot; he led the Politburo and the Central Committee by persuasion and even by bad-tempered cajoling, but not by fear. Moreover, he placed the Party unequivocally at the apex of the political process. There was no ambiguity about which institution headed the

Soviet state order. State terror was practised in Lenin's time – and not only in the years of the Civil War. In any case, the rampant barbarities of the Great Terror of 1937–38 were not constant while Lenin was yet alive. Similarly, the Communist leadership lost its features of personal despotism after Stalin's death in 1953. The winner of the succession struggle, Nikita Khrushchev, certainly came to dominate the politics of the USSR; but he and his associates continued to debate the great affairs of state. The Party was re-installed at the apex of political life even though from the late 1950s he lessened the Party's tutelage over governmental institutions. Khrushchev also significantly reduced the number of Gulag inmates.

And yet there always existed interpretations which tended in the opposite direction. Several authors argued that the continuities of the Soviet state order were more important than the discontinuities. From the early years of the October Revolution, several constant features were already evident. A one-party dictatorship was a reality within months of the Communist seizure of power. Freedom of expression was being severely restricted even before the establishment of the preventive censorship authority Glavlit in 1922. Arbitrary application of legal norms was openly professed from October 1917. Nor did the Communists hide the fact that they regarded society as a human mass to be indoctrinated, mobilised and, if circumstances appeared appropriate, sacrificed for the good of the cause. Among such interpretations there were many disputes. Some writers resorted to 'totalitarianism' as a model or ideal type which best described the Soviet state order. Other designations included communist autocracy, bureaucratic socialism, state socialism and a deformed workers' state. Still other historians confined themselves to describing the phenomena without feeling constrained to opt for a specific term. But common to many exponents of each terminology was the idea that the history of the USSR displayed basic continuities.[1]

There is really no need to choose definitively between the notion that Stalin's rule had its peculiarities and the notion that the entire Soviet period displayed basic continuities. Stalin's rule had peculiarities and the Soviet period had continuities. What is more, some of the peculiarities were not only an expression of Stalin's unique personality and inclinations, but also a reaction to problems inherent in the basic continuities which pre-dated his rule. This becomes clear when a searchlight is shone on the extraordinary difficulties encountered by successive rulers, from Lenin to Gorbachev, in their efforts at political and economic reform in the USSR. Soviet history, from the origins of the state in the October 1917 Revolution to the collapse at the end of 1991, abounds in such efforts. The word 'reform' was seldom used. Yet although it was anathematised in the Communist lexicon as a phenomenon characteristic of a bourgeois-democratic order, the introduction of reforming measures was a frequent phenomenon in the USSR. This recurrence invites explanation. The obligation arises to account not only for the motives for successive reforms, but also for the failure of each reform to satisfy the ascendant party leadership. Why were reforms undertaken and why were they undertaken so frequently?

The answers tell us much about the motivations and nature of Stalinism and demand that we should start with an analysis of the early Soviet order. The fundaments of this order were cemented into position in the first year-and-a-half after the October Revolution. By March 1919, when the Party held its 8th Congress, the Communists ruled a one-party state. Their Party was organised on centralist principles with a commitment to hierarchy and discipline; it was essentially the supreme agency of state and relayed its directives and appointed its personnel to the government and all other public institutions.[2] Control over the mass media was tight and the beginnings of a one-ideology state were being realised. At the same time the Party, while issuing decrees, was negligent about the rule of law. The Communist dictatorship's survival took precedence over judicial procedure. Police-state methods were inaugurated; a legal nihilism prevailed. Meanwhile the state acted on the premise that it had the political right and ideological duty to command, indoctrinate and mobilise society for the ends prescribed by the ascendant Party leadership. The Soviet order was the basic form of state and society for the next seven decades. Invented under Lenin, it lasted until the final couple of years of Mikhail Gorbachev's general secretaryship.

This is not to say that absolutely every brick in the fundaments had been laid by 1919. Rival parties continued to exist, however frailly and fitfully, in open politics. The Mensheviks contested some elections to the soviets in the Civil War, and the show-trial of the Socialist-Revolutionaries did not occur until 1922. The Soviet state was not strictly a one-party state until these parties had been eliminated. Similarly it took until 1922 for a comprehensive censorship, Glavlit, to be established.[3] Until then, the Communist authorities had relied on sporadic intervention by the Cheka and on the vetting of authors by government-owned publishing houses which discouraged approaches from writers overtly hostile to the October Revolution.[4] Not even all judicial institutions were immediately subverted by Communist rule. And the administrative framework of Communist power in the Civil War was shaky in the extreme. The Kremlin leadership concentrated its resources on the conscription and deployment of Red Army soldiers and the extraction of food supplies from the countryside; the mobilisation of society for more complex tasks of 'socialist construction' were to a large extent postponed until peacetime – and even in the 1920s this was an ambition fraught with technical and social difficulties.

All this notwithstanding, the months from 1917 to March 1919 are reasonably designated as the period when the fundaments of the Soviet order were introduced and consolidated. Stalin did not need to invent that order from the late 1920s. As a member of Lenin's Politburo, he took part in building the order without being its main political figure; and he observed the recurrent difficulties which arose in the Civil War. But it was years after Lenin's death before he decisively moulded most official policies in the USSR.[5]

Thus Stalin was not the initiator of the reform decided by the Politburo in February 1921 and approved by the 10th Party Congress in March. This was Lenin's New Economic Policy (NEP). Its main feature involved concessions to private enterprise and tightening of political control inside and outside the Party. The NEP lasted less than seven years and was subject to internal revision for its entire duration. Despite facilitating economic recovery, it failed to convince many Communist leaders about its long-term prospects of ensuring rapid economic development, solving political and national problems and achieving a socialist society. In January 1928 Stalin pounced while investigating food-supply deficits in the Urals and western Siberia. A second great reform was imposed by him, and the resultant trauma was immense. Forced-rate industrialisation; forcible agricultural collectivisation; political terror in town and village; the extension of Party and governmental dominance over virtually the entire economy: such were the features of Stalin's rejection of the NEP. They are not usually mentioned as a project of reform. But if the analysis is accepted that the features were formulated within the framework of the existing state order, the description is apt. While emasculating much of 'Lenin's legacy', Stalin was trying in his own way to conserve and strengthen it.

More generally, Stalin was striving to energise and stabilise the whole Soviet order. Things did not work out as intended, and – after various attempts to rectify problems as he understood them – Stalin geared up the machinery of state terror. Among his developing purposes was the reduction of the Party's capacity to impede his despotic power and, more generally, to rid politics of the informal methods of obstruction.[6] The bloody mass purges of 1937–38 were the result. Stalin's despotism was confirmed, but the informal methods proved hard to eradicate; and Stalin subsequently limited himself to occasional attacks on particular groups in public and social life.[7] Whether he was planning a second Great Terror in 1953 is still unclear. Probably a terror of some kind was in the offing, but he went to his death keeping his precise plans, if such they were, close to his chest. Be that as it may, it is evident that the reform of the late 1930s had failed to eliminate some of the underlying problems Stalin had identified. In the last years of his rule, he opted for a conservative consolidation of his institutional re-arrangements; he felt compelled to accept that the Soviet order imposed restriction on even him as a despot to transform state and society.

In subsequent years, the Communist Party leadership undertook measures to gouge out the cement of such arrangements in various sectors. The Party was re-elevated to the apex of the Soviet state. Arbitrary state violence was abandoned (although there was no effort to install genuine constitutionalism and the rule of law). Greater attention was paid to the needs of Soviet consumers. The boundaries of public discussion were widened. Eventually, at Khrushchev's behest, several institutional re-modellings were undertaken. Regional Economic Councils (*Sovnarkhozy*) were established. The Party was bifurcated. Turnover of Party and governmental personnel was deep and frequent.[8]

This process of reforms was accomplished within the framework of the Soviet order inaugurated in 1917–19. But Khrushchev was dismissed in 1964, and his successor, Leonid Brezhnev, tried to sedate Party and government by means of a policy of 'stability of cadres'. Tighter controls over political and cultural criticism were introduced. Partial reforms for the economy were announced by Alexei Kosygin, but then dropped because they derogated from the Party's authority. Brezhnev's measures led to the quietening of politics; but although a reversion to Stalinism was not seriously contemplated, the project of making the post-1953 regime operate merely by removing the Khrushchevite idiosyncrasies was unsuccessful: a large number of profound political, social, economic and national difficulties accumulated.

Finally in 1985 a reform programme was initiated which went still further than Khrushchev. Gorbachev, elaborating his policies as he went along, introduced ever-wider freedom of expression. He installed electoral competition in the Party and, in 1989, reorganised the state through the Congress of People's Deputies. A year earlier, there had been reforms in the economy permitting a degree of private enterprise. This reform was so drastic that it shattered the linkages of the entire Soviet order. The USSR, placed under recurrent strain, collapsed more with a whimper than with a bang in December 1991.

Campaigns for large-scale reform recurred across the existence of the Soviet Union, and the question arises why they were undertaken so frequently. One possible answer lies in the importance of the supreme leaders. Lenin in 1921 argued, plausibly, that the regime would fall without the inception of a NEP. But for Lenin, it is doubtful that the reform would have been accepted at that time by the Party.[9] Likewise there can be little doubt but that the Great Terror of 1937–38 was largely the product of the personal choice and determination of Stalin. It was he who started it and he who brought it to an end. With Khrushchev the case is a strong one that several reforms after 1953 were affected by his preferences. And it would be difficult to deny Gorbachev his essential importance in the introduction of reform-communist measures in the 1980s. Rival politicians would never have ruled the state in those periods in exactly the same way if they had been in power.

This kind of explanation has much merit. But it would be foolish to overlook the significant pressure exerted by contemporary circumstances. In 1921 a peasant revolt in Tambov, paralleled in an increasing number of regions, lit up reality for the Politburo. Refusal to abandon forcible grain expropriations would have the likely consequence of the collapse of Communist power.[10]

In 1928 there was also an enormously difficult environment for the regime. War scares; the moderate pace of industrial growth; the rise in social and nationalist hostility: all these factors had an impact on policy-makers. And in 1937 the regime was confronted by a wave of resentment at its policies over the previous few years; there was also the widespread sense that the country needed to prepare itself for the outbreak of a European war.[11] After Stalin's death, moreover, there was a growing crisis in the Communist leadership's desire to 'normalise' political life, raise economic output and avoid a further deterioration in relations with the US. Always the policy-makers acted against the background of immense problems. After Gorbachev acceded to power, he talked of 'pre-crisis' phenomena in state and society. The Party had lost all verve. The economy was in the doldrums. Regional and national embitterment had grown. The rivalry between the USSR and the US remained dangerous.

Thus successive reforms were not provoked exclusively by the whim of rulers. In fact, the rulers were usually responding to a specific internal and external environment and were developing measures to tackle it. The historiography of reform has attracted many works based on the premise that each period can be understood separately. For some scholars, for example, the Lenin of 1917 was entirely different from the Lenin of 1921 – and different again from the Lenin of 1922.[12] Equally popular has been the insistence that Leninism and Stalinism are completely dissimilar modes and theories of revolutionary practice. Khrushchev's attack on Stalin has been widely interpreted as a comprehensive programme of 'de-Stalinisation'. In short, several outstanding works of Sovietology have taken it as axiomatic that a particular period is best studied as a discrete entity.

This is indeed a productive mode of investigation. The history of the Soviet Union offers a remarkably compressed sequence of important stages, each of which contrasts in various ways with the others. Without sensitivity to each period's uniqueness there can be no convincing evaluation. Reforms make sense only when the inherited problems they were meant to solve are put under investigation.

Yet often the pre-occupation with a given period has excessively reduced attention to the chronic problems. From beginning to end, in fact, the Soviet order was put under strain by them. The problems existed quite independently of period, environment or leader. From Lenin to Gorbachev, the Politburo had difficulties in obtaining the approval of most citizens. Marxism-Leninism was constantly a minority taste.[13] Furthermore, the Politburo was always aware that the administrative stratum in all public institutions – and Soviet communism was essentially an administrative form of politics and economics – was corrupt and untrustworthy. Central and indeed local rulers could never rely on the information coming to them from below. Disobedience of directives, even if it took a passive form, was permanent. The Politburo could not even be sure of the reliability and talent of the administrators it directly appointed, and such uncertainly pervaded the whole administrative system.

These were internal problems. But the USSR also existed in a hostile world from which, as its rulers always recognised, it needed to attract technology and political support as well as to borrow ideas. The problem existed of how to do this while insulating administrators and society in general from the corrosive effects of contact with the blandishments of capitalism, religion and rival political creeds to communism.

It is through this prism, too, that the successive reforms of the Soviet order need to be examined. The methods used by the rulers were remarkably similar across the decades. The basic problems were permanent and, because of the constraints of the one-party dictatorship, the attempted solutions were akin to each other. Purges did not start with Stalin. They began with the expulsion of undesirables from the Party in 1918.[14] The process continued through the 1920s, and the criteria for purges included political as well as social and moral qualities. The difference in the late 1930s was that an individual's expulsion from Party or government involved denunciation as an enemy of the people and either execution or dispatch to the Gulag. Purges became peaceful again after 1953 – and they were designated differently: exchange of Party cards was the favourite term. But purging by whatever name it was known remained a recurrent practice of the Soviet order.

Another method was ideological invocation. Lenin called for 'European Socialist Revolution', Stalin for 'Socialism in One Country', Khrushchev for a 'Return to Lenin'. In each case, the summons was sounded for people to aid the state in building the new economy and society within a framework of political consensus maintained by the one-party dictatorship. Not material self-interest but political commitment and ideological belief were proclaimed as the reason for rallying behind the Communist leadership. Even in the lethargic years of Brezhnev the regime laid claim to an ideology superior to anything provided abroad. Under Gorbachev the people of the Soviet Union were – at least initially – told that Marxism-Leninism constituted an indispensable key to the door of a better state and society.

Then there were all the experiments with industrial forms. Exasperated by an unreliable state administration, Lenin introduced the Workers' and Peasants' Inspectorate (*Rabkrin*), and his Testament stipulated the desirability of re-jigging the inter-relationships of higher Party bodies. Later, in the 1930s, Stalin reduced the powers of the Party in favour of governmental agencies.[15] But he never quite settled the relations between Party and government – and several further reorganisations took place before 1953. Yet the master of institutional tinkering was Khrushchev. His establishment of *sovnarkhozy* and his bifurcation of the Party were examples. So, too, was his fiddling with the rules for holding Central Committee plenums. Even Brezhnev was not averse to rearranging the institutional forms of governmental oversight of the economy. And scarcely a month passed in the late 1980s without some initiative from Gorbachev for changes in the structure of state power.

Two further methods deserve consideration. One is the tendency of the Soviet state to effect change by the launching of 'campaigns'. Typically this was done by announcing a particular policy as the current official priority. From the Civil War through to the period of *glasnost* and *perestroika* this enabled the Kremlin to identify matters that lower administrators were obliged to regard as needing urgent attention. There were party recruitment campaigns in the 1920s. There were campaigns for raising steel production in the 1930s as well as for arresting 'enemies of the people'. In the late 1950s there were campaigns to plant maize and to increase recruitment to the Party. In the 1970s there were occasional campaigns to eradicate particular forms of corruption; and in the last half-decade of the Soviet order there were campaigns across the entire range of public policy. Along with this campaigning over the decades, moreover, went a fostering of 'socialist competition'. It began in the Civil War and was never abandoned. Factory was pitched against factory, province against province, republic against republic. Administrators everywhere were put on notice that careers would be enhanced or damaged by their effectiveness in competing to put official measures into practice.

These and other measures constituted an arsenal of militant techniques to make the Soviet order operate effectively. In the short term, whether individually or collectively, they worked to a certain degree. But across the seven decades of Communist rule they never – not even once – worked sufficiently well for further measures to be deemed unnecessary. The problem was that lower-level administrators learned how to cope with the pressure from above. They pretended to comply while refining and strengthening the very methods that the Kremlin wished to eradicate. They formed cliental groups.[16] They set up local 'nests'. They gave misleading information to the higher levels of the hierarchy. They looked after their own sectional interests at the expense of the officially designated public good – and, with few exceptions, they refused to take the ideology seriously. The rest of society, observing the privileges of the members of élites, became unamenable to official cajoling to work harder and more conscientiously. Soviet citizens were exploited and oppressed, and they knew it.

Sometimes the leadership responded by increasing the sharpness of such measures. After Stalin felt baulked in 1935–36, he threw the country into the Great Terror in 1937. When the early measures of Khrushchev turned out unsatisfactorily, he instigated deeper measures of reform in the late 1950s. When Gorbachev discovered the inadequacy of his initial programme of 1985–87, he drove faster and further into a campaign of transformation.

Yet this was not the sole mode of recurrent reaction. The emergencies set off by the pressurising campaigns sometimes threatened the survival of the Soviet order. The most striking case is the Great Terror, which came near to dissolving the cement of all public institutions. Probably, too, Khrushchev's associates felt that dissolution would follow if he were to be allowed to pursue his increasingly unpredictable policies. As for Gorbachev, there were many in his entourage who sought to deflect him. For some months, in winter 1990–91, he yielded to them. But then in spring 1991 he allied himself with Yeltsin. The consequence was that the entourage mounted the coup attempt of August 1991.[17] Although the coup failed, the doom of the Soviet order was sealed. These are just the starkest instances of pressures being relieved – or of attempts being made to relieve them – when the central Communist leadership took fright at the scale of the threat to the Soviet order's existence.

Yet such relief of pressure has also been a frequent phenomenon on a more mundane plane. A cyclical trend was observable. When militancy failed, compromise was sometimes tried out. After the turbulence of the Civil War, the Kremlin relaxed its pressure on Party functionaries and let them get on with the management of local public life as they saw fit. Stalin, too, felt obliged to attract the trust of his functionaries when he brought the Great Terror to an end in late 1938. The use of repressive methods did not cease, but it was much more carefully targeted than previously. Political, economic and military élites were given comfortable, secure conditions of life and work. Stalin had to settle for a more conservative and informal framework for the Soviet order than he had once envisaged.

After 1964, under Brezhnev, the indulgence to incumbent post-holders became a cardinal political doctrine: 'stability of cadres'. It became virtually impossible for an individual to lose a post unless he or she had criticised Brezhnev, the Politburo or their policies. Only a few unlucky persons were exceptions. Thus the Georgian Party first secretary Mzhavanadze was sacked for corruption; but his dismissal was the exception that proved the rule. Even old age was an insufficient reason for removal from office. From the Politburo downwards, functionaries of pensionable age were left in post. When Andropov briefly held power in 1982–84, there was a swift, peaceful purge of some of the gerontocrats, and many notoriously corrupt officials were sacked. But Chernenko, his successor, tacitly restored the doctrine of stability of cadres. Only with his death was the chronic indulgence to administrative personnel revoked.

Other manifestations of compromise across the seven decades included the tolerance of 'tails' and 'nests'. Despite his determination to expunge them in 1937–38, Stalin had to relent. He found in fact that the USSR was ungovernable without them. Unless the patronage system was allowed to survive, the entire administrative mechanism of Party and government was going to be put at risk. The tolerance was greater at some times than at others. Obviously it was highly developed in the period from 1964, when stability of cadres was eulogised and practised. But it was a lasting phenomenon. And in such troughs of compromise, the opportunity was more than usually propitious for 'the localities' to get on with affairs undisturbed. Centralism remained the Kremlin's proclaimed objective; but during the NEP and throughout the Brezhnev period there was a resurgence of obstruction from the republics and the provinces. In the Soviet republics there was a creeping 'nationalisation' of public life as the élites of the titular nationality gave preferment to their co-nationals.[18] In the 'Russian' provinces, too, there was local self-assertion. The *obkom* Party secretary became a law unto himself, behaving like a little general secretary – or indeed like a little tsar. The inundation of the Soviet order in the late 1980s had been welling up steadily in the years before Gorbachev came to power.

Compromises, moreover, did not have an exclusively internal aspect. In various periods of Soviet history, the rulers sought to ease their problems by means of international reconciliation. In the NEP years, the Politburo signed dozens of trade treaties. In the 1970s, the Politburo tried to secure permanent détente with the US. This was done in part to reduce the necessary commitment to high military expenditure. It was also undertaken simply as a quick means of acquiring advanced technology: even Stalin did this in the 1930s when pursuing the objective of 'Socialism in One Country'.[19] Under Brezhnev, not only technological transfer but also grain imports were facilitated by more cordial relations with the West until the Soviet invasion of Afghanistan in 1979.

The cycle of pressurisation and compromise was structurally determined. So long as the Soviet order endured, the alternation continued. Indeed there was no choice for rulers except to try either pressurisation or relaxation and to use roughly the sort of methods used from Lenin to 'early' Gorbachev. What is evident is that the Soviet order imposed limits on what each ruling group could do in the way of reform unless it was willing to risk the dissolution of the state. The primary features of that order were unchanging: one-party dictatorship; centralised party; one-ideology state; legal nihilism; state economic ownership; mass mobilisation; police intrusiveness; insulation from the foreign models of state and society. Such features fitted together in a tight architecture. Attempts to remove any pillar of the building would risk bringing everything tumbling down. The architecture of liberal-democracy and capitalism in most countries has been looser and opportunities for reform wider. But in the USSR, deep reform was always going to be an exercise of great jeopardy.

Undoubtedly the reform processes begun in 1921, 1937 and 1953 each had their dangers – and sooner or later these dangers were recognised as such. The difference from Gorbachev's *glasnost* and *perestroika* was twofold in nature. First, Gorbachev went faster and deeper than any other reformer of the USSR; second, his associates failed to stop the process before the ultimate stage of dissolution came about.

Gorbachev's record as a reformer was impressive. What he did, he did consciously as a reform-communist believer. Yet he did not understand the basic architecture of Soviet state and society. He was a 'holy fool' for communism. Eventually he paid the price of his miscomprehension. Looking back in Soviet history, he identified himself with two figures, Lenin and Bukharin. He failed to understand that neither Lenin nor Bukharin was a humanitarian. It would be difficult to imagine even Bukharin risking the overthrow of the entire Soviet order on the basis of a romantic notion of what kind of reform was practically feasible. But the point here is not to award marks for intellectual perspicacity to past Soviet rulers. Gorbachev's focus was on the task of making fundamental alterations to a building that was rotten and tottering. This at least ought to be recognised as a great achievement. Eventually recognising that adequate reform was ultimately impossible in the USSR, he pushed the logic of his career to its conclusion and dedicated himself to his country's transformation. Sad to say, reform since 1991 has not proved much easier than under communism. Constraints of politics, economics, society and culture do not disappear with revolutions. They did not vanish immediately after 1917; they certainly persist in the twenty-first century.

It is in this framework that Stalin and 'Stalinism' have to be considered. No one is likely to deny that much that happened between the late 1920s and 1953 was the product of Stalin's murderous idiosyncrasies. While contentedly following him into the rupture with the NEP, most Communists were unaware of the scale and violence of the policies he would introduce. (Quite possibly, even probably, he himself did not anticipate them in 1928.) They would never have supported him if they had known what was about to happen. They themselves were to be the most prominent victims in the Great Terror of 1937–38. The mayhem of quota-based arrests, beatings, confessions and punishments were more the work of Stalin's hands than of anybody else's. Indeed it has become clear that even some of his closest associates, including Molotov and Kaganovich, had to be intimidated into accepting his argument in favour of sustained and expanded state terrorism. Not only terror but also culture was a reflection of the Leader's idiosyncrasies. The *Short Course of the History of the All-Union Communist Party (Bolsheviks)* and the official biography of Stalin expressed the imperatives he had set the regime's propagandists. Economic, social and foreign policy were largely in his hands. Such institutional re-modellings as occurred were instigated either at his command or with his active approval. Stalin dominated Soviet politics in his time.

But he did not act in a void. He had inherited a very specific kind of state order. Founded by Lenin, it had its own basic features long before Stalin's despotism commenced. Stalin could order the killing of any individual or group in society he pleased. He could alter policy at whim; his word was unchallengeable law for his subordinates even though he continued to cloak his powers with formal obeisance to internal Party norms.

Yet his objective in the First Five-Year Plan and the Great Terror to remove all obstacles to the operation of the Soviet state order under his command was only partially successful. The system of patronage networks and local 'nests' proved ineradicable. Stalin destroyed some of them, but could not eliminate the general phenomenon. Furthermore, the additional political pressure exerted by the Kremlin in the 1930s proved incapable of creating a dependable channel of accurate information for him. Officials further down the hierarchy of Party and state had a reinforced interest in providing the Kremlin only with such reportage as would serve the cause of their physical survival and material well-being. Indoctrination had a substantial effect. But its impact was nowhere near as satisfactory as Stalin required; even many of his loyal officials, including those who owed their promotion to him directly, held private doubts about his ideas and policies (as the de-Stalinisation programme after 1953 was to demonstrate beyond peradventure). The workings of the economy proved enormously resistant to central political intervention despite the efforts made to persuade, reorganise and intimidate. Stalin was the great jailer of the USSR; he was also imprisoned by the necessities of the state order he had come to lead.

In these circumstances he had a restricted list of options. Not once did he contemplate a reversion to the democracy and market economy of the months between February and October 1917: Stalin was a proud defender of the Soviet state order and wished to consolidate what had been bequeathed to him. Unlike Gorbachev in the late 1980s, he was not going to risk tampering with the political, social and cultural underpinnings of the USSR. In his own bizarre way Stalin was a communist believer. He also understood that fundamental reform of the state order would endanger the interests of himself, his Party and government.

This order, however, required constant attentiveness if it was not to undergo the entropy suffered when the complacent Brezhnev came to power in 1964. It needed the rulers to agitate and energise it. The Politburo had to be feared, and its members had to deal severely with those sectors of public life where non-compliance and even opposition were growing. The resources for such a purpose had to come from within the regime. Liberal-democratic states have an advantage here. Multi-party competition, for all its manifest weaknesses, keeps the governing party aware that alternative governments are possible. The press and other media also have a positive function in alerting public opinion to wrong-doing, even though they themselves are hardly without political prejudices in a capitalist economic system. The Communist leaderships in general, and Stalin in gross particular, had to discover other ways to introduce a lively efficiency to the Soviet state order. These modalities had been concocted within a few years of the October Revolution. They included several methods of pressure:

turnover of personnel; quota-based commands; campaigns and mobilisations; invocations to Communist duty. They also embraced accommodation. Communist rulers offered perks and privileges to the officials of Party and state. Pressure and accommodation took a mainly cyclical pattern; but there were few periods between the October Revolution and the collapse of the USSR when both sets of modalities were not functioning to a greater or lesser extent.

What Stalin did was to pick up these modalities and apply them in an outrageous fashion. Instead of just sacking opponents, he also arrested and killed them; and he killed potential opponents too in his surgical attacks of the 1930s. He did not merely give out targets for industrial production: he applied targeting to the running of the political system by indicating to the NKVD how many arrests and executions he demanded. He ran military-style campaigns throughout society, dragooning most citizens into them and enforcing the most dreadful sacrifices in the current generation for the supposed benefit of later ones. He also rewarded officials egregiously. 'Egalitarianism' became literally a dirty word in official discourse and the network of privileged access to shops, hospital, social services as well as nannies, servants and chauffeurs was drastically expanded.[20]

Stalin's activity was despotic and homicidal, and the contrasts with Lenin and Khrushchev are rightly made. But Stalin and Stalinism cannot properly be comprehended without reference to the kind of state order he inherited. The course of his career illustrates this. He was always a restless politician. But something had needed to be done in the late 1920s about the NEP. The policy had helped with economic recovery. But it had done this at a price, and most Communist leaders, when asked to choose between Stalin and Bukharin, enthusiastically preferred Stalin; even many oppositionist leaders were willing to recant and come over to his side. The NEP had led to a growth of political, economic, cultural and national phenomena which in course of time would have undermined the Soviet state order. Stalin's apparent solution consolidated the order in his lifetime. The solution was not without its weaknesses. Such was the hatred of him and his policies in the 1930s that many peasants prayed for the *Wehrmacht* to invade.[21] Behind the façade of political unity the USSR seethed with societal discontent. But Stalin's rule was largely effective nevertheless in consolidating the Soviet state order.

Yet it caused as many problems in the longer term as it alleviated at the time – and, let it be added, it caused huge short-term problems too.

The rigidities of Stalinism were resistant to the quarter-measures of reform applied by Khrushchev and the half-measures promoted by Gorbachev until he decided that a fuller transformation was essential. Stalin therefore deserves to be remembered as one of those Soviet leaders who had a lasting fundamental impact. The point, however, is that he did this more restrained by the chains of a state order than is usually suggested.

NOTES

This chapter is a development of the ideas, based on further empirical material, laid out in the author's article, 'Architectural Problems of Reform in the Soviet Union: From Design to Collapse', *Totalitarian Movements and Political Religions* 2/2 (Autumn 2001), pp.7–17.

1. R. Service, *A History of Modern Russia from Nicholas II to Putin* (London: Penguin, 2003), pp.1–6.
2. R. Service, 'Polyarchy to Party Hegemony', *Sbornik* 10 (1984), pp.79–90.
3. A. Blyum, *Za kulisami 'Ministerstva Pravdy': Tainy istorii sovetskoi tsenzury, 1917–1929* (St Petersburg: Akademicheskii proekt, 1994), p.79.
4. C. Read, *Culture and Power in Revolutionary Russia* (London: Macmillan, 1990), chs.2–3.
5. R. McNeal, *Stalin: Man and Ruler* (London: Macmillan, 1985); R. Tucker, *Stalin in Power: The Revolution From Above* (New York: Norton, 1990).
6. O.V. Khlevnyuk, *1937-i: Stalin, NKVD i sovetskoe obshchestvo* (Moscow: Respublika, 1992), p.77.
7. *Vosemnadtsatyi s'ezd VKP(b). 10–21 marta 1939 goda. Stenograficheskii otchet* (Moscow: Gosizdat, 1939), pp.143–4, 229.
8. S. Pons, 'La politica organizzativa nel apparato del PCUS', in F. Gori (ed.), *Il XX Congresso del PCUS* (Milan: F. Angeli, 1988), pp.200–4.
9. R. Service, *Lenin: A Political Life, Vol.3, The Iron Ring* (London: Macmillan, 1991), pp.205–13.
10. *Rossiiskii gosudarstvennyi arkhiv sotsial'no-politicheskoi istorii* (Russian State Social and Political History Archive), f.17. op.3, d.127, items 1–2.
11. O.V. Khlevnyuk, 'The Objectives of the Great Terror, 1937–1938', in J. Cooper, M. Perrie and E.A. Rees (eds.), *Soviet History, 1917–1953* (London: Macmillan, 1995), p.173.
12. M. Lewin, *Lenin's Last Struggle* (London: Faber, 1969); S.F. Cohen, *Bukharin and the Russian Revolution: A Political Biography, 1888–1938* (London: Wildwood House, 1974).
13. S. White, *Political Culture and Soviet Politics* (London: Macmillan, 1979), chs.1–2.
14. *Pravda*, 22 May 1918.
15. F. Benvenuti and S. Pons, *Il Sistema di Potere dello Stalinismo: Partito e Stato in URSS, 1933–1953* (Milan: F. Angeli, 1988).
16. T.H. Rigby, *Political Elites in the USSR: Central Leaders and Local Cadres from Lenin to Gorbachëv* (London: E. Elgar, 1990).
17. A. Brown, *The Gorbachev Factor* (Oxford: Oxford University Press, 1996).
18. G. Hosking, *The Awakening of the Soviet Union*, 2nd edn. (London: Heinemann, 1991).
19. A.C. Sutton, *Western Technology and Soviet Union Economic Development, 1930–1945* (Stanford: Hoover Institution, 1973).
20. N. Timasheff, *The Great Retreat: The Growth and Decline of Communism in Russia* (New York: Arno Press, 1972).
21. S. Fitzpatrick, *Stalin's Peasants: Resistance and Survival in the Russian Village After Collectivisation* (Oxford: Oxford University Press, 1994).

3

Stalinism, Totalitarian Society and the Politics of 'Perfect Control'

FELIX PATRIKEEFF

Introduction: The Riddle of Stalinism

Can Stalinism be adequately defined? Elaborate early attempts were made to explain the phenomenon and its period, ranging from the crude model-making of Friedrich and Brzezinski (linking it to the genus of totalitarianism), to Sartre's intricate politico-philosophical analysis.[1] None of these was especially successful, as most of these efforts were ultimately limited by the inability to find the balance between the man, the system that he presided over and the practical aspects of the exercise of power during this distinctive period. More recent work on the subject has added important dimensions to our understanding of the riddle of Stalinism, but the riddle nonetheless remains. The study of Stalinism has, beyond the work of the older totalitarian school and distinctive treatments such as that by the existentialist Sartre, split into the 'traditionalists', 'neo-traditionalists' and 'revisionists'. 'Which one of these', concludes Sheila Fitzpatrick (a scholar very much at the heart of recent scholarly debate on Stalinism in the post-Soviet era), 'will become the dominant paradigm of scholarship … is anybody's guess'.[2] Invariably, an examination of Stalinism boils down to essences, for, as Ian Kershaw and Moshe Lewin put it, 'in human affairs *only* entities with a history are subject to theorization and are definable'.[3] The historical tableau associated with Stalin and his regime is vast, and touches on virtually every aspect of human existence in the Soviet Union. And yet frustratingly simple questions still arise in studying it, such as, for example, 'How did Stalin rule?'[4]

This essay explores the core nature of Stalinism's relationship with, and place in, Soviet society, focusing especially on the notion of the politics of 'perfect control', as it is here that much of the debate still resides: was it the dictator or Soviet society that provided the all-important framework for Stalinism and the extreme forms of political conduct this brought with it? The implications are considerable, as this inevitably reverts to the issue of how to reconcile the excesses of Stalinism with the immense nation-building process that was at its heart.

One of the more interesting and concise efforts to disentangle the web of explanations for the phenomenon of Stalinism remains that of Mary McAuley in her *Politics and the Soviet Union*.[5] Her conclusion, on the basis of a thorough reading of the various theoretical perspectives then available to her (her book was first published in 1977), is that economic and political characteristics of Stalinist Russia cannot be separated in the search for a definition of Stalinism:

> Implicit in the analysis is the suggestion that they cannot be understood one without the other or, to put it more strongly, that in talking about Stalinism one is talking about a phenomenon in which the 'political' cannot be separated from the 'economic'. If one tries to separate the two, one runs into problems of trying to explain how Stalinism worked or what provided the system with its momentum.[6]

However, McAuley tends to undermine the principle she herself lays down, when she eventually succumbs to the temptation of accounting for the 'cult of personality' in purely political and historical terms:

> Stalin and his subordinates assiduously cultivated the Stalin myth in a manner reminiscent of Louis XIV and his court. Stalin was thanked, praised for each and every event; all achievements were attributed to him. If one reads the hymns to Stalin, the references to his greatness and goodness by any public speaker or writer, one is forcefully reminded of the eulogies made, at all levels, to the Sun King. This phenomenon, that of sincere adulation by large sections of society, is something that is hard to comprehend; something that seems to fit, in some sense, into a period when people still believed in the Divine Right of Kings, but is out of place in twentieth-century Europe. Yet it happened, and added another dimension to the strange combination of old and new ideas that made up the theory of time.[7]

Hers is a Stalinism that represents a 'revolution from above', much like the form given to it by Roy Medvedev (the earliest of the examples of critical scholarship on Stalinism that emerged from the Soviet Union) when he asks, 'How did [Stalin] manage to carry out his criminal plans? Why did the party allow so much bloodshed? Why was it powerless to resist such enormous tyranny? What was inevitable in this frightful tragedy, and what was accidental?'[8] However, unlike McAuley's use of the court of Louis XIV as an analogy, Medvedev prefers the use of church-laden imagery and allusions to Greek mythology to answer his own rhetorical questions:

> The deification of Stalin justified in advance everything he did, everything connected with his name, including new crimes and abuses of power. All the achievements and virtues of socialism were embodied in him. The activism of other leaders was paralyzed. Not conscious discipline but blind faith in Stalin was required. Like every cult, this one tended to transform the Communist Party into an ecclesiastical organization, with a sharp distinction between ordinary people and leader-priests headed by their infallible pope. The gulf between the people and Stalin was not only deepened but idealized. The business of state in the Kremlin became as remote and incomprehensible for the unconsecrated as the affairs of the gods on Olympus.[9]

According to such interpretations, filled as they are with classical symbolism, Stalinism has an historical distinctiveness to be accounted for, but also implicit in it is a tangible geometric shape: that of a triangular formation of power, with the masses at the base and the all-powerful *vozhd'* (the *dux*) at the pinnacle. By giving it this shape, writers such as McAuley and Medvedev revert to the framework of the totalitarian school, despite being critical of the latter.[10] Looked at in another way, they seek to define the essence of Stalinism,[11] and yet in doing so resort to describing and elaborating the relationship between the pinnacle and base of an overblown, but nevertheless conventional, dictatorship. This linear, and essentially two-dimensional, treatment serves to depict the phenomenon in such a way as to force even the most painstaking strokes and careful choice of hues in Medvedev's depiction of Stalinism to resemble little more than a caricature of a 'Stalin dictatorship'. As such, it joins the many other hangings in a gallery whose display suggests that an image of the Stalinist period may be skilfully rendered, but with the subject remaining sphinx-like to the understanding of the artist.[12]

The list of such 'artists' is, as suggested in the introductory remarks, long and would be more profitably left to a definitive bibliographical study of the subject (which, quite remarkably, even 50 years after the demise of the *vozhd'*, remains to be written). This essay is concerned with a single, albeit crucial, methodological strand common to most, if not all, of the major studies of Stalinism: how the latter can be approached in a multi-dimensional fashion. It is suggested that, through a general failure to deal adequately with this aspect of the problem, the majority of analyses falter – almost as one – at a single hurdle and thereby resign themselves to the two-dimensional representation of Stalinism described above.

It is curious, albeit understandable, that such a politically disparate group of writers, which includes Trotsky, Tucker and Nove as well,[13] would resort to the pinnacle–base configuration when imparting a physical form to Stalinism in their work, even though this does little to convey what it is that differentiated Stalinism from less distinctive forms of dictatorship.[14] Setting aside the concurrent Cold War dimension, which in many ways underpinned the totalitarianist approach to the study of the Soviet Union,[15] the need to explain Stalinism and its elusive essence nonetheless remained an important element of even this school's work. However, if the arrangement of the pinnacle and base in their triangular relationship is studied closely, the conceptual shortcomings of this approach readily come to life. Two-dimensional views of Stalinism were precisely those that caused Khrushchev so much trouble in his Secret Speech: the entire scheme of excesses during the Stalinist period being laid at the feet of a single dictator was both difficult to sustain *and* elicited widespread resistance and criticism.[16] Furthermore, they explained little, if anything, of the dynamic that lay at the heart of the phenomenon and, in a politically convenient fashion, excluded society from the analysis, except as the unwitting, helpless victim of the excesses of totalitarian power.[17]

Giving Shape to the Concept: The Relationship between Pinnacle and Base, and the Locus of Power

With the revisionism that appeared in the 1970s, a third line was added to the triangle, giving it a third dimension, with Stalin (the dictator) sitting on top of a pyramidal structure, in which society was seen as 'more than just a passive object of the regime's manipulation and mobilization ...'.[18] Depth was thereby added to the dimension of breadth in the visual representation of the Stalinist polity. A significant problem still remained, however. For this image to maintain its logical validity, and to add to the understanding of social structure and its contributions to the political realm in *any* context, let alone in such a complex form of dictatorship, it had to be certain that the relationship between the pinnacle and the base was both fixed and constant, and that it was the precise one implied by the commonly accepted notion of dictatorship.[19] Such a relationship is, however, never entirely clear-cut (and notably so under Stalinism), given the uncertainty of the frames of reference of how politics is played out within society. In Stalinism, the fact that arrests, 'crimes' and reports made on peers (the most striking example being the potential for children to report on their own parents) became more frequent, and random, suggests that a more intricate set of political relations emerged within Soviet society at that time.[20]

Without taking these important dimensions into consideration, the configuration of base and pinnacle remains problematic, and a nuanced appreciation of society's role difficult; the traditional perspective perforce resulting in a static representation of society. In history, the act of defining the texture of society, which in effect promises to provide the pyramid of power relations with its substance and orientation, is far from being constant, let alone an absolute, as Raymond Aron makes clear in his answer to Sartre's *Critique de la Raison Dialectique*:

> The historian selects facts the same way that he constructs them. 'Even though history aspires to signification, it is condemned to choose its regions, its epochs, its groups of men, its individuals within these groups. And it must make them emerge again as discontinuous figures against an historical continuum, which is appropriate to serve as a backdrop.'[21]

In short, there are no fixed referents according to which the construction of a totality-in-miniature can take place.[22] Not even the nebulous notion of an historical continuum can serve this purpose, for its infinitude of historical facts provides an expectation of and, as Aron concludes, the backdrop to, rather than the substance or foundations of, the structure. The latter, as he indicates, must rely on *written* history's chosen region, epoch, groups of people and the

individuals within these groups. This is not necessarily a nihilistic
view. Rather, it is an interpretation made flexible and dynamic by
acknowledging the limitations of written history: the removal of the
notion of the existence of, or need for, a fixed base and imposed,
homogenised society leaves the analysis with a *fourth* dimension; an
impression of ferment and change *within* society, dictated not by the
vozhd', but emerging from society itself. This, in turn, forms a
base–pinnacle relationship unfettered by the rigidity of a framework
characterised by the crude hierarchy implicit in 'dictatorship'.

According to such an interpretation, Stalin's 'revolution from
above', handing down directives through a rigid hierarchy, loses
meaning because it is no longer certain that the 'dictator' is necessarily
at the pinnacle; he could, instead, be issuing proclamations which
travel *across* rather than *down*. Such an approach would, it may be
argued, then provide an all-important dynamism to the study of
Stalinism.

In this way, the pinnacle might be occupied by local administrators
who would be receiving, interpreting and adapting general policy lines
coming across their local and regional boundaries of power. Thus
when Roger Pethybridge, in his adaptation of the theories of Arendt
and Aron,[23] states that Russia under Stalin became a totalitarian
political regime 'in which the atomised masses face their ruler without
the protection of adequate intermediary institutions',[24] he seems to
ignore a vital factor: the recondite and, ironically, diffuse nature of
power and political relations during Stalinism. Aron himself hints at
how difficult it is to pinpoint the locus of political power in a general
context, let alone a relationship that is both direct and *total* between
the one and the many:

> I am busy writing at my desk and I look through the open
> window; I see a labourer in the garden and a roadworker in the
> street. Each of us sees the world through the totalization of his
> own project. Each of us can also communicate with the other
> two, and exclude the third from this relation. The third man, in
> turn, can constitute himself as mediator between the other two.
> The gardener and the roadworker may communicate by the
> intermediary of the writer. The roadworker and the writer may
> find a common language by the intermediary of the gardener.
> The gardener and the roadworker may cast the writer back
> towards the solitude of the intellectual, outside the labourers'

society. Each in turn can be the third-man mediator without being elevated, at this moment of critical experience, into a leader or a judge ...[25]

Aron's thoughts on the way in which power, consensus and political alignment are arrived at are ones marked by great fluidity. The terms of reference for the people involved are not formalistic, nor are they harnessed by the strictures that institutions, steely hierarchies and social status usually bring with them. There is a mobility, not only in the social sense, but in the way power is constructed and tactically employed.

Of course, the presence of a distant, somewhat aloof dictator is part of the fluid state of society, and this is undoubtedly an important element to the whole equation. Percy Chen, a Chinese citizen who spent some time in Moscow with the VEO (the All-Union Electrical Organisation) at a time when Stalinism was first finding its form, provides an insight into this dimension of the problem. Chen, son of the Trinidad-born Republican Chinese Foreign Minister Eugene Chen, recalled how he used a vaguely known channel to the nascent dictator's personal power base to correct an unacceptable situation he found himself in with a superior at the VEO. He had received a notice from this person, instructing him to attend a meeting for a threatened purge of the organisation. He did not want to go because, as a Chinese citizen, he thought that he should remain aloof from such unpleasantness. He approached Mikhail Borodin, a one-time adviser to the Chinese government and, at that point, editor of the *Moscow Daily News*, who advised him simply, 'Tell Stalin'. This Chen did:

> I went home, wrote a letter in Russian, and enclosed the notice. In the letter I wrote that this probably originated from F– [his superior] and that I wanted her to be directed to cease all such activities: otherwise I would have to leave Russia.
>
> At one of the gates in the Kremlin wall there was a small wooden box which was Stalin's 'hot line'. Ordinary Moscow citizens could write a letter addressed to him, and drop it into this small box, and the letter would reach Stalin. This is what I did with my letter.
>
> I felt that dealing directly with Stalin would bring the swiftest action. And so it did. Nothing further was heard about my attending any more meetings of this nature. I also learned later that F– had sent a letter to the *Mestkom* of VEO in which an

accusation had been made against me. In essence it stated that I
had been the owner of large cocoa estates in Trinidad and
therefore was a landowner. Thus I found out that, to put it
mildly, F– did not like me.[26]

But in many respects, such direct intervention was secondary to the
elaboration of politics on the ground, in which employing vague
prescriptions passed down by the dictator and his party both novelly
and inventively provided underlings with the power to savage
politically their peers and superiors, or to begin to carve out
distinctive niches for themselves. Each person could, with skillful
manipulation of 'the word' or the interpreted 'correct line', in effect
become the 'leader' or 'judge' that Aron writes of in his philosophical
contemplations.

The lines of political interplay and power relations are, in short,
not straightforward ones. The unfolding of local politics remains
peculiar to local conditions, making a direct relationship between the
local power nexus and the 'all-encompassing personality' at best
notional, and at worst a whimsical idealisation. 'Authority' must be
regarded as an abstraction and its actualisation very much dependent
on its perception *in situ*.[27] The Stalinist period gave full body to such
a formulation, and Stalin its intentionally vague prescription: 'Don't
spare individuals, no matter what position they occupy; spare only the
cause, the interests of the cause'.[28]

It might be argued, as indeed Friedrich and Brzezinski did, that
totalitarian rule is distinct from autocracy and simple dictatorship, in
that totalitarianism is a technologically based near-complete control of
the individual.[29] This, however, would be a very difficult position to
hold, because for most of Stalin's period in power the chief
preoccupation was with the primitive accumulation needed to launch
and sustain massive industrialisation; an environment in which the
sophisticated forms of control suggested by Friedrich and Brzezinski
would have been impossible, the conditions being chaotic.
Pethybridge, not surprisingly, chooses to account for his version of
totalitarianism in a different way:

> Rural culture was overrun by the towns with scant regard for
> indigenous traditions of long standing. The fact that town
> workers had to play the major role in the task of enforcing
> collectivization illustrates in social terms the complete failure of
> *smychka* in NEP.[30]

Discarding the technical sophistication of Orwell's *1984* (with its Big Brother), strongly resonating in Friedrich and Brzezinski's work, Pethybridge prefers instead to confer the grand title of 'totalitarianism' on a Soviet Union characterised by the savagery of that writer's *Animal Farm*. There is, in effect, a considerable difference between the intervention of the city in the countryside for the purposes of achieving a higher gearing in the search for development and the sustained, minute control of the masses by the 'all-powerful' centre.

This is not to say that the intervention by the 'shock troops' during collectivisation is not significant; it is, but for different reasons from that of Stalin achieving a personal hegemony over the country. In this respect, Aron neatly sums up the argument against the over-simplification of the nature of relations in Stalinism to the point that they represent a chain of command and response linked to the whim of a single individual:

> Relations ... must depend on dialectical Reason and therefore must appear as internal relations at the same time as relations constitutive of organic totality. But simultaneously, the totality of these relations will never exist save in the totalization effected by an individual: society is never identical with an organic totality.[31]

The ultimate significance of this reasoning is the conclusion that the majority of those who attempt to represent the meaning of Stalinism find themselves in some important respects doing so through the dictator's own *Weltanschauung*; their totalisation being that of Stalin himself. It is this paradox that allows Trotsky to write, 'Aided by accommodating foreign correspondents in Moscow, the Stalin propaganda machine has been systematically deceiving public opinion the world over about the actual state of affairs in the Soviet Union. The monolithic Stalinist government is a myth'.[32] But only a few lines later he adds, 'The totalitarian state ... has encompassed the entire economy of the country as well. Stalin can justly say ... "La Société, c'est moi"'.[33] Such a lapse would normally be attributed to Trotsky's penchant for the sweeping historical metaphor. In the case of his biography of Stalin, from which these lines are taken, there is often an additional reason given: Trotsky was 'too close to the subject'; his normally lucid train of thought hindered by his personal involvement in the events that led to his own catastrophic political end.[34] This curiosity, especially when viewed in light of later writings by a host of scholars from a variety of points on the political spectrum, but who all exhibit a similar tendency, can most fruitfully be described as a form of 'historical parallax', with the apparent change in the position and nature of the object – Stalin – actually being caused by a change in the position of the observer. Employing a static frame of reference, the resulting inconsistency can hardly be avoided. This phenomenon is summed up best by McAuley when she likens the 'Stalinist' view of Stalinism to that put forward by the totalitarian school:

> Both depicted the Soviet period from 1917 to 1953 as one in which aims remained unchanged, both saw the party as somehow still the same party because its 'ideology' (that is, the rhetoric of Marxism-Leninism) remained the same; both emphasized the guiding nature of something called 'Marxist-Leninist ideology' and granted Stalin almost superhuman powers of control over society.[35]

In a chapter devoted to the 'Social Ingredients of Stalinism', Pethybridge shows how severely the parallax view – and in his case *multi*-parallax – can hamper an assessment of the subject. First of all, he cites Plekhanov from the latter's essay on the role of the individual in history, 'every man of talent who becomes a *social force* is the product of *social relations*. Since this is the case, it is clear why talented people can ... change only individual features of events, but not their general trend'.[36]

In short, while social relations were forming Stalinism, the latter was making a mark on them to some extent. Pethybridge, having at first described the essay as brilliant, then proceeds mercilessly to demolish it and, along with it, its author's intellectual credentials:

> Plekhanov's generalisation holds less water when Stalin's later career as sole dictator is examined. After 1928 his margin of manoeuvrability widened, so that he could and did change the general trend of events. Plekhanov was a Marxist and thus committed to underplaying the influence of the individual. He also wrote prior to the epoch of modern totalitarianism, and it probably appeared inconceivable to a thinker of his era that one man could make such a bold imprint on mass society in the way Stalin and Hitler did.[37]

It is a response that is understandable in the context of historical parallax: Pethybridge wishes to introduce an explanation to account for the social basis for the formation of Stalinism, and therefore employs Plekhanov's insightful dictum to further our understanding of the phenomenon. However, it is equally important for Pethybridge to underline Stalin's unique place in it, and this can only be done by methodologically shifting ground by questioning Plekhanov's own credentials. Because the latter was a Marxist, his observations lose a certain amount of validity through the inevitable innate dogmatism; because he wrote before the time of Stalin and Hitler, his *generalisations* lose further validity. In doing so, Pethybridge gradually moves in his own right to the position of seeing Soviet society through the veil of the historical greatness of one man. The irony is, of course, that although modern historians like Pethybridge have been ready to invalidate, or at least question, the thinking of their intellectual forebears by means of stressing the latter's inability to see accurately into the future, they themselves resort to comparing Stalin with historical personalities such as Louis XIV and Napoleon Bonaparte (both of whom were to their particular period, and subsequent historiography, as imposing as Stalin and Hitler are to our own era, and were well-known to Plekhanov when he wrote his essay). Political theorists and sociologists, on the other hand, are forced to follow Wittfogel's lead in employing the metaphor 'Oriental despotism' to explain the phenomenon of 'total power', but using this in the context of the modern period. By shifting the point of reference away from the social conditions that were Stalinism, these theorists, directly or indirectly, inadvertently pay homage to the unique facets of personality; facets to which the glories achieved, and crimes perpetrated, by the Soviet state are directly attached.

Stalinism: An Alternative Perspective

Is there an alternative approach to the problem of defining the social origins of Stalinism in such a theoretical context? A possible line of analysis is the following: Stalinism is, rather than the Leviathan-like form normally depicted, the evolution and fruition of a popular consciousness. In this respect, although 1917 is an important stage in this evolution, it cannot be taken – for reasons already discussed – as the key point for the emergence of this consciousness,[38] with its general focus being the system of government 'inherited' and 'shaped' by Stalin and his cohorts. It is a dictatorship, but not necessarily one based solely and simply on persona.[39] Within this consciousness emerges a newly found sense of freedom, unhindered by traditional constraints: it becomes, for instance, a far simpler task to topple an immediate superior or peer through the presentation of evidence of 'ideological inconsistency' on the part of the latter, this being based on a politically convenient reading of the latest tendency in a *living* ideology. That the ideology should be prefaced by 'living' is most important, for this popularises and democratises the ideology, making it a vital practical form and readily accessible to those who might otherwise view such a body of doctrine as something removed from their daily lives; their own struggles on the shop-floor, in the office, on the farm. With the direct inclusion of individuals in the ideological process within these spheres, words such as 'bureaucrat', 'wrecker', 'traitor' and 'kulak' are charged with a vast amount of political energy; particularly when they are open to the broadest of possible interpretations and, in effect, made accessible to all.

The very notion of freedom within a dictatorship is, at first sight, a complete nonsense. Yet it should become clear that in a vital society within which tensions become heightened, outlook agitated, and with a social environment that is internally bound for a dramatic rearrangement of its socio-economic order, the idea of political freedom is nothing short of awesome. It is difficult in our own political environment, where the value-laden concept of freedom is generally synonymous with good, to appreciate fully the terrifying prospect of living in a near-Hobbesian state of nature, in which freedom is freedom to survive and prevent one's own extinction at the whim of another. In such a state, politicisation is the inevitable result at all levels of society, with the normal restraints (such as police force, security service and law itself) no longer elements of mediation, but weapons responsive directly to the ideological strains current in random pockets of society, and weapons to be used, or, if not, then possibly to fall victim to oneself. Within such a context the question might be raised as to *why* these restraints and bodies normally associated with the enforcement of a set of laws become, virtually in every sphere of society, the generators of an idiosyncratic body of 'law'? Here might be added the nature of the immense trigger mechanism which allowed Stalinism to flower. It is insufficient to cite Stalin's view that Communists, like any other party, developed and grew by means of internal struggle,[40] to explain the intensity of, as Khrushchev described it, the 'moral and physical annihilation' which gripped the Party and State at the height of Stalinism.[41] Nor can the lack of faith expressed by Stalin in the private agricultural sector fully account for the emergence of the massive preconditions necessary for the violence of collectivisation.[42]

The pronouncements and reflections are no more than ephemera, produced by the underlying conditions which evolved from dramatic changes in consciousness, the ossification of traditional forms of power relations and, finally, the distinct and virile lines of confrontation that emerged from these contradictory forms. Firing these lines of confrontation was the general disillusionment engendered by a period of economic stasis and an inability to define paths of personal or collective advancement. Under such conditions the society might initiate a process of severe self-correction or realignment, requiring – as the conditions were more than ripe – no more than a signal from the self-appointed political focus: the ruler/ruling party.

That a single individual, and his ideas, should emerge to personify changing attitudes within Party and State is symptomatic of two separate factors, the first of these being the evolution of the Bolshevik Party and one-man direction. The other factor is a more general one which rests, again, on how one approaches the study of history, and is directly related to the nuances of the earlier-examined tendency to equate Stalinism with persona. In his introductory essay to the 1888 edition of *Oliver Cromwell's Letters and Speeches*, Thomas Carlyle noted that:

> Working for long years in those unspeakable Historic Provinces [the original letters and papers left by Cromwell] ... it becomes more apparent to one, that this man Oliver Cromwell was ... the soul of the Puritan Revolt, without whom it had never been a revolt transcendently memorable, and an Epoch in the World's History; that in fact he, more than is common in such cases, does deserve to give his name to the Period in question, and have the Puritan Revolt considered as a *Cromwelliad* ...[43]

These are lines which might have been taken from any one of a number of scholarly depictions of Stalin. However, Carlyle does not stop there, but continues by giving elucidation to the *relationship* between the epoch and persona:

> Even if false, [his] words, authentically spoken and written by the chief actor in the business, must be of prime moment for

understanding of it. These are the words this man found
suitablest to represent the Things themselves, around him, ... of
which we seek a History. The newborn Things and Events, as
they bodied themselves forth to Oliver Cromwell from the
Whirlwind of passing Time, – this is the name and definition he
saw good to give them. To get at these direct utterances of his, is
to get at the very heart of the business; were there once light for
us in these, the business had begun again at the heart of it to be
luminous![44]

Tapping the very core of the consciousness, his reflections, conclusions
and, ultimately, his very personality give voice and form to it. Thus, at
a point in history when the Party had for some time been involved in
the narrowly intellectual confines of reconciling the monolithic Party
with the *desiderata* of Party democracy, Stalin turned to the question
of the blatant incompetence of the Communist cells in rural areas,
suggesting that if they would spread a little more instruction in good
farming practices among the peasants, production would reflect this
positive contribution. As an example he stated that a ten *pood* increase
in yield per *desyatina* would be possible *without* necessitating the
introduction of new machinery. Bringing this matter closer to the
futility of philosophical discussion, Stalin asked, 'Is this really less
important than conversations about Curzon's politics?'[45] With an
atmosphere of economic and political uncertainty permeating the very
fabric of Soviet society,[46] such logic presents itself as the reflection of
its very soul, and phrased in its own potent language: in Carlyle's
words, 'to get at these direct utterances of his, is to get at the very
heart of the business ...'.[47] It is therefore understandable how, in the
subsequent turbulent years of unchecked capital accumulation and
Party 'reorganisation', this persona would come to represent an
increasingly steady anchor to which all members of the population at
large came to be tied while they were tossed by, but also agitated, the
troubled political sea. Accordingly, Stalin's public image was shaped to
represent him as 'good-humoured and fatherly, plainspoken with no
airs or pretensions, the human leader mingling easily with the
people'.[48] A similar phenomenon, and perhaps in an even more
concentrated and vivid form, was in evidence in the People's Republic
of China during the Cultural Revolution. The parallel is worth
drawing for the purposes of the present excursus in that it
demonstrates the nature of political freedom when it is realised and

released. In a talk presented at the Central Work Conference, Mao
Zedong described the interaction in the following way:

> [T]he Great Cultural Revolution wreaked havoc after I approved
> Nieh Yüan-tzu's big character poster in Peking University, and
> wrote a letter to Tsinghua University Middle School, as well as
> writing a big-character poster of my own entitled 'Bombard the
> Headquarters'. It all happened within a very short period, less
> than five months ... The time was so short and the events so
> violent. I myself had not foreseen that as soon as the Peking
> University poster was broadcast, the whole country would be
> thrown into turmoil.[49]

A further indication of what happens in such a charged atmosphere,
and the heightening of political consciousness that goes on *in situ*
under conditions which are more than ripe for sweeping change, is the
explanation that, 'Even before the letter to the Red Guards had gone
out, Red Guards had mobilized throughout the country, and in one
rush they swept you off your feet ... It has only been five months.
Perhaps the movement may last another five months, or longer'.[50]

Just as it would be inaccurate to identify the severity of the
Cultural Revolution with the *imposition* by the 'Great Helmsman' of
the Red Guard bands on an unwilling countryside, so too would it be
to ascribe the 'excesses' of collectivisation – and later, in the 1930s, its
replication in the cities and Party – solely to the crimes of dictatorship,
let alone to those of a single personality. The levels of internecine
strife, coupled with the sudden appearance of great potential for social
mobility after years of ossification and disillusionment, are enough to
suggest that the answer to the origins of Stalinism, especially in its
most brutal forms, lies somewhere apart from the direct
dictator–masses relationship usually depicted, in which dictates are
'handed down' through an all-powerful and all-encompassing
hierarchy. Some, such as R.W. Thurston, express a degree of doubt as
to the proposition that upward mobility was a source of support for
Stalin's regime during the period 1937–38. However, it might equally
be argued that in periods of great upheaval, such as the Cultural
Revolution in the People's Republic of China and at the height of
Stalinism in the Soviet Union, support for the regime is, in a profound
sense, relatively unimportant, as the society is struggling within
(indeed, *with*) itself, and the ability to get ahead becomes more an act
of opportunism and localised personal initiative than a process of

relatively orderly social mobility. The government is therefore in some important respects simply 'holding the ring', while these processes find their own levels and forms.[51]

De-Stalinisation

A final dimension to the broader problem, and one that is directly related to the tentative conclusion reached here, is that of de-Stalinisation. Here the images of Stalinism come into brightest relief because, in analysing the path of Soviet politics and society from the time Stalin died, historians have also to reveal their deep-seated thoughts on the nature and origins of the phenomenon. It is here too that the majority come to methodological grief in trying to explain the phenomenon of Stalinism in terms of excesses of the few against the innocence of the many. Suffice it to say that in most writings which touch on the subject, de-Stalinisation consists of a process by which the contaminated bark of 'Stalinists' will be removed from the *apparat* responsible for smothering a long-suffering population beneath it. Although Stalin ultimately relied on the masses, to paraphrase Medvedev's argument in this regard, the latter were deluded; the victims of 'religious psychology: illusions, autosuggestion, the inability to think critically, intolerance towards dissidents, and fanaticism. Perceptions of reality were distorted'.[52] This veil of deceit had been anticipated by Isaac Deutscher when he recognised, at a very early stage, what he regarded as having been instrumental in initiating its lifting. Jean-Paul Sartre,[53] in a piece of political soul-searching after the events in Hungary in 1956, added to this picture by suggesting that those who were lifting the veil were, in fact, Stalinists themselves.[54] Implicit in these thinkers' writings is the sacred abstraction of the Revolution and the formation of the Socialist People, which must at all costs be excluded from taking a share of the guilt associated with Stalinism. But who then were the Stalinists, and what was Stalinism? Sartre, predictably, offered a tortuous explanation for this:

> [T]he Plan is only a hypothesis which is subject continuously to the test of experience and which it must be possible to correct without bias, as a function of actual experience. The urgency of correction implies total agreement among the organisers; this agreement alone will prevent a temporary deviation from being adopted for its own sake, from changing the trend; it alone will

make possible the cancellation of all harmful measures, even one that has just been stopped; it alone makes the leaders conform constantly to objectivity. On the other hand, there is no doubt about the threats from abroad; in spite of which the dumb, hostile mass of country folk refuses to rally; compulsion therefore has to be increased. Now, a dictatorial group must first of all impose dictatorship on itself. Thus, external danger and internal resistance exact indissoluble unity from the leaders. Without deep roots, without real support, the group of 'organizers' can maintain its authority and ensure national security only if it first of all works out from the inside, by itself and through itself, its own security; events oblige it to push its own integration to the limit. But the limit is never reached, for the biological and mental unity of the individual supplies the best image of it ... Thus the cult of the personality is above everything the cult of social unity in one person. And Stalin's function was not to represent the indissolubility of the group, but to be that very indissolubility, and to forge it as a whole.[55]

Deutscher, on the other hand, in attempting altruistically to exonerate the People, finds himself in a position whereby he appears to be producing, at least in part, an apologia for Stalinism:

[T]he cultural significance of Stalinism cannot be judged merely by the way it ravaged letters and arts. It is the contradiction between Stalin's constructive and destructive influences that should be kept in mind. While he was mercilessly flattening the spiritual life of the intelligentsia, he also carried ... the basic elements of civilization to a vast mass of uncivilized humanity. Under his rule Russian culture lost depth but gained in breadth. The prediction may perhaps be ventured that this extensive spread of civilization in Russia will be followed by a new phase of intensive development, a phase from which another generation will look back with relief upon the barbarous antics of the Stalinist era.[56]

Such thorny issues, it may be concluded, cannot be adequately addressed without reverting the masses – the People – to a full and active role at the very heart of Stalinism. The ideas that came to symbolise Stalinism may have been derived from the intelligentsia and *apparatchiki*, but the lines of conflict which gave sustenance, and indeed life, to these ideas grew out of a massive swell of popular consciousness.[57]

Conclusion: Bringing the People Back In

Trotsky, in his characteristic fashion, described the ebb and flow of the masses in revolutionary history by noting that:

> Revolution crushes and demolishes the machinery of the old state. Therein is its essence. Crowds fill the arena. They decide, they act, they legislate in their own unprecedented way; they judge, they issue orders. The essence of the revolution is that the mass itself becomes its own executive organ. But when the masses leave the social arena, retire to their various boroughs, retreat into their sundry dwellings, perplexed, disillusioned, tired, the place becomes desolate. And its bleakness merely deepens as it is filled with the new bureaucratic machinery. Naturally, the men in charge, unsure of themselves and of the crowds, are apprehensive.[58]

If such an analysis is applied to post-1917 Russia, the Stalinist period (especially its early segment of collectivisation and industrialisation, together with the purges) must be regarded as at least the second flow: the direct challenge of the masses to the ebb of the New Economic Policy. The prophetic element in Trotsky's observations, and for Deutscher's analysis the irony, is that the latter part of the quotation, and the ebb, is more representative of the Khrushchevian period and the attempts at de-Stalinisation. The masses, quite to the contrary of Deutscher's view, embodied Stalinism and gave life and direction to it. Finally, the crowds, before withdrawing from the arena, internalised the drama of the Stalinist Leviathan they had created while the new leadership apprehensively proffered a new and unwanted path of de-Stalinisation and bureaucratic order.

To this end, in contrast to the idealisation of the People employed by Deutscher and others in their work, there is the image presented by Ante Ciliga, the Yugoslav communist who experienced at first hand a very broad cross-section of Soviet society between 1926 and 1936.[59] His observations reveal areas generally ignored by the theorists who produce highly coloured, stylised renditions of the People in Stalinism. Ciliga's People are by comparison a far more mundane and cynical grouping; reflecting the nature of shifting political and economic relations in post-1917 Russia. They are amorphous as a category: specific units rooted in crude, harsh reality and caught in the economic brier of the land. There is no suggestion that these individuals should be lumped together and lifted to lofty heights of abstraction while, at the same time, obscuring the yawning chasms of contradiction represented by a mass of humanity fragmented and re-fragmented by attitude, aspiration and regional variation. Although the following extract is based on Ciliga's visit to the Caucasus, and therefore geographically quite specific, the conclusions he reaches are generally representative of the broader character of transformation of social relations apparent then:

> The villages of Ingushetia are miserable and backward. At first sight, no social differentiation can be perceived. On looking more closely, however, one sees poor and rich. Here one learns the relativity of our concepts of wealth and poverty. The curious fact about it was that this social differentiation had developed only after the revolution, during the NEP. The more prosperous elements of the village were very much at one with the Soviet system; they had acquired their prosperity through the posts they occupied in that system. The chairman of the rural Soviet, the manager of the co-op (the ex-leader of the insurgent band), the contractor for public works, the lorry owner, the peasant who hired out premises to the Soviet administration – these were 'Soviet patriots', but a touch of uncertainty showed through their patriotism. Vague rumours about the new rural policy reached them. They were in favour of a free commerce in wheat, of a consolidation of the markets, of an unrestricted development of small private economy. As to the poor, they were of a contrary opinion and upheld the new Government policy in the hope of a better future.[60]

It is a passage heavy with the portents of struggle, portraying the new lines of division which will go on to provide the true 'excesses' of Stalinism. In such circumstances directives and Stalin's pronouncements are the metaphorical nod for the latent energy and violence to break through long-standing barriers which have caused, and continue to cause, such widespread frustration. The paradox of the Russian Revolution is that while the superficial frames of reference altered dramatically, the nature of Russian life, with its explicit economic conditions and implicit power relations, had not:

At Vladicaucasus, a small detail recalled me to the realities of Soviet life; at the municipal park, an entrance fee had to be paid in order to enter the well-kept gardens. 'A budgetary matter', a local Communist told me, by way of justification. In fact, the municipal policy of Czarist days had remained unchanged; today, as yesterday, the people, the poor, were not allowed to walk in the best part of the park.[61]

The social origins of Stalinism therefore lay not in the 'seeds' of dictatorship and a personality cult, but in a widespread popular desire to break away from this oppressive continuity of the old order, dictated by conventional and *localised* relations of power, coupled with the all too familiar faces of scarcity and deprivation. Stalinism was, in this sense, the emergence and execution of a general will intent on finding solutions to problems (both economic and political) which lay at the core of this paradox. The 'crimes' and 'mistakes' often attributed to Stalinism are, by this definition, nothing more than euphemisms used to explain away the excesses generated in, and by, all spheres of a society bound for an extreme form of self-correction.

NOTES

1. See M. McAuley, *Politics and the Soviet Union* (London: Penguin, 1977), esp. pp.116–48; R.V. Daniels, *The Stalin Revolution* (Lexington, MA: Heath, 1972), esp. the section by C.J. Friedrich and Z. Brzezinski, pp.198–213; J.-P. Sartre, *The Spectre of Stalin* (London: Hamish Hamilton, 1969); see also note 56 below. See also Jean Elleinstein, *The Stalin Phenomenon* (London: Lawrence and Wishart, 1976), esp. ch.7.
2. S. Fitzpatrick (ed.), *Stalinism: New Directions* (London and NY: Routledge, 2000), p.11. Sheila Fitzpatrick's status in this debate was established somewhat earlier, arguably with the publication of her essay 'New Perspectives on Stalinism' in the early Gorbachev period, *Russian Review* 45/4 (October 1986), pp.357–413. This drew much commentary and discussion from a variety of scholars of Stalinism, see *Russian Review*, 46/4 (October 1987), forming the nub of discussion that further intensified with the collapse of the Soviet Union.
3. I. Kershaw and M. Lewin (eds.), *Stalinism and Nazism: Dictatorships in Comparison* (Cambridge: Cambridge University Press, 1997), pp.1–2.
4. R.G. Suny, 'Stalin and his Stalinism: Power and Authority in the Soviet Union, 1930–53', in ibid., p.12.
5. McAuley (note 1), esp. pp.116–48.
6. Ibid. p.142.
7. Ibid. p.146. The theme of gratitude is a most important one, and is explored by Jeffrey Brooks in his book, *Thank You, Comrade Stalin!* (Princeton: Princeton University Press, 2000), and an article, 'Stalin's Politics of Obligation', in the present collection of essays.
8. R. Medvedev, *Let History Judge* (London: Macmillan, 1972), p.358; see also idem, *On Stalin and Stalinism* (Oxford: Oxford University Press, 1979).
9. Medvedev, *Let History Judge* (note 8), p.362.
10. See C.J. Friedrich and Z. Brzezinski, *Totalitarian Dictatorship and Autocracy*, 2nd rev.

edn. (Cambridge, MA: Harvard University Press, 1965); for typology and model (or for a broader coverage of the literature), see C.J. Friedrich, M. Curtis and B.R. Barber, *Totalitarianism in Perspective: Three Views* (London: Pall Mall, 1969), esp. Barber's 'Conceptual Foundations of Totalitarianism', pp.3–52.

11. The totalitarian school, because of the need to link Stalinism with fascism qualitatively (and it is with respect to the essence that Friedrich's argument fails to convince); Medvedev fails to explain why the tears that fell from 'hundreds of millions of eyes' in March 1953 were sincere; McAuley, by stating the purpose of her study to be the raising of questions rather than the provision of answers to them, ensures that the onus is not on her to answer the riddle. However, McAuley does volunteer a tentative solution: namely that it lies in the morass of the political economy of the period (the same, of course, could be concluded of fascism, too).

12. At times, in the attempt to understand, the artist resorts to a flood of miniatures in place of the Great Portrait: 'Stalin was not simply a dictator, he stood at the peak of a whole system of smaller dictators; he was the head bureaucrat over hundreds of thousands of smaller bureaucrats', Medvedev, *Let History Judge* (note 8), p.416.

13. For Alec Nove, see his *Stalinism and After*, 3rd rev. edn. (London: George Allen & Unwin, 1989):

   Society as a whole required to be mobilized, individual convenience was unimportant. By all his actions Stalin showed that he believed in Hierarchy and Discipline as essential virtues. Privilege too, but privilege was dispensed to those who served well, and was not, under Stalin, a secure right. Stalin was many things, but surely not the expression of the narrow self-interest of the bureaucratic elite. He feared their consolidation, and punished them without mercy. They were proportionately the principal victims of the great terror. Their lives, property and privilege depended on Stalin's whim and everyone knew it. (p.60)

   Tucker describes Stalin's place in the following way:

   In high Stalinist culture, heroes had a leader and teacher, a higher hero: Stalin. There was a hierarchy of hero cults with Stalin's, or Lenin-Stalin's, at the apex. Below the apex were cults of deceased leaders like Sverdlov, Dzerzhinsky, and Kirov, and then small cults of living comrades of Stalin, notably Voroshilov. Below these were the much publicized heroes from the common folk: labor heroes and heroines like Stakhanov and Maria Demchenko, heroic Polar explorers like Otto Schmidt ... Stalinist falcons like Chkalov who set new world records for long-distance flights, heroic scalers of heretofore unclimbed mountain peaks, and others ... As befitted the figure at the apex of the hero pyramid, Stalin – along with the mummified Lenin down below – came now into the zenith of scripted glory. The heroism of this fearful man ... became a dominant cultural motif.

   R.C. Tucker, *Stalin in Power* (New York: W.W. Norton, 1990), pp.564–5. For Trotsky, see his *Stalin* (New York: Stein & Day, 1967), for example: 'Stalin is a past master of the art of tying a man to him not by winning his admiration but by forcing him into complicity in heinous and unforgivable crimes. Such are the bricks of the pyramid of which Stalin is the peak'. (p.421)

14. As J.F. Hough, *Democratization and Revolution in the USSR, 1985–1991* (Washington, DC: Brookings Institution Press, 1997), p.143, puts it, 'Western scholars who distinguished between totalitarian and authoritarian dictatorships emphasized this absence of limitations on government, although they allowed their point to be obscured by their insistence on the crucial role of irrational terror and a one-man dictatorship'.

15. Stephen F. Cohen observes of American scholarship in his excellent *Rethinking the Soviet Experience: Politics and History since 1917* (New York and Oxford: Oxford University Press, 1985), pp.9–10, 'The cold war intruded into [American] academic Sovietology politically and intellectually. It began by shaping the field's institutional

development in ways that made scholarship ("applied research") in America's national interest, rather than more detached academic pursuits, the main purpose of Soviet studies'.

16. R.V. Daniels, *The Conscience of the Revolution: Communist Opposition in Soviet Russia* (New York: Clarion (Simon & Schuster), 1960), p.392, makes this point well by citing the 'highly unsettling' effects of the speech both in the Soviet Union itself and amongst Communists worldwide, and pointing out that, with the riots that occurred in Tiflis as a consequence of the Secret Speech, 'this was the ultimate irony, that the most serious civil disturbance in Soviet Russia since collectivization days should come as a demonstration in *support* of the late dictator'.

17. Such an analysis was commonplace in earlier writings, but extends to more recent work on totalitarianism, too. Edgar Morin, 'The Anti-Totalitarian Revolution', in P. Beilharz, G. Robinson and J. Rundell (eds.), *Between Totalitarianism and Postmodernity: A Thesis Eleven Reader* (Cambridge, MA: MIT Press, 1993), pp.88–9, for example, concludes that totalitarianism 'is a system based on the monopoly of a party which is unique not only because it is a most unusual sort of party. It is a party in which all spiritual and temporal powers are concentrated in the apparatus which governs, controls and administers'. Robert Conquest, *Stalin: Breaker of Nations* (London: Weidenfeld, 1993), p.315, goes so far as to employ Soviet historian Natan Eidelman's conclusion that under Stalinism, 'a significant part of the Soviet population "was living under a hypnotic spell"'.

18. Fitzpatrick, *Stalinism* (note 2), p.6.

19. The power of conforming to traditional perceptions is strong, as vividly shown in Dmitri Volkogonov's biography, *Stalin: Triumph and Tragedy*, trans. and ed. H. Shukman (London: George Weidenfeld & Nicholson, 1991), p.xxiii, '[Stalin's] voice would resound from time to time from the pinnacle of the pyramid, while millions listened in holy terror at its foot'.

20. For an examination of this, see S. Fitzpatrick, 'Signals from Below: Soviet Letters of Denunciation of the 1930s', in S. Fitzpatrick and R. Gellately (eds.), *Accusatory Practices: Denunciation in Modern European History, 1789–1989* (Chicago and London: University of Chicago Press, 1997), pp.84–120, esp. pp.105–6.

21. R. Aron, *History and the Dialectic of Violence* (Oxford: Blackwell, 1975), p.139; the quote is from C. Lévi Strauss, *The Savage Mind* [*La pensee sauvage*] (London: Weidenfeld and Nicolson, 1972, 1966), pp.257–8.

22. Indeed, Aron doubts the possibility of constructing a totalisation when he concludes that Sartre 'wants a totalization of total History to be possible, which is just what the concept of a totalization defined on the basis of individual *praxis* seems to exclude', Aron (note 21), p.224. See below for the elaboration of this position in light of the present study.

23. See Roger Pethybridge, *The Social Prelude to Stalinism* (London: Macmillan, 1974), pp.196–251.

24. Ibid., p.241.

25. Aron (note 21), pp.30–1.

26. P. Chen, *China Called Me: My Life Inside the Chinese Revolution* (Boston: Little, Brown, 1979), p.210.

27. A literary representation of this point can be found in Gogol, *Revizor* and Vladimir Voinovich, *The Life and Extraordinary Adventures of Private Chonkin*.

28. J.V. Stalin, *Sochineniia*, 16 Vols. (Moscow: Gos. izd-vo politicheskoi literatury, 1946–67), Vol.4, p.368.

29. Totalitarianism in its ascribed meaning was, arguably, only ever possible in a sectoral context. The press, for example, is one area where totalitarianism could be seen in something of a 'pure' form, as Victor Serge suggests in his analysis of Stalin's place in it:

> [Stalin] is 'brilliant,' 'beloved as the firstborn child,' 'radiant as the sun.' And they [the newspapers] print nothing else. Everything revolves around the new Imperator

cult. And never will the paean of praise attain a higher pitch of exaltation than the day after the leader has massacred his oldest comrades in struggle, the men who had worked with Lenin. The totalitarian press functions to perfection.

Victor Serge, *From Lenin to Stalin* (New York: Monad Press, 1973), p.82.
30. Pethybridge (note 23), p 241.
31. Aron (note 21), p.31.
32. Trotsky (note 13), p.421.
33. Ibid.
34. See Bertram D. Wolfe's explanation in his introduction to the biography of Stalin by Trotsky (note 13), p.5 of introduction.
35. McAuley (note 1), p.148.
36. Pethybridge (note 23), p.312.
37. Ibid.
38. Such views are reinforced by writers such as Stephen Kotkin, who view Stalinism not as a post-revolutionary form, but the genuine revolution itself. See Stephen Kotkin, *Magnetic Mountain: Stalinism as a Civilization* (Berkeley, CA: University of California Press, 1995), esp. pp.5–6.
39. Already mentioned – but nonetheless worth restating – is the extent to which historians, who do not, generally speaking, subscribe to the 'great man in history' notion, willingly make Stalin an exception and ascribe a staggering amount of the social and attitudinal change taking place in Soviet society to his personality. The examples are numerous. Alec Nove, 'Was Stalin Really necessary?', *Encounter* (April 1962), pp.86–92, attempts to fathom Stalin's responsibility for the evils perpetrated during the 1920s and 1930s, producing a clear distinction between evils springing from policy choices (indirect) and 'evil actions' (direct). His conclusion, however, is that, 'Of course, these categories shade into one another, as do murder and manslaughter. In the first case, the evils were in a sense situation-determined, *but Stalin had a large hand in determining the situation*. In the second, his guilt is as clear as a politician's guilt can be' (emphasis added). The fact that Nove enters the brutality of collectivisation and the 'madly excessive pace of industrial development' under the first heading leaves Stalin responsible directly (or indirectly) for an overwhelming proportion of the guilt.
40. See, for example, 'The Foundations of Leninism', in B. Franklin (ed.), *The Essential Stalin: Major Theoretical Writings, 1905–1952* (London: Croon Helm, 1973), pp.179–80.
41. N.S. Khrushchev 'On the Cult of Personality and its Consequences', Report delivered to the 20th Congress of the CPSU, 25 February 1956, in T.H. Rigby (ed.), *The Stalin Dictatorship: Khrushchev's 'Secret Speech' and Other Documents* (Sydney: Sydney University Press, 1968), p.29.
42. Bauman, the Moscow Party Secretary, stated in June 1929 that the Moscow *oblast'* (province) was preparing to collectivise 25 per cent of peasants in five years and that, in general, 20 years would be required to collectivise all, *Pravda*, 16 June 1929 (Stalin's comments on the private sector were made at the plenum in April 1929). For a graphic depiction of the elemental nature of the collectivisation process, see S. Fitzpatrick, *Stalin's Peasants: Resistance and Survival in the Russian Village after Collectivization* (Oxford and New York: Oxford University Press, 1994), pp.49–59.
43. T. Carlyle, *Oliver Cromwell's Letters and Speeches* (London: Chapman & Hall, 1888), Vol.I, p.11.
44. Ibid., pp.11–12.
45. *Pravda*, No.277, 6 December 1923.
46. In summary, the situation in the first half of the 1920s was as follows: on the question of internal Party democracy the debate had been raised so far above the heads of the population that not even the Party rank-and-file had a clear image of the differences between the positions of the opposition and leadership. One railway worker at the Moscow Party meeting of 11 December 1923 declared, 'The workers will ask me what

46 REDEFINING STALINISM

your fundamental differences are; to speak frankly, I do not know how to answer', D. Law, 'The Left Opposition in 1923', *Critique* 2 (n.d.), p.44. While economic recovery continued through the mid-twenties, there were serious problems still unsolved. With the Scissors Crisis having revealed stresses on the *smychka* between town and country, the position of the proletariat became precarious. As late as 1927, Bukharin warned that, 'If there were a fall in the relative weight of the working class in its political and its social and class power, ... this would subvert the basis of the proletarian dictatorship, the basis of our government', quoted in A. Nove, *Was Stalin Really Necessary?* (London: George Allen & Unwin, 1964), p.21. The ruble had fallen: the purchasing power of 1,000,000 rubles in 1914 was estimated to be 0.00002 of a ruble by March 1924, E. Zaleski, *Planning for Economic Growth in the Soviet Union, 1918–1932*, trans. and ed. M.C. MacAndrew and G.W. Nutter (Chapel Hill, NC: University of Carolina Press, 1971), p.23. These were the immediate problems; on the horizon loomed much larger questions concerning the development of heavy industry and the process of capital formation.

47. Carlyle (note 43), p.11.
48. Fitzpatrick (note 42), p.275.
49. From a speech to the Central Work Conference, 25 October 1966, in S. Schram (ed.), *Mao Tse-tung Unrehearsed* (London: Pelican, 1974), p.271. An eloquent, and most perceptive, rendition of this period is provided by J. Spence, *Mao* (London: Phoenix, 1999), pp.183–6.
50. Schram (note 49), p.271.
51. See R.W. Thurston, *Life and Terror in Stalin's Russia, 1934–1941* (New Haven and London: Yale University Press, 1996), p.147.
52. Medvedev, *Let History Judge* (note 8), p.363.
53. I. Deutscher, *Russia in Transition* (New York: Coward-McCann, 1957), pp.6–7, 'in its original phases de-Stalinisation has been or was primarily the work of the intelligentsia. Writers, artists, scientists, and historians have been its pioneers'.
54. Sartre (note 1), p.77, 'And it serves no good purpose to repeat that those who are carrying out de-Stalinisation are Stalinists. What else could they be?' The essay originally appeared in *Les Temps Modernes* (Paris: Gallimard 1956–57). In a book of essays compiled in Deutscher's honour, Louis Menashe expresses this point in a slightly different way: 'the leading proponents of de-Stalinization were themselves good Stalin men, moulded by the habits of rule prevailing during the epoch of collectivization, rapid industrialization, and the purges', Louis Menashe, 'The Dilemma of De-Stalinization', in D. Horowitz (ed.), *Isaac Deutscher: The Man and His Work* (London: Macdonald, 1971), pp.141–2.
55. Sartre (note 1), pp.56–7.
56. I. Deutscher, *Stalin* (London: Penguin, 1974), p.364.
57. As Geoffrey Hosking concludes in his novel interpretation of a totalitarian society, it 'is neither demonic, nor unchanging, nor totally manipulated from above. Actually, it is "human, all too human"', Geoffrey Hosking, *The Awakening of the Soviet Union*, enlarged edn. (Cambridge, MA: Harvard University Press, 1991), p.7.
58. Trotsky (note 13), p.41.
59. His account was first published in England by Routledge as *The Russian Enigma* (the first part only) in 1940, as an edition in the Labour Book Service. Before that it was available only in its French edition, *Au pays du grand mensonge* (Paris: Éditions Champ Libre, 1938). These quotations are drawn from the finally published complete version, Ante Ciliga, *The Russian Enigma* (London: Ink Links, 1979).
60. Ibid., p.41.
61. Ibid., p.43.

4

Stalin's Politics of Obligation

JEFFREY BROOKS

The fall of communism in Russia has brought no Commissions of Truth and Reconciliation; no trials or punishments of the perpetrators of some of the worst atrocities of the twentieth century. Nor have surviving victims received apologies or more than minimal compensation.[1] Even Jews who elsewhere have proven energetic in demanding an historical accounting are strangely quiet. The examination by Russians and others of their experience, victimisation, culpability, resilience and resignation during the time that Stalin reigned is oddly missing from today's historical discourse. Where one would expect a cacophony of accusations, denunciations, demands, denials and individual condemnations, one hears instead a ringing silence.

The lack of attention to a traumatic and fairly recent past derives in part from an understandable preoccupation with the demands of the present, but it also owes much to the key defining features of Soviet culture under Stalin's regime. Among these was the cumulative theft of agency from all other actors in society, and its concentration in the Party, the State and ultimately in Stalin himself. The theft of agency took place through the development of a complex set of inter-relationships based on the politics of obligation. By promoting Stalin as the source of accomplishments and benefactor of society, he and his supporters reinforced the aspiration to totalitarian control and undercut the moral standing of their opponents. At the same time, the acceptance of Stalin as the

prime agent in society exonerated other actors for crimes and
outrages that are known to have taken place. One of the historical
legacies of this political culture appears to be a constraint on the
full examination of culpability that has taken place in many other
societies emerging from traumatic internecine predation. The roots
of this present quandary can be seen in the cultural development of
the 1930s.

To define the relationship between government and society,
Soviet publicists in the mid-1930s used the slogan 'Thank You,
Comrade Stalin, for a Happy Childhood'. Exemplary citizens
thanked Stalin for their well-being in pictures and newspaper
articles, outdoing each other in avowing how much they owed the
State and leader. The 'economy of the gift', as I have called this
cultural construct, reflected and reinforced many aspects of Soviet
life.[2] Those who crafted it invoked Stalin and the leadership as
selfless providers and represented the citizenry as deserving
recipients. Stalin's regime used the notion of obligation to shape
Moscow's ties with the empire and later, after the Second World
War, to formulate relations with the new communist countries and
the wider world. Thus Russians became the benefactors of other
peoples, and the Soviet Union became the patron of other nations.

Many aspects of Soviet society changed between the mid-1930s,
when the slogan 'Thank You, Comrade Stalin!' first appeared, and
Stalin's death in 1953, but the Soviet government's reliance on a
sense of obligation remained constant. After Stalin's death, his
successors restated the politics of obligation by positing the
existence of a debt of young people to the wartime generation. As
the economy stagnated in the 1970s, the younger generation was
denied a moral platform from which to protest because they owed
their elders a debt of gratitude for the victory over fascism. Within
the Soviet bloc, East German communists adopted this Soviet
practice to justify a variety of sacrifices by their citizens for
international communist causes, as did the Soviets themselves.[3]

Stalin's cult and the preoccupation with obligation differed
markedly from the cult of Lenin. The Bolsheviks mummified Lenin
amid the ambiguities of the NEP, the struggle for power after his
death, and the crisis of legitimacy that ensued. Lenin's cult was
more constant than Stalin's. It ran in the background of daily life
almost as unobtrusively as a computer operating system, and it was
equally important for imposing meaning on the Soviet historical

experience. Under Stalin, Soviet authorities used Lenin's cult to convince people that the founder was good and therefore so was the system. Stalin's heirs used Lenin's cult similarly to remind people that, regardless of what Stalin had done, the system was still good because it was founded on Lenin's benevolence.

The obligation that Stalin perpetuated was not a feature of Lenin's cult. No one had to thank Comrade Lenin 'for a happy childhood'; no one had to attribute his or her own good acts and accomplishments to Lenin as the founder of Soviet society. Though Lenin was portrayed occasionally as a giver of presents to children, no one was indebted to him and no one deluged him with gifts. In contrast, Stalin claimed to have nearly single-handedly transformed the country and won the Second World War. Yet Stalin's economy of the gift resembled Lenin's cult in one respect: despite its archaic features, it belonged to a modern mass political culture in which the representation of the leader was an art.[4]

Stalin's politics of obligation in part grew out of the Bolsheviks' attempts to legitimate themselves and motivate workers by turning economic relationships into moral relationships. Treating goods and services as benefits dispensed from above rather than as normal objects of economic transactions served to obligate the population, since all gift-giving implies reciprocity, as the French anthropologist Marcel Mauss argued in his classic essay, *The Gift*.[5] Yet as Mauss' critics noted, reciprocity must be concealed or a gift is not a gift. Stalin and his promoters utilised each aspect of giving. Portraying Stalin as the chief architect of the Soviet system and source of its benefits, they placed a heavy burden of reciprocity upon all citizens. Nevertheless they disguised this obligation as spontaneous gratitude. In primitive societies, those who orchestrate such unequal exchanges seek primarily to accumulate obligations or 'symbolic capital'.[6] Stalin and his colleagues extracted material goods and services from the population, but they also used the symbolic capital that accrued to create his cult and legitimate his leadership. The French sociologist Pierre Bourdieu wrote succinctly about the political implications of great gifts in primitive societies:

> An unbroken progression leads from the symmetry of gift exchange to the asymmetry of the conspicuous redistribution that is the basis of the constitution of political authority. As one

moves away from perfect reciprocity, which assumes a relative
equality of economic situation, the proportion of counter-
services that are provided in the typically symbolic form of
gratitude, homage, respect, obligations or moral debts
necessarily increases.[7]

Stalin and his colleagues struggled to affirm their political authority
during the terrible years of the First Five-Year Plan (1928–32) and
forced collectivisation, when the Stalinist economy of the gift was
born. The politics of obligation filled a need when the officially
sanctioned image of the world diverged sharply from the actualities
of daily life. The media celebrated the success of a minority who
flourished in the expanding state administration, while beyond its
purview living standards plummeted and famine stalked the land.
Public speech became a grotesque form of theatrical recitation as
true believers affirmed the official picture of the world, while those
with doubts either persuaded themselves to believe or simply
performed the necessary rites as a means of self-protection. Stalin
cunningly directed the show and played his part, well aware of the
actors' varying convictions. He was the chief agent in the
formulation of the economy of the gift.[8] He made *Pravda* the apex
of the media and his mouthpiece and within its pages no one could
tinker with his image without his approval.

A chorus of official voices credited Stalin with triumph after
triumph while ignoring the terrible results of collectivisation and
the chaos of the plan, and justifying the slaughter and deportation
of alleged 'kulaks' and others. *Pravda*'s front page on New Year's
Day 1931 shows Stalin beside factories, while European
interventionists point a menacing canon. On 6 November 1933,
Krest'ianskaia gazeta (*The Peasant Newspaper*) featured Stalin in a
Napoleonic pose, with tractors and smiling collective farmers in the
background. The first issue of the humour magazine *Krokodil*
(*Crocodile*) in January 1934 displays a cover picture of a *kolkhoz*
family in a large house with a samovar and a sumptuous spread of
food. The caption is 'the new village'. A picture of Stalin graces the
wall, reminding all to whom they owed homage.

The ritual of thanking Stalin was not entirely without precedent
in Russian life. Stalin and his advocates drew on a Russian past of
gift-giving, bribery, official favours and, on another plane, the
revolutionary movement and Orthodox Christianity, including the

gift of the sacraments through which the believer can attain eternal life.[9] Russian political tradition conflated the monarchy with the Orthodox Church, and the proverb, 'Without the Tsar the land is a widow; without the Tsar the people is an orphan', expresses the Tsar's assigned place in the popular imagination, although these views faded in the last decades of the old regime.[10] The Bolsheviks' first appeals to gratitude grew out of the disastrous economic consequences of the October Revolution, the Civil War and early Soviet policies. Borrowing asceticism albeit unwittingly from Orthodox Christianity and the populist tradition, they legitimated their rule in a situation in which the benefits of the revolution were far from obvious by representing themselves as selfless servants of a greater good.[11] Not accidentally, they used their monopoly of the press to withhold information about their personal lives from the public and therefore to hide the perquisites they enjoyed as the country's new rulers.

The concealment was striking enough at a time when ordinary people suffered extreme deprivation. *Pravda*'s obituaries provide a revealing example of the new rulers' pose of selfless service and the renunciation of personal life, albeit masked in part by the official ideology of collectivism.[12] 'Comrade Nesterenko had no personal biography and no personal needs', reads a routine memorial to a functionary on 15 March 1925. In the same year, I.S. Unshlikht, a high military official, praised the deceased Army chief M.V. Frunze in similar terms. 'Comrade Frunze did not know any personal life', he observed.[13] Local activists quickly seized upon this conceit in their public presentation of themselves. In *Pravda*'s reports on exemplary cadres, there was praise for a factory manager who 'completely forgot about himself' (29 March 1923), a teacher who had 'no personal concern for himself' (13 April 1923), and a 'teacher ascetic' (4 May 1923). Stalin adopted the image of the revolutionary ascetic, promising, on the front page of *Pravda*'s special birthday issue on 22 December 1929, to give 'if need be, all my blood, drop by drop' to the cause. Editors of *Literaturnaia gazeta* (*The Literary Gazette*) even included in their special issue a description of his suffering from typhus in prison in 1908. 'His temperature was very high and he momentarily fell into delirium', recalled an old Bolshevik who had once shared his cell.[14]

Russia's new rulers recast the object of sacrifice in both the Orthodox and revolutionary traditions. Orthodox saints served

God and populist revolutionaries served the people. In each case
the ascetic personally assumed a debt, whether to Christ for his
suffering on the Cross or to the people for their difficult lives.[15]
'We are debtors of the people', the populist theorist N.K.
Mikhailovsky wrote in 1873, 'the debt lies on our conscience, and
we wish to pay it'.[16] Once in power, the Bolsheviks retained the
sentiment but replaced the people as the creditor, first by such
vague entities as the revolution, the proletariat and socialist ideals,
then in the mid-1920s by the Party, and finally, during the 'great
change' of the First Five-Year Plan and collectivisation, by Stalin.
Although the rulers still claimed the ideal of selfless service, they
made themselves the creditors and the ordinary citizens the
debtors. In the complicated calculus of who owed what to whom,
ordinary people moved full circle before and after the revolution,
morphing from creditors to debtors of the Party, and ultimately of
Stalin.

The official rituals of public obligation to Stalin also owed
something to parallel exchanges of obligation that existed largely
outside the public culture. These included the networks of
influence and acquaintances (*blat*) as well as patronage that were
used to obtain scarce goods and services and to command
reciprocity. Whereas the rituals of thanking Stalin were largely
confined to the artificial world of the press and media, *blat* and
patronage were features of everyday life. The public ritual of
obligation to Stalin expressed the official understanding of
citizenship and social identity, but it hardly figured in the day-to-
day practices of ordinary Soviet citizens. If mentioned at all in the
press, *blat* networks and patronage were objects of scorn and
derision. This schizophrenia in which real practices were largely
ignored in favour of idealised ones was the rule for Soviet public
culture and was typical of the political theatre of Stalinism.

Parallel worlds of obligation did not arise accidentally. The
reliance on *blat* and networks of influence also grew out of the
early Bolshevik experience, when money lost its value and access to
goods was secured through connections.[17] References to *blat* and
the trading of influence appear in such publications as *Krokodil* in
the 1920s.[18] Since the distribution of ordinary goods and services
depended on rationing rather than pricing, people often attained
what they wanted through an influential friend to whom they then
owed a reciprocal favour or a gift. This struggle to gain life's

benefits undercut the official distribution system but reinforced the power and authority of the hierarchy, since those with power or access to scarce goods were best placed to reward their friends and acquaintances, and hence to secure favours and gifts in return. Networks of *blat* increased the cohesion of Russian society, since those who used them often cloaked their transactions and mutual dependence in expressions of friendship or affection.[19]

Patronage (*pokrovitel'stvo*), like *blat*, fundamentally permeated Soviet society. Patronage was a vertical system of exchange, whereas *blat* was horizontal as well as vertical, since favours were traded among equals as well as between superiors and inferiors. Stalin and his supporters used patronage as a tool, but ordinary people used it like *blat* to circumvent the system in gaining access to scarce goods, opportunities and services.[20] Evidence suggests that such networks characterised all communist systems. China under Mao developed an economy of moral obligations equivalent to *blat* (*guanxi*), and so did Poland.[21]

Stalin rose to power as a patron, advancing the careers of his supporters from whom he required personal loyalty rather than a commitment to abstract norms or values.[22] During the Civil War he was simultaneously Commissar of Nationalities, of the Workers' and Peasants' Inspectorate, and one of five members of the Politburo. He was also the Politburo's only liaison with the Organisation Bureau (Orgburo), responsible for Party personnel. In each case he controlled appointments at the apex of a pyramid of patronage. From April 1922 as General Secretary his reach grew. What was true at the top was true down the hierarchy. Recommendations from existing members were needed to join the Party, so new members gained patrons. Sheila Fitzpatrick notes that 'patronage relations were ubiquitous in Soviet society'.[23] Graeme Gill cites the 'personalist principle' in the Soviet power structure, according to which people sought help or protection from superiors.[24] Thus bosses of all sorts acted as patrons, from factory directors and Party secretaries to rural officials, and collectivisation institutionalised these practices among the peasantry. An early official link between city and countryside that Lenin himself promoted was a form of patronage (*shefstvo*), under which working-class organisations aided rural counterparts. Many of the urban activists, the so-called '25,000ers' who carried out forced collectivisation, had worked in these brigades.[25]

The practice of patronage reinforced the official public culture of the gift through the commonly accepted expectation that the leaders and patrons would confer benefits on those below them. This expectation is revealed in complaints, pleas for assistance and other unpublished letters to Soviet leaders. Rank-and-file citizens often used family terms typical of patron–client relationships. 'Nearest and dearest and most esteemed leaders of the people', a collective farm couple addressed Stalin and Mikhail Kalinin, the head of the Central Executive Committee, in the mid 1930s, 'We express our tremendous gratitude ... that you have warmed the millions of hearts of many family women', they wrote with reference to the Stalin Constitution.[26] They contributed 150 rubles to the state loan. 'Comrade Kalinin!, my own true father!', wrote a worker, complaining in 1928 about deportations to Siberia.[27] 'Uncle Vyacheslav! [Molotov]', wrote an inhabitant of Krasnodar, who was so moved by the crash of the propaganda plane, the *Maxim Gorky*, that she enclosed five rubles to build another.[28]

Other terms of affection were also common. A group of Cossacks wrote 'to our beloved Stalin' to convey 'great enthusiastic thanks' for a public statement he made about Cossacks.[29] 'Uncle Kalinin', a great favourite among petitioners was also addressed as 'Dear friend of the toilers'.[30] Even A.V. Lunacharsky, the People's Commissar of Culture, received such letters, particularly from schoolchildren, one of whom hopefully addressed him as 'a golden uncle'.[31] Writers of these letters invoked a fundamental feature of patronage, the personal link between patron and client. Thus a minor official in Krasnoyarsk concluded a letter in 1939 advising Stalin how to reorganise internal trade: 'I am boundlessly devoted to the Great cause of the Party and to you personally'. Significantly, eager to establish a link, he pleaded for a response even if his suggestions proved uninteresting.

Such requests ranged widely but shared a common rationale, that is, an expectation that Stalin and his colleagues were a source of bounty. The father of a large family who wrote to Kalinin in March 1937 exemplifies the connection between patronage and the economy of the gift. The author captioned it, 'Our leaders' concern for those with large families'. Identifying himself as a 46-year-old candidate member of the Party, the author gave thanks for a sum of 2,000 rubles that he had received, presumably for his large family. He noted that until the money arrived his children had been barefoot and naked. He wrote that he bought clothes, sat the children at the table, gave them their outfits, and announced, 'Here is your gift from our government, from the Central Executive Committee, from the Communist Party, and from the comrades, from our leaders who are concerned about people; that is, Stalin and Molotov and Kaganovich, Voroshilov and Kalinin, Ordzhonikidze, Zhdanov, Andreev, Chubar, Postyshev'.[32]

Stalin and his promoters reconfigured patronage in the public culture so as to present him as the patron of particular groups and outstanding individuals. His public demands for reciprocity were more encompassing than those of ordinary patrons or contacts in *blat* networks. Stalin emerged as a super-patron during the first half of the 1930s, when he cast himself as the 'father' of the nation. He had himself photographed surrounded by young people and children. He was even shown on 30 December 1936 as Grandfather Frost, the Russian Santa Claus, surrounded by joyful children, dancing around a newly approved 'New Year's tree'. Entry into the patron–client relationship with Stalin required participation in the Stalinist political theatre. Non-participants remained almost invisible in Soviet public culture.

In the years of the great change, ordinary people were incorporated into the rhetoric. On 7 November 1930, the All-Union Conference of Rural Shock Worker Correspondents credited Stalin in *Krest'ianskaia gazeta* for the successes of industrialisation and collectivisation, and promised in return 'to struggle still harder for collectivisation, and still more forcefully to beat the kulaks on the basis of complete collectivisation and their liquidation as a class'. The Stalinist social contract was personal, as were other patron-client relationships. *Krest'ianskaia gazeta* featured an article on 23 June 1930 captioned, 'the Gratitude of Comrade Stalin to workers, technical personnel and the leading staff of the Rostov Rural Mechanisation Centre (*Ressel'mash*)'. A group of 875 elderly workers at the Red Three Corner factory who made galoshes addressed Stalin on the front page of the trade union newspaper *Trud* (*Labour*) on 6 February 1937 in terms typical of the symbolic relationship between the leader and the ordinary working citizen. A passage reads:

> Our own Iosif Vissarionovich, you are the human being who is closest and dearest to us. We are obligated to you for the fact

that we now work and live in an entirely different fashion, that
our labour has changed from being involuntary to being an
affair of honour and valour. We have achieved this under your
wise leadership.

The authors concluded with the promise: 'To the end of our days
we will carry in our hearts the greatest love and thankfulness to
you, our dear father and teacher'.

The economy of the gift depended on notions of honour and
shame that had long traditions in Russia.[33] Codes of honour in
duels, honours dispensed by the rulers, and legal protection of
honour all figured in Russia's pre-Soviet past. The Soviet
government distributed honours, and such gifts served to create a
community of honoured citizens. Official honours ranged from
Stalin Prizes to 'the board of honour' for exemplary pupils, who
were treated in this respect as workers. In each case, honouring was
a public ritual for those with authority to reward those who
excelled at assigned tasks. In a typical cartoon in *Krokodil* on 30
March 1949, a smiling teacher turns from 'the board of honour' on
which are listed the names and grades of excellent students to smile
at a be-medalled student who is reading his report card. Those who
fulfilled their obligations belonged to the honourable community,
and those who behaved dishonourably in the eyes of the
government were lumped with the enemies of the people. The
possibility of dishonour was inherent in the notion of a gift, since
like an insult or a challenge, a gift can be refused or inadequately
reciprocated.[34] The trade union newspaper *Trud* played on this
threat in its lead editorial of 28 March 1937, 'On an Honourable
and Dishonourable Attitude toward the State'. The editors
highlighted the workers' 'holy obligation' to do a good job and
follow rules, and warned that those with a 'dishonourable attitude',
that is those who did not properly reciprocate by working hard,
would end up 'in that muddy water in which the people's enemies
catch their fish'.

Throughout the 1930s, celebrities and groups paraded across
the stage of Soviet life, invoking the social contract according to
which Stalin was the benefactor and they were his clients. By the
mid-1930s, Soviet newspapers were featuring individuals, such as
the prize-wining collective farmer Mariya Demchenko, who was
quoted in *Pravda* on 8 March 1936: 'What more can I give the

homeland to repay her as a true daughter for my training and for all her attention and love?' In *Pravda* on 15 November 1935, Stakhanov, the super-achieving coalminer, thanked Stalin more directly: 'To him, to the great Stalin, we are all obligated for the happy life of our country, for the joyfulness and glory of our beautiful homeland'. In 1938, *Krokodil* peopled its front page with a merry crowd holding up placards with the current slogans, 'Long Live the Stalin Constitution', 'Life Has Become Better, Comrades – Life Has Become Merrier', and 'Thank You, Comrade Stalin, for a Happy Life!' Amidst the slogans was a large picture of Stalin smiling.

Scientists, pilots and explorers became favoured heroes of Soviet public life during the 1930s, and the press subordinated their successes to the economy of the gift. The hero of the decade was flyer V.P. Chkalov, who performed record flights in 1936 and 1937 and died in a crash in 1938. After one successful flight, *Pravda* quoted his wife, who voiced her 'limitless feeling of gratitude' toward Stalin.[35] In 1937, a *Pravda* columnist imagined the flyer's thoughts after a flight to Oregon: 'It seemed that he himself had still done little, too little for the country, for the Party, for Stalin who raised him and to whom he owed everything'.[36] *Pravda* published a letter from the parents of another flyer on 30 June 1938: 'With all our hearts we thank the Party and our beloved Comrade Stalin, who raised our son as a proud falcon of the country of socialism'. Scientific celebrities, such as I.P. Pavlov and the space visionary K.E. Tsiolkovsky, as well as functionaries and pseudo-scientists such as Trofim Lysenko, who almost single-handedly destroyed Soviet biology, and the plant hybridiser I.V. Michurin were lionised as luminaries whose success derived from the State rather than their own unique qualities.

The non-Russian nationalities were gradually brought into the network of public patronage and assumed a special burden of debt. *Pravda* largely ignored the nationalities throughout the 1920s, despite the government's intense interest in them.[37] Under the banner first of 'the brotherhood of peoples', and then in the mid-1930s of 'the friendship of peoples', Russian cultural dominance became Stalin and the Party's gift to the non-Russian nationalities. After the government abandoned the policy of promoting native cultures at the expense of Russian culture, the non-Russians were required, in the words of Terry Martin, 'to express repeatedly and ritualistically their gratitude to the Russians for their "brotherly" help and their admiration and love for the great Russian culture'.[38] On 30 December 1936, the 15th anniversary of the formation of the Soviet Union, *Trud* featured a front-page picture of Stalin standing above a crowd of joyous people in various national costumes who are offering him flowers. On the third page of the same paper, under the caption 'Brotherly Thanks', the Chairman of the Central Executive Committee of the Uzbek Republic praised the transformation of his republic from an ill-educated backwater into a flourishing and prosperous land. He concluded:

> On this day of the fifteenth anniversary of the Union of Soviet Socialist Republics the Uzbek people express the feeling of the deepest brotherly gratitude to the Russian people, to the Bolshevik Party, and to the beloved leader of the toilers of the whole world, Comrade Stalin.

No group was as deeply enmeshed in Soviet client–patron ties as the intelligentsia, and particularly the creative intelligentsia. Bolshevism's first cultural titan, Maxim Gorky, patronised favourites like a Renaissance prince. Later, other officials, including even satraps such as the NKVD chiefs G.G. Yagoda and N.I. Ezhov, patronised the cultural élite. The writer Mikhail Bulgakov, according to one account, captured the situation in which Stalin's minions, patrons in their own right, were reduced to clients in a sketch in which he pictured himself arriving barefoot before Stalin and his court. When Stalin asked why his feet were unclad, the author replied that he owned no boots. Stalin then quipped, 'What is this? My writer going without boots? What an outrage! Yagoda, take off your boots, give them to him'.[39]

Patronage was close to mentorship, which was prevalent among the cultural élite in the early twentieth century.[40] Isaac Babel invoked Gorky as his mentor, and other authors and artists identified themselves with notable predecessors, as did Gorky with Leo Tolstoy. The prevalence and acceptability of mentorship in intellectual circles and an appreciation of the mentor's role may have made Stalin's cult appear more acceptable to intellectuals, since Stalin presented himself as the nation's teacher. The First Congress of Soviet Writers, which convened in Moscow in August 1934, provided the occasion for writers and artists to join the Stalinist performance as public figures.

Journalistic commentaries on the conference were full of references to Stalin's personal patronage of Soviet literature. The editors of *Literaturnaia gazeta*, in their lead article on 17 August, the day on which the First Congress of Soviet Writers opened, provided what amounted to a list of Stalin's gifts to Soviet literature. 'Soviet literature owes its flowering to Comrade Stalin's concern, his personal instructions, and his help, and many Soviet writers owe [him] their creative biographies', read one such statement. 'Comrade Stalin gave [Soviet writers] the brilliant definition of the method of Socialist Realism', read another.

Not surprisingly, reciprocity and obligation were important themes of the conference. Fedor Gladkov, author of the early Soviet classic *Cement*, which was later claimed as a classic precursor of Socialist Realism, emphasised this in *Literaturnaia gazeta* a few days before the conference opened. 'We should justify the hopes put in us by the great Party and our beloved leader', he wrote.[41] Andrei Zhdanov, Stalin's boss of culture, also stressed reciprocity when he asked towards the end of his lengthy speech: 'Comrade Stalin called our writers engineers of the human soul. What does that mean? What duties does that impose on you?'[42]

One of the most often repeated phrases at the congress was the demand that writers, in the words of the propagandist and Stalinist historian E. Yaroslavsky, create works 'worthy of our glorious epoch'.[43] In this vein, Leonid Leonov expressed his desire to work harder so 'we are worthy to be contemporaries of Stalin'.[44] One feature of the congress was the conspicuous presence of writers from the nationalities and their testimony to the wonderful transformation of their lands. Alexander Shirvanzade, a writer from Armenia, expressed his regret that Armenia's 'literature still lags behind socialist reality'.[45] The final statement issued by the writers at the congress to the Central Committee exemplified this moral calculus in which reciprocity bulked so large:

> We feel the deepest gratitude to the Communist Party and the Central Committee and particularly Comrade Stalin for his untiring concern and attention to us, Soviet writers.
> We writers have done less than we could do and ought to do. We affirm to the Central Committee that we will do everything to tie our literature still more closely with life and with the struggle of the peoples of the USSR, so that our craft

will be greater, so that the extraordinary life of our country
will shine in art in all the richness of its colours.[46]

Members of the creative intelligentsia who understood and
accepted the mutual obligations of Stalinist patronage were wooed
and rewarded with dachas, vacations and other privileges.
Construction began on the artists' settlement of Peredelkino in
1935 and access to its dachas become a sought-after privilege,
enjoyed by hacks as well as serious writers. On the short list of
those who received the first country houses, in addition to literary
functionaries, were Isaac Babel and Boris Pasternak.[47] Under the
carrot-and-stick regimen, even independently minded writers could
not escape the politics of obligation. In late 1945, Kornei
Chukovsky, the famous children's writer and critic, wrote to the
Council of Peoples Commissars to request an automobile: 'All my
immediate neighbors in Peredelkino (Konstantin Simonov, N.
Pogodin, P. Pavlenko, Valentin Kataev and others) have got cars at
their dachas'.[48]

Stalin used gifts large and small to remind writers and artists of
their absolute obligation, while celebrating his generous
patronage.[49] The experience of the Ukrainian film-maker Alexander
Dovzhenko is a good example. Stalin met with Dovzhenko in May
1935 and urged him make a film about the hero of the Civil War,
N.A. Shchors, showing Ukrainians' role in the revolution and
Russians' 'fraternal' aid. He capped his request with the gift of a
phonograph so that the director could hear a recording of
Ukrainian folksongs. The film-maker avowed in an interview
published after the meeting that he would cherish the gift as long as
he lived. 'In what other country could workers and artists, scholars
and authors feel such a direct intimacy with their beloved leader?'
he asked. He later told friends that the gift was to remind him of
his nationalist past and therefore of his special obligation to satisfy
Stalin.

The conceit that Stalin and the State conferred unique benefits
on writers by providing an opportunity to describe Soviet life
undercut the very notion of the modern artist. Since the Romantic
era, writers had imagined themselves Promethean figures whose
unique gifts were both personal and divine. When Stalin and the
Party claimed to provide the very opportunity to create, writers lost
their aura. Vladimir Nabokov, writing in exile at the end of the

Stalin era, titled his convoluted novel about a lonely émigré author almost without readers *The Gift* (1952), meaning the gift of creativity. In a foreword to the English edition he noted that he wrote it in Berlin in 1935–37; that is, directly after the promulgation of the Stalinist creed in the arts at the Congress of Soviet Writers.[50]

Writers did more than engage in the ritual of thanking. They incorporated the economy of the gift into their writing and in the limits they imposed on their characters. A world, even an imagined one, in which the State and its leader were the prime movers offered little space for self-assertive heroes to achieve their own objectives. The most popular novel and film of the 1930s was D.A. Furmanov's *Chapayev* (1933). Readers knew that Furmanov, who describes his life as Chapayev's commissar, was almost as famous as Maxim Gorky. Yet Furmanov represents himself in the novel as someone without a personal life and with no desires, even though he is shown to be responsible for his commander's victories. Chapayev is defeated and killed when the Party sends the commissar, who represents Furmanov, elsewhere. Yet readers learn nothing more of this true hero's adventures because he is not an individual agent, but a surrogate for the Party-State and its leader. Even when Soviet writers granted their heroes stardom they were careful to demonstrate subservience to the State and Party. Hence Nikolai Ostrovsky's disabled hero in *How the Steel was Tempered* (1932–34) triumphs by finishing his novel and gaining the Regional Party Committee's approval.

Confinement of heroism suited the Stalinist system of the 1930s, but was not appropriate for a country at war. The Nazi invasion and the threat of defeat had a powerful impact on the public representation of agency. Before the Second World War, publicists used the social contract based on the moral economy of the gift as a rhetorical device to enlarge the persona of the leader at the expense of other actors in the theatre of Soviet politics. This formulation was a casualty of the Nazi onslaught. As the Red Army collapsed, Stalin withdrew into the background of public life, the old rhetoric of obligation vanished, and the press consigned the country's fate to the officers, soldiers and civilians at the front. The soldiers' obligation was no longer to Stalin, but instead to their families, towns and villages, and to the nation. The press in turn stressed the population's debt to the Red Army and published stories of citizens' gifts to ordinary soldiers.[51] As soon as the tide of war turned, however, Stalin and his supporters reinstated the economy of the gift with vigour. 'Thank you, dear Marshal, for our freedom, for our children's happiness, for life', became the mantra of all who wished to celebrate publicly the nation's victories.[52]

In fiction, the return to heroes who were subordinated to the Party and State was complete. Statements such as 'your life is no longer your own, but belongs to the Party and the whole people', from A. Fadeev's *The Young Guard* (1946), appeared frequently in Soviet literature.[53] This emotional effacement figures ludicrously in early Cold War propaganda fiction. Andrei, a border guard and the hero of A.O. Avdeenko's *Nad Tissoi* (*By the Tissa*) is on heightened alert. His dying mother writes begging him to come to her bedside. When he confesses his grief to his superior, the officer tells him that if his mother knew of the alert, 'she would apologise for troubling you!' She would say, he added, 'Forgive me, and again forgive me. Grip your gun firmly'.[54] Then he asks, 'Do you agree or not agree with your mother?'

The belittling of fictional heroes as well as actual citizens culminated in Stalin's last decade when Soviet propagandists made him the benefactor of the entire world.[55] In September 1944, American Ambassador Averell Harriman cabled Harry Hopkins from Moscow: 'That it is our obligation to help Russia and accept her policies because she has won the war for us appears to be the general attitude'.[56] Soviet publicists soon took up the refrains of the Cold War, however, and, instead of demanding thanks from the West, orchestrated a chorus of gratitude from the People's Republics and supporters elsewhere in the world. A columnist in *Literaturnaia gazeta*, comparing disinterested Soviet aid to Eastern Europe with the bondage of the Marshall Plan, observed: 'In their struggle for socialism the People's Democracies depended on the aid and experience of the powerful Soviet Union'.[57] Although Soviet policy in the immediate post-war period was to extract value from Eastern Europe, the press told a different story. 'The Soviet Army brought us not only freedom ... Now this people has given us its dearest treasure – the Soviet peasantry's rich thirty-year experience', visiting Hungarians told *Pravda* on 27 July 1949.

The affirmation of Stalin's cult and the corresponding emphasis on obligation reached an apotheosis on his 70th birthday in December 1949, when he was thanked by admirers and supplicants.

STALIN'S POLITICS OF OBLIGATION

In the weeks before the birthday, newspapers carried declarations from enterprises and sites that had over-fulfilled their plans. 'Everyone who toils strives to commemorate the seventieth birthday of Comrade Stalin with new labour victories; with new contributions to the Five-Year Plan', *Trud* editorialised on 16 December. In *Literaturnaia gazeta*, under the caption, 'In Honour of the Beloved Leader', A. Mariyamov described the gathering at a Leningrad factory that over-fulfilled its norm as a 'gift to Stalin':

> A gift to Stalin is linked with work for the good of the people in the toilers' great and noble impulse because the very name of their beloved leader is the greatest symbol of the selfless struggle for the general welfare of all Soviet people and for the happiness of all humanity.[58]

At a special ceremony in the Bolshoi Theatre, the poet A.A. Tarkovsky read a poem from Soviet writers praising Stalin's labours and thanking him 'for leading us from great darkness to where there is light and happiness'.[59] There seemed to be no limit to the praise and no restraint on the corresponding obligation. Captions from the trade union newspaper on 21 December tell the story:

The Peoples' Love for Comrade Stalin
The Person and Family Member Closest to Us
The Thanks of the Oil Workers
The Creator of the People's Happiness
Stalin Raised Us
The Teacher and Friend of the Entire World

Stalin's aura eclipsed those around him, and fed resentment and bitterness within the leadership. The memory of Stalin's claim that he alone had organised the victory in the Second World War grated on Nikita Khrushchev, who expressed his ire at the closed session of the 20th Party Congress in February 1956. Yet despite his anger, Khrushchev may have owed his old boss gratitude for one gift: Stalin's theft of agency from all other actors in Soviet society was also a theft of responsibility. Khrushchev astounded his colleagues with a catalogue of Stalin's crimes; comforted them with the promise of overdue glory for past accomplishments; and then absolved them of responsibility for heinous acts committed under the leader they had served faithfully. 'Not Stalin, but the Party as a

whole, the Soviet government, our heroic army, its talented leaders
and brave soldiers, the whole Soviet nation – these are the ones
who assured the victory in the Great Patriotic War', he assured his
audience.[60] Khrushchev assigned responsibility for 'the crimes of
the Stalin era' only to Stalin and a few others. 'Stalin put the Party
and the NKVD up to the use of mass terror', he explained.[61] In
answer to his own rhetorical question, 'Where were the members of
the Political Bureau of the Central Committee?', he emphasised
'how difficult it was for any member of the Political Bureau to take
a stand'.[62]

On the field of historical memory, those who have not rejected
the mythology of the gift are doomed to see both the
accomplishments and horrors of the Communist era as the work of
the leader. This limited vision has posed difficulty in separating
Stalin and also Lenin from positive aspects of Soviet history. The
concentration of agency in the leader deprived other actors both of
their share of accomplishments and their accountability for
misdeeds. The lingering thrall of this mythology may explain some
of the nostalgia for the old days, as evidenced by truck drivers who
continued to carry Stalin's picture in their cabs, and a more general
lack of interest in the causative factors that brought the Soviet
Union down. Although the legacies of Stalin's cult may appear
immutable, over time other powerful mythologies have been
overcome through freedom of the press and ballot. The French
after a long delay are dismantling the myth of the resistance and the
scaffolding of memory that once shielded perpetrators of Vichy.[63]
The import of free discussion is also apparent in the former East
and West Germany. Whereas the West's confrontation with the past
proceeded haltingly, it moved, while in the East, historical
accounting had to await the election of a democratic parliament in
1990. As the American historian of Germany Jeffrey Herf observes,
the East's about-face was 'a stunning confirmation that an honest
effort to face the Nazi past was inseparable from the development
of democracy'.[64]

For three-quarters of a century, advocates of the Soviet regime
bent the trajectory of memory around the metaphor of the path, the
leaders' path, the Marxist-Leninist-Stalinist path to communism,
imposing a futuristic vision that obscured past and present.[65]
Exceptional and creative people countered with images of the path
to judgement. Boris Pasternak concluded his final poem in *Doctor*

Zhivago with the lines, 'So shall the centuries drift, trailing like a caravan/ Coming for judgment, out of the dark, to me'.[66] Anna Akhmatova wrote in 'Requiem', 'I shall go creep to our wailing wall/ Crawl to the Kremlin towers'.[67] Such voices heard then and anew now, promise the reprise of agency and a kind of redemptive accounting that their authors imagined and craved. Ten years is a short period for a people collectively preoccupied with economic survival and with crafting a new understanding of their place in the world. It is not surprising that the historical reckoning that Pasternak and Akhmatova foretold has not yet begun in earnest, but one can expect it in the near future, if Russia continues to develop as a democracy supported by an active examination of historical experience.

NOTES

I benefited from a mini-conference organised by Sheila Fitzpatrick at the University of Chicago on 'Gift-Giving in Communist and Post-Communist Societies' in September 2001. I thank Karen Brooks, Georgiy Cherniavskiy, Michael David-Fox, George Liber, Lary May, Harry Shukman and Olga Velikanova for helpful comments and suggestions. I also thank the Kennan Institute and the Wilson Center for support during my residence there in 1999–2000.

1. Those pardoned during Khrushchev's de-Stalinisation received a payment related to their salary, and surviving victims in the 1990s received an addition to their pension. Jews who emigrated in the 1970s had to compensate the government for their secondary and higher education.
2. Jeffrey Brooks, *Thank You, Comrade Stalin! Soviet Public Culture from Revolution to Cold War* (Princeton: Princeton University Press, 2000), pp.83–105. For a bibliography, see also Alan D. Schrift (ed.), *The Logic of the Gift: Toward an Ethic of Generosity* (New York: Routledge, 1997).
3. Sandrine Kott, *Le communisme au quotidien: Les entreprises d'Etat dans la societé est-allemande* (Paris: Berlin, 2001), pp.271–93.
4. See George L. Mosse's classic, *The Nationalization of the Masses* (New York: New American Library, 1975), pp.21–46.
5. Marcel Mauss, *The Gift: Forms and Functions of Exchange in Archaic Societies*, trans. Ian Cunnison (New York: Norton, 1967); Katherine Verdery, *What was Socialism and What Comes Next* (Princeton: Princeton, University Press, 2001), p.26, explains that in Soviet-type systems goods were often distributed at low prices, 'effectively given away'.
6. Pierre Bourdieu, 'Marginalia', in Schrift (note 2), p.234.
7. Pierre Bourdieu, 'Selections', in ibid., p.215.
8. I discuss Stalin's role in his cult in Brooks (note 2), pp.61–70.
9. On bribery, see Alena Ledeneva, Stephen Lovell and Andrei Rogachevskii (eds.), *Bribery and Blat in Russia: Negotiating Reciprocity from the Middle Ages to the 1990s* (Basingstoke: Macmillan, 2000); on sacramentalism, see George P. Fedotov,

Collected Works, Vol.3, *The Russian Religious Mind: I: Kievan Christianity. The 10th to the 13th Centuries* (Belmont, MA: Norland Publishing Company, 1975), pp.31–5.

10. Quoted in Elena Hellberg-Hirn, *Soil and Soul: The Symbolic World of Russianness* (Aldershot: Ashgate, 1998), p.62, see also pp.57–78. I show the decline in *When Russia Learned to Read: Literacy and Popular Literature, 1861–1917* (Evanston: Northwestern University Press, 2003, 1985), pp.214–45.
11. Avram Brown, 'The Bolshevik Rejection of the "Revolutionary Christ" and Dem'ian Bednyi's *The Flawless New Testament of the Evangelist Dem'ian*', in *Kritika: Explorations in Russian and Eurasian History* 2/1 (Winter 2001), pp.5–44, describes the Bolsheviks' abhorrence of Christian morality.
12. N.K. Mikhailovskii, *Literaturnaya kritika i vospominaniya* (Moscow: Iskusstvo, 1995), p.79.
13. *Pravda*, 3 November 1925.
14. *Literaturnaya gazeta*, 23 December 1929.
15. On the religious tradition, see Yu. M. Lotman, *Izbrannye stat'i* (Tallin: Alekasndra, 1993), pp.345–55.
16. Mikhailovskii (note 12), p.79.
17. On this, see J. Kornai, *The Socialist System: The Political Economy of Communism* (Princeton: Princeton University Press, 1992); Julie Hessler, 'Culture of Shortages: A Social History of Soviet Trade 1917–1953', unpublished Ph.D. dissertation, University of Chicago, 1996; on the origins of the term from the Polish and Yiddish, see Ledeneva et al. (note 9), 'Introduction', p.18.
18. Alena V. Ledeneva, *Russia's Economy of Favours*: *Blat, Networking and Informal Exchange* (Cambridge: Cambridge University Press, 1998), pp.11–22.
19. Sheila Fitzpatrick, '*Blat* in Stalin's Time', in Ledeneva et al. (note 9), pp.178–9.
20. Ledeneva (note 18), p.3; see also Fitzpatrick (note 19), pp.166–82, and Alena Ledeneva, 'Continuity and Change of *Blat* Practices in Soviet and Post-Soviet Russia', in Ledeneva et al. (note 9), pp.183–205.
21. Mayfair Mei-hui Yang, *Gifts, Favors, and Banquets: The Art of Social Relationships in China* (Ithaca: Cornell University Press, 1994), pp.86–7.
22. On patromonialism, see Vadim Volkov, 'Patromonialism versus Rational Bureaucracy: The Historical Relativity of Corruption,, in Ledeneva et al. (note 9), pp.35–47.
23. Sheila Fitzpatrick, *Everyday Stalinism: Ordinary Life in Extraordinary Times: Soviet Russia in the 1930s* (Oxford: University Press, 1999), p.110; see also idem, 'Patronage and the Intelligentsia in Stalin's Russia', in Stephen G. Wheatcroft (ed.), *Challenging Traditional Views of Russian History* (Basingstoke: Palgrave Macmillan, 2002), pp.92–111. On patronage by institutions, see Michael David-Fox, 'From Illusory "Society" to Intellectual "Public": VOKS, International Travel and Party-Intelligentsia Relations in the Interwar Period', *Contemporary European History* 11/1 (2002), pp.7–32.
24. Graeme Gill, 'Stalinism and the fall of the Soviet Union', in Wheatcroft (note 23), p.223.
25. On *shefstvo* and patronage during collectivisation, see Lynne Viola, *The Best Sons of the Fatherland: Workers in the Vanguard of Soviet Collectivization* (New York: Oxford University Press, 1987), pp.18, 43–4, 157, 173.
26. A.Ya. Livshin, I.B. Orlov and O.V. Khlevnyuk, *Pis'ma vo vlast', 1928–1939: Zayavleniya, zhaloby, donosy, pis'ma v gosudarstvennye struktury i sovetskim vozhdyam* (Moskva: ROSSPEN, 2002), p.13.
27. Ibid., p.363.
28. Ibid., p.270.

29. Ibid., p.299.
30. Ibid., p.373.
31. Ibid., p.68.
32. Ibid., pp.332–3.
33. Nancy Shields Kollmann, *By Honor Bound: State and Society in Early Modern Russia* (Ithaca: Cornell University Press, 1999); Yurii Lotman, 'O semiotike ponyatii "styd" i "strakh" v mekhanizme kul'tury', in idem, *Semiosfera* (St Petersburg: Iskusstvo-SPB, 2000), pp.664–6.
34. Pierre Bourdieu, 'Selections from the Logic of Practice', in Schrift (note 2), p.193.
35. *Pravda*, 25 July 1936.
36. Ibid., 21 June 1937.
37. Brooks (note 2), pp.75–6.
38. Terry Martin, *The Affirmative Action Empire: Nations and Nationalism in the Soviet Union, 1923–1939* (Ithaca: Cornell University Press, 2001), pp.130–2, 455.
39. Quoted in Fitzpatrick, *Everyday Stalinism* (note 23), p.111, from Vasilii Shentalinskii, *Raby svobody. v literaturnykh arkhivakh KGB* (Moscow: Parus, 1995), p.120.
40. Barbara Walker describes mentoring among the intelligentsia in *Maximilian Voloshin and the Russian Literary Circle: Culture and Survival in Revolutionary Times* (Bloomington: Indiana University Press, 2003).
41. *Literaturnaya gazeta*, 12 August 1934.
42. Ibid., 20 August 1934.
43. Ibid., 26 August 1934.
44. Ibid., 22 August 1934.
45. Ibid., 22 August 1934.
46. Ibid., 2 September 1934.
47. D.L. Babichenko, *Pisateli i tsenzory: Sovetskaya literatura 1940-x godov pod politicheskim kontrolem TsK* (Moscow: Rossiya Molodaya, 1994), p.12.
48. Quoted in Vera Tolz, 'Cultural Bosses as Patrons and Clients: the Functioning of the Creative Unions in the Post-War Period', in *Contemporary European History* 11/1 (2002), pp.87–105.
49. The following is based on George O. Liber, *Alexander Dovzhenko: A Life in Soviet Film* (London: British Film Institute, 2002), pp.157–8.
50. Vladimir Nabokov, *The Gift* (New York: G.P. Putnam's Sons, 1963), p.9.
51. Brooks (note 2), pp.159–94.
52. *Pravda*, 1 September 1943.
53. A. Fadeyev, *The Young Guard*, trans. Violet Dutt (Moscow: Foreign Languages Publishing House, 1958), p.485.
54. A.O Avdeenko, *Nad Tissoi (Iz pogranichnoi khroniki)* (Moscow: Voennoe izdatel'stvo Ministerstva Oborony Soyuza SSR, 1955), p.62.
55. Brooks (note 2), chs.7, 8 and epilogue.
56. Navy cable from Moscow, 9 September 1944, Harriman papers, Library of Congress. I discuss US–Soviet relations in 'Stalin's Ghost: Cold War Culture and U.S.–Soviet Relations', in Klaus Larres and Kenneth Osgood (eds.), *After Stalin's Death: The Cold War as International History* (London: Rowman and Littlefield, forthcoming).
57. Andrei Simoi, 'We Live in a Stalinist Epoch', *Literaturnaya gazeta*, 5 November 1946, p.5.
58. A. Mar'yamov, 'V chest' lyubimogo vozhdya', *Literaturnaya gazeta*, 10 December 1949, p.1.
59. A.A. Tarkovsky, 'Slovo sovetskikh pisatelei k tovarishchu Stalinu', *Literaturnaya gazeta*, 24 December 1949, 1.

60. Nikita S. Khrushchev, *The Crimes of the Stalin Era: Special Report to the 20th Congress of the Communist Party of the Soviet Union*, annotated by Boris I. Nicolaevsky (New York: New Leader, 1956), p.43.
61. Ibid., p.25.
62. Ibid., pp.60–1.
63. See Henry Rousso, *Le syndrome de Vichy de 1944 á nos jours* (Paris: Éditions du Seuil, 1990, 1987).
64. Jeffrey Herf, *Divided Memory: The Nazi Past in the Two Germanies* (Cambridge, MA: Harvard University Press, 1997), p.390.
65. Brooks (note 2), pp.48–9, 79–81, 125.
66. Boris Pasternak, *Doctor Zhivago*, trans. Max Hayward and Manya Harari (New York: Random House, 1991), p.559.
67. Anna Akhmatova, *Selected Poems*, trans. D.M. Thomas (London: Penguin, 1988), p.89.

5

Stalin and Foreign Intelligence

CHRISTOPHER ANDREW and JULIE ELKNER

Ever since the collapse of the Soviet Union, the *Sluzhba Vneshnei Razvedki* (SVR), successor to the KGB's First Chief [Foreign Intelligence] Directorate, has continued to celebrate the achievements of Stalin's foreign intelligence services, of which it sees itself as the direct descendant. In 1995, it marked the 75th anniversary of the foundation of the *Inostrannyi Otdel* (INO), the foreign intelligence arm of the Cheka and its inter-war successors, by publishing a volume which celebrated the careers of 75 leading intelligence officers and agents of the Soviet era in a style which differed little from the uncritical hagiographies previously produced by the KGB.[1] In 1995, the SVR also began the publication of a multi-volume official history of Soviet foreign intelligence operations which, at the time of writing, has reached the end of the Great Patriotic War.[2] Though a mine of mostly reliable factual information, it too presents a heroically sanitised view of Soviet intelligence history. The videos on foreign operations in the Stalin era recently produced by the SVR's Television Information Service take a similar approach.[3]

No inter-war Western prime minister or president came close to matching Stalin's appetite for secret intelligence from both home and abroad.[4] Though it has as yet been little researched, that appetite was evident even under Lenin. As Lenin's health declined in 1922, the head of the GPU (from 1923 the OGPU), Feliks Dzerzhinsky, turned increasingly to Stalin for support. Documents in the Dzerzhinsky collection in the former Party archives show that on some occasions he acted as intermediary between Stalin and the ailing Lenin. Following Lenin's incapacitation after his third stroke in March 1923, Stalin turned increasingly to Dzerzhinsky to keep him informed on 'the moods of the masses'.[5] This is unwelcome evidence for both the SVR and the internal Russian security service, the *Federal'naya Sluzhba Bezopasnosti* (FSB), which still attempt to preserve Dzerzhinsky's spotless Soviet reputation as the 'knight of the revolution', *sans peur et sans reproche*. To mark the 125th anniversary of Dzerzhinsky's birth in 2002, the FSB published evidence that before his death he became an opponent of Stalin. He is said to have told Aleksei Rykov in June 1926, 'I do not share the policy of this government. I do not understand it and see no sense in it'.[6] At Dzerzhinsky's funeral a month later, however, Stalin eulogised him as 'terror of the bourgeoisie, devout knight of the proletariat [and] noble-blooded fighter for the Communist Revolution'.[7]

Stalin continued to pay close attention to intelligence reports from Dzerzhinsky's successor, the increasingly infirm Vyacheslav Menzhinsky.[8] His personal confidence in Menzhinsky, however, steadily declined. On 14 November 1932, Menzhinsky wrote to Stalin and the Politburo on behalf of the OGPU Collegium, requesting the institution of a 'Feliks Dzerzhinsky' medal to mark the 15th anniversary of the founding of the Cheka. He enclosed a draft decree and a description of the medal. Stalin wrote 'Opposed. St[alin]' in blue pencil on the request, and the issue was not raised again.[9] Genrikh Yagoda, who became head of the NKVD (which absorbed the OGPU) after Menzhinsky's death in 1934, was an opportunist, prepared to throw in his lot with Stalin to advance his career but never willing to give him the unconditional support which Stalin demanded.[10] On occasion Yagoda proved willing to take on the entire Politburo to defend his departmental interests. According to Sergei Konstantinov, in August 1934, only a month after taking office, Yagoda published a circular on the creation in the NKVD camps of *krai*- and *oblast*-level courts for investigation of crimes committed in NKVD labour camps, which contradicted a whole series of laws and previous instructions of the Politburo, and succeeded in having his way.[11] By contrast, Nikolai Ezhov, who succeeded Yagoda as head of the NKVD in 1936 at Stalin's behest, was unswervingly sycophantic and gained an access to Stalin which was second only to that of Vyacheslav Molotov. During the Terror in 1937–38, Ezhov called on Stalin 278 times in the Kremlin for lengthy meetings lasting on average three hours (a total of 834 hours).[12] Lavrenti Beria, who replaced Ezhov late in 1938 and remained the dominating figure in state security (even when not formally its head) for the remainder of the Stalinist era, struck Stalin's daughter, Svetlana, as 'a magnificent modern specimen of the artful courtier, the embodiment of oriental perfidy, flattery and hypocrisy'.[13] He became closer to Stalin than any other member of his entourage, acting as unofficial toastmaster at his long, late-night, heavy-drinking dinner parties.[14]

The FSB historian, Professor Aleksandr Plekhanov, declares it 'completely inadmissible to rank Dzerzhinsky with Yagoda, Ezhov and Beria'. A recent article by him reveals that in 1921 Dzerzhinsky ordered the arrest of Beria for crimes committed in Azerbaijan. According to Plekhanov, Beria was saved from prison (or worse punishment) only by the personal intervention on his behalf of Stalin and Ordzhonikidze.[15] After Yagoda, Ezhov and Beria were removed from office, all were executed (in 1938, 1940 and 1953, respectively). By an appropriately black irony, the crimes for which all three were condemned to death included the imaginary offence of working as British secret agents. In reality, no British intelligence operations against Stalinist Russia came close to achieving such spectacular successes.

Though the SVR version of foreign intelligence operations in the Stalin era is both sanitised and uncritical, there is no doubt that Soviet intelligence collection in the West completely outclassed that of Western agencies in the Soviet Union. Stalin's foreign intelligence system had two decisive operational advantages over its Western rivals. First, while security in Moscow was obsessional, much Western security remained feeble. Second, the Communist parties and their 'fellow-travellers' in the West gave Soviet intelligence a major source of committed ideological agents, who were seduced by the myth-image of the world's first worker-peasant state proceeding rapidly along the path of socialist construction under the wise leadership of Comrade Stalin.

The Soviet spy mania of the 1930s, which reached its apogee in the Great Terror and made Western intelligence operations in Moscow almost impossibly difficult, derived not simply from the general sense of insecurity within the Soviet system generated by its encircling capitalist neighbours, but also from what Khrushchev later famously described as Stalin's 'pathologically suspicious personality': 'Everywhere and in everything he saw "enemies", "two-facers" and "spies"'. Most of the Soviet population accepted the official doctrine that they were threatened by a major conspiracy of spies and saboteurs in the pay of foreign secret services. In every factory, NKVD officers lectured workers on the dangers from non-existent imperialist agents in their midst.[16] Films at Soviet cinemas, comedies included, invariably contained their obligatory quota of spies.[17] On 10 October 1937, undoubtedly at Stalin's wishes, the Politburo approved NKVD operational order No.00693, classing all embassies and consulates as bases of foreign intelligence agencies, and instructing KRO (counter-espionage) staff 'to arrest immediately all Soviet citizens linked with the personnel of diplomatic representations and visiting their offices and homes'. 'Ceaseless surveillance' was to be maintained over all staff of major embassies. Unsurprisingly, a whole series of foreign consulates closed down.[18]

The Soviet Union in the Stalin era was thus a more difficult intelligence target than anywhere else in Europe – so difficult indeed that both the pre-war Foreign Office and the State Department believed that any attempt to set up intelligence stations in their Moscow embassies would do more harm than good.[19] In 1938 the British ambassador in Moscow, Viscount Chilston, complained that 'it is impossible to gain even an inkling of what is discussed within the [Kremlin's] walls', but continued to veto a proposal to establish a Secret Intelligence Service (SIS) station on the grounds that 'the disadvantages, in the form of increased suspicion and general hostility, would far outweigh any practical advantages which might be secured by [its] presence'.[20] There was no British intelligence station in Stalin's Russia until August 1941, when the Special Operations Executive (SOE) established a liaison mission in Moscow in the aftermath of the German invasion.[21] The United States was even slower to establish an intelligence presence. Because of continued opposition from the State Department, the CIA was not allowed to set up its first Moscow station until after Stalin's death.[22]

By comparison with Moscow, both London and Washington were soft targets. Until the Second World War, the Foreign Office did not possess a single security officer, let alone a security department. Security in many British embassies was also remarkably lax. In Rome, according to Sir Andrew Noble, who was stationed there in the mid-1930s, it was 'virtually non-existent'. Embassy servants had access to the keys to red boxes and filing cabinets containing classified documents, as well as   probably – to the number of the combination lock on the embassy safe. Among the servants was Francesco Constantini, who was recruited as a Soviet agent in 1924 and for more than a decade provided his controllers with a remarkable quantity of classified British diplomatic documents.[23] Soviet recruits in the Foreign Office during the 1930s included two of the 'Cambridge Five', Donald Maclean and John Cairncross, and two cipher clerks, Ernest Oldham and Captain John King.[24]

For most of the inter-war period, Britain was the main foreign target of Soviet intelligence collection. Stalin seems to have been an avid consumer of both the British documents obtained by Soviet agents and the diplomatic traffic successfully decrypted with the help of the cipher material they supplied. An NKVD report of 15 November 1935 notes, for example, that no less than 101 of the British documents obtained from Francesco Constantini (or his brother Secondo) since the beginning of the year had been judged sufficiently important to be 'sent to Comrade Stalin': among them the Foreign Office records of talks between Sir John Simon, the British Foreign Secretary, Anthony Eden, junior Foreign Office Minister (who became Foreign Secretary at the end of the year), and Hitler in Berlin; between Eden and Maksim Litvinov, the Soviet Commissar for Foreign Affairs, in Moscow; between Eden and Jozef Beck, the Polish Foreign Minister, in Warsaw; between Eden and Eduard Beneš, the Czechoslovak Foreign Minister, in Prague; and between Eden and Mussolini in Rome.[25]

A striking omission from NKVD headquarters' (the Centre) list of the most important Foreign Office documents supplied to Stalin was Eden's account of his talks with him during his visit to Moscow in March 1935 – despite the fact that this document was sent to the Rome Embassy and was probably among those obtained by Constantini.[26] Since this was Stalin's first meeting with a minister in a Western government, their talks were of unusual significance. The most likely explanation for the Centre's failure to send the British record of the meeting to the Kremlin is that the head of foreign intelligence, Abram Slutsky, feared to pass on to Stalin some of

Eden's comments about him. INO would have been unembarrassed to report the fact that Eden was impressed by Stalin's 'remarkable knowledge and understanding of international affairs'. But it doubtless lacked the nerve to repeat Eden's description of Stalin as 'a man of strong oriental traits of character with unshakeable assurance and control whose courtesy in no way hid from us an implacable ruthlessness'. The Centre was probably also nervous about reporting some of the opinions attributed by Eden to Stalin – for example, that he was 'perhaps more appreciative of [the] German point of view than Monsieur Litvino[v]'.[27]

The United States did not become a priority Soviet intelligence target until the Second World War. Wartime Washington proved an even softer target than London. Every major branch of the Roosevelt administration was successfully penetrated by Soviet intelligence. Among the easiest of all US targets was its embassy in Moscow, which was penetrated virtually continuously from the beginning of Soviet–American diplomatic relations in 1933 until at least the mid-1960s. For over a decade it did not occur to the embassy to search for Soviet bugs. When a US Navy electrician conducted the first electronic sweep of the embassy in 1944, he discovered 120 hidden microphones. For a time, according to a member of the embassy staff, more 'kept turning up, in the legs of any new tables and chairs that were delivered, in the plaster of the walls, any and everywhere'.[28]

The failure to discover further bugs during the early years of the Cold War was due more to the increasing sophistication of Soviet electronic eavesdropping than to improvements in embassy security. In 1952 the new American Ambassador, George Kennan, ordered a thorough search of both the embassy and his own residence. The security experts sent from Washington asked him to dictate the text of an old diplomatic despatch in his study in order to help them discover any voice-activated listening device. As he continued his dictation, one of the experts suddenly began hacking away at the wall behind a wooden replica of the Great Seal of the United States. Finding nothing in the wall, he then attacked the Seal itself with a mason's hammer and triumphantly extracted from it a pencil-shaped bug which had been relaying Kennan's every word (and no doubt those of previous ambassadors) to Soviet eavesdroppers. Next morning Kennan noted a 'new grimness' among the Soviet guards and embassy staff: 'So dense was the atmosphere of anger and hostility that one could have cut it with a knife'.[29] Studies of US–Soviet relations in the Stalin era have yet to take account of the large amounts of intelligence obtained by bugging the American embassy.

The official SVR history fails to acknowledge the remarkable contrast between the success of intelligence collection in the Stalin era and the often miserable quality of intelligence analysis. In all one-party states, intelligence analysis is distorted by the insistent demands of political correctness. Few analysts are willing to challenge the views of the political leadership. Foreign intelligence in authoritarian regimes thus often acts as a mechanism for reinforcing rather than correcting the regimes' misconceptions of the outside world. In Stalinist Russia, the distortions produced by political correctness were made worse by a recurrent tendency to conspiracy theory (another common characteristic of authoritarian regimes), of which Stalin himself was the chief exponent. The tendency to substitute conspiracy theory for evidence-based analysis when assessing the intentions of the encircling imperialist powers in the 1930s was made worse by Stalin's increasing determination to act as his own intelligence analyst. Stalin, indeed, actively discouraged intelligence analysis by others, which he condemned as 'dangerous guesswork'. 'Don't tell me what you think', he is reported to have said, 'give me the facts and the source!' As a result, INO had no analytical department. Soviet intelligence reports throughout, and even beyond, the Stalin era characteristically consisted of compilations of relevant information on particular topics with little argument or analysis.[30]

Stalin's 'pathological suspiciousness' was one of the dominant characteristics of his self-appointed role as the Soviet Union's leading intelligence analyst. Molotov later recalled being told by Stalin:

> I think that one can never trust the intelligence. One has to listen to them but then check on them. The intelligence people can lead to dangerous situations that it is impossible to get out of. There were endless provocateurs on both sides. This is why one cannot count on the intelligence without a thorough and constant checking and double-checking.[31]

One of the main priorities of the intelligence officers who trawled through the Centre's treasure trove of British diplomatic

documents and decrypts was to discover the anti-Soviet
conspiracies which Comrade Stalin, 'Lenin's outstanding pupil, the
best son of the Bolshevik Party, the worthy successor and great
continuer of Lenin's cause', knew were there.

A characteristic example of the Centre's politically correct
distortion of important intelligence was its treatment of the Foreign
Office record of the meeting in March 1935 between Sir John
Simon, Anthony Eden and Adolf Hitler in Berlin. Copies of the
minutes were supplied both by Captain King in the Foreign Office
and by Francesco Constantini in the Rome Embassy.[32] Nine days
before the meeting, in defiance of the post-war Versailles Treaty,
Hitler had announced the introduction of conscription. The fact
that the meeting – the first between Hitler and a British Foreign
Secretary – went ahead at all was, in itself, cause for suspicion in
Moscow. On the British side the talks were mainly exploratory – to
discover what the extent of Hitler's demands for the revision of the
Treaty of Versailles really was, and what prospect there was of
accommodating them. Moscow, however, saw grounds for deep
suspicion.

While disclaiming any intention of attacking the Soviet Union,
Hitler told his British visitors that there was a distinct danger of
Russia starting a war, and declared himself 'firmly convinced that
one day co-operation and solidarity would be urgently necessary to
defend Europe against the ... Bolshevik menace'. Simon and Eden
showed not the slightest interest in an Anglo-German, anti-
Bolshevik agreement, but their fairly conventional exchange of
diplomatic pleasantries had sinister overtones in Moscow.
According to the Foreign Office record, 'The British Ministers were
sincerely thankful for the way in which they had been received in
Berlin, and would take away very pleasant memories of the
kindness and hospitality shown them'.[33]

The British record of the talks runs to over 23,000 words. The
Russian translation circulated by the Centre to Stalin and others in
the Soviet leadership came to less than 4,000. Instead of producing
a conventional précis, the Centre selected a series of statements by
Simon, Eden, Hitler and other participants in the talks, and
assembled them into what appeared as a continuous conversation.
The significance of some individual statements was thus distorted
by removing them from their context. Probably at the time,
certainly subsequently, one of Simon's comments was

misconstrued as giving Germany *carte blanche* to take over Austria.[34]

Doubtless in line with Stalin's own conspiracy theories, the Centre interpreted the visit by Simon and Eden to Berlin as the first in a series of meetings at which British statesmen sought not merely to appease Hitler but also to give him encouragement to attack Russia.[35] In reality, although some British diplomats would have been content to see the two dictators come to blows of their own accord, no British Foreign Secretary and no British government would have contemplated orchestrating such a conflict. The conspiracy theories which were born in Stalin's Moscow in the 1930s, however, have – remarkably – survived the end of the Soviet era. The SVR official history of Russian intelligence insists that neither the many volumes of published Foreign Office documents nor the even more voluminous unpublished files in the Public Record Office can be relied upon. The British government, it maintains, is still engaged in a conspiracy to conceal the existence of other top-secret documents which reveal the terrible truth about the real aims of British foreign policy before the Second World War:

> Some documents from the 1930s having to do with the negotiations of British leaders with the highest leadership of Fascist Germany, including directly with Hitler, have been kept to this day in secret archives of the British Foreign Office. The British do not want the indiscreet peering at the proof of their policy of collusion with Hitler and spurring Germany on to its Eastern campaign.[36]

The British diplomat, R.A. Sykes, later wisely described Stalin's world view as 'a curious mixture of shrewdness and nonsense'.[37] Stalin's shrewdness was apparent in the way that he out-manoeuvred his rivals after the death of Lenin, gradually acquired absolute power as General Secretary, and later out-negotiated Churchill and Roosevelt during their wartime conferences. Historians have found it difficult to accept that so shrewd a man also believed in so much nonsense. But it is no more possible to understand Stalin without acknowledging his addiction to conspiracy theories about both Western statesman and his Russian opponents (Trotsky chief among them) than it is to comprehend Hitler without grasping the passion with which he pursued his even more terrible and absurd conspiracy theories about the Jews.

At a number of critical moments Stalin's 'pathologically suspicious' approach to intelligence analysis deluded him into believing that all the Soviet Union's best German and British agents were part of an elaborate conspiracy to deceive him. During the first half of 1941, the NKVD networks in Germany headed by Arvid Harnack, an official in the Economics Ministry, and Harro Schulze-Boysen, a lieutenant in *Luftwaffe* intelligence, provided vitally important intelligence on Hitler's preparations for Operation 'Barbarossa', the invasion of Russia. On 16 June, the deputy NKVD resident in Berlin, Aleksandr Korotkov, cabled Moscow that intelligence from the two networks indicated that, 'All of the military training by Germany in preparation for its attack on the Soviet Union is complete, and the strike may be expected at any time'.[38] Similar intelligence arrived from NKVD sources as far afield as China and Japan. The head of foreign intelligence, Pavel Fitin, had been appointed in 1939 at the age of only 31, owing his unprecedentedly rapid promotion largely to the liquidation of so many more senior intelligence officers during the Terror. His willingness to pass on so many reports of the impending German attack to a sceptical Stalin, though doubtless prompted chiefly by grave concern for the threat to Mother Russia, also showed an unusual degree of moral courage. KGB historians later counted 'over a hundred' intelligence warnings of preparations for the German attack forwarded by Fitin to Stalin between 1 January and 21 June 1941.[39] Other reports came from military intelligence. All were wasted.

Though many NKVD officers shared, if usually to a less grotesque degree, Stalin's addiction to conspiracy theory, the main blame for the catastrophic failure to foresee the surprise attack on 22 June belongs to Stalin himself, who continued to act as his own chief intelligence analyst. Stalin not merely ignored a series of wholly accurate warnings. He denounced many of those who provided them. His response to an NKVD report from Schulze-Boysen on 16 June was the obscene minute: 'You can tell your "source" in German air force headquarters to go fuck himself. He's not a "source", he's a disinformer. J. Stalin'.[40] Stalin also heaped abuse on the GRU (Soviet military intelligence) illegal, Richard Sorge, later posthumously recognised as one of the heroes of Soviet intelligence, who sent similar warnings from Tokyo, where he had penetrated the German embassy and seduced the ambassador's wife. Sorge's warnings of Operation 'Barbarossa' were denounced by Stalin as disinformation from a lying 'shit who has set himself up with some small factories and brothels in Japan'.[41]

Stalin was much less suspicious of Adolf Hitler than of Winston Churchill, the evil genius who had preached an anti-Bolshevik crusade in the Civil War 20 years earlier and had been plotting against the Soviet Union ever since. Behind many of the reports of impending German attack, Stalin claimed to detect a disinformation campaign by Churchill designed to continue the long-standing British plot to embroil him with Hitler. Churchill's personal warnings to Stalin of preparations for 'Barbarossa' only heightened his suspicions. From the intelligence reports sent by the London residency, Stalin almost certainly knew that until June 1941 the Joint Intelligence Committee (JIC), the body responsible for the main British intelligence assessments, did not believe that Hitler was preparing an invasion. It reported to Churchill as late as 23 May that 'the advantages ... to Germany of concluding an agreement with the USSR are overwhelming'.[42] The JIC assessments were probably regarded by Stalin as further proof that Churchill's warnings were intended to deceive him. Stalin's deep suspicions of Churchill and of British policy in general were cleverly exploited by the Germans. As part of the deception operation which preceded 'Barbarossa', the *Abwehr*, German military intelligence, spread reports that rumours of an impending German attack were part of a British disinformation campaign.

By early June, reports of German troop movements towards the Soviet frontier were too numerous to be explained, even by Stalin, simply as British disinformation. At a private lunch in the German embassy in Moscow, the ambassador, Count von der Schulenberg, revealed that Hitler had definitely decided on invasion. 'You will ask me why I am doing this', he said to the astonished Soviet ambassador to Germany, Vladimir Georgievich Dekanozov: 'I was raised in the spirit of Bismarck, who was always an opponent of war with Russia'. Stalin's response was to tell the Politburo, 'Disinformation has now reached ambassadorial level!'[43] On 9 June, or soon afterwards, however, Stalin received a report that the German embassy had been sent orders by telegram to prepare for evacuation within a week, and had begun burning documents in the basement.[44]

Though Stalin remained preoccupied by a non-existent British conspiracy, he increasingly began to suspect a German plot as well

– though not one which aimed at surprise attack. As it became
increasingly difficult to conceal German troop movements, the
Abwehr spread rumours that Hitler was preparing to issue an
ultimatum, backed by some display of military might, demanding
new concessions from the Soviet Union. It was this illusory threat
of an ultimatum, rather than the real threat of German invasion,
which increasingly worried Stalin during the few weeks and days
before 'Barbarossa'. He was not alone. A succession of foreign
statesmen and journalists were also taken in by the planted rumours
of a German ultimatum.[45]

Beria sought to protect his position as head of the NKVD by
expressing mounting indignation at those inside and outside the
NKVD who dared to send reports of preparations for a German
invasion. On 21 June 1941 he ordered four NKVD officers who
persisted in sending such reports to be 'ground into labour camp
dust'. He wrote to Stalin on the same day with his characteristic
mix of brutality and sycophancy:

> I again insist on recalling and punishing our ambassador to
> Berlin, Dekanozov, who keeps bombarding me with 'reports'
> on Hitler's alleged preparations to attack the USSR. He has
> reported that this attack will start tomorrow ...
> But I and my people, Iosif Vissarionovich, have firmly
> embedded in our memory your wise conclusion: Hitler is not
> going to attack us in 1941.[46]

Beria probably also intended to liquidate Fitin for daring to
'bombard' Stalin with false reports of impending German attack.
An SVR official biography concludes, probably correctly, 'Only the
outbreak of war saved P.M. Fitin from the firing squad'.[47]

Recently declassified documents show that the Soviet
ambassador to Britain, Ivan Maisky, considered it prudent to
censor unpalatable news from his wartime reports to Stalin. Thus
Maisky's report on his discussions with Eden and Churchill on 4
September 1941 omitted the fact, which Maisky noted in his
private diary that evening, that Churchill had estimated that a
second front could not be opened until 1944.[48] Maisky was
eventually recalled to Moscow in August 1943, reportedly because
Stalin believed him to be too accommodating in his dealings with
the English, who were 'sabotaging' the opening of a second
front.[49]

It did not, however, occur to the Cambridge Five (Kim Philby, Donald Maclean, Guy Burgess, Anthony Blunt and John Cairncross), probably the ablest group of Soviet wartime agents, to imitate Maisky's political correctness. From 1942 to 1944 they were to be seriously suspected by the Centre of being double agents controlled by British intelligence simply because their voluminous and highly classified intelligence sometimes failed to conform to Stalin's and the Centre's conspiracy theories. In particular, the Five became discredited by their failure to provide evidence of a wartime British plot against the Soviet Union. Of the reality of that non-existent conspiracy, Stalin, and therefore his chief intelligence advisers, had no doubt. In October 1942, Stalin wrote to Maisky, 'All of us in Moscow have gained the impression that Churchill is aiming at the defeat of the USSR, in order then to come to terms with the Germany of Hitler or Brüning at the expense of our country'.[50] Always in Stalin's mind when he brooded on Churchill's supposed wartime conspiracies against him was the figure of Hitler's Deputy Führer, Rudolf Hess, whom, he told Maisky, Churchill was keeping 'in reserve'. In May 1941 Hess had made a bizarre flight to Scotland, in the deluded belief that he could arrange peace between Britain and Germany. Both London and Berlin correctly concluded that Hess was somewhat deranged. Stalin, inevitably, believed instead that Hess's flight was part of a well-laid plot by British intelligence. His suspicions deepened after the German invasion in June. For at least the next two years he suspected that Hess was part of a British conspiracy to abandon its alliance with the Soviet Union and sign a separate peace with Germany.[51]

On 25 October 1943 the Centre informed the London residency that it was now clear, after long analysis of the voluminous intelligence from the Five, that they were double agents, working on the instructions of SIS and MI5. As far back as their years at Cambridge, Philby, Maclean and Burgess had probably been acting on instructions from British intelligence to infiltrate the student Left before making contact with the NKVD. Only thus, the Centre reasoned, was it possible to explain why both SIS and MI5 were currently employing in highly sensitive jobs Cambridge graduates with a Communist background. The lack of any reference to British recruitment of Soviet agents in the intelligence supplied either by 'Söhnchen' (Philby) from SIS or by 'Tony' (Blunt) from MI5 was seen as further evidence that both were being used to feed disinformation to the NKGB: 'During the entire period that S[öhnchen] and T[ony] worked for the British special services, they did not help expose a single valuable ISLANDERS [British] agent either in the USSR or in the Soviet embassy in the ISLAND [Britain]'. There was, of course, no such 'valuable agent' for Philby or Blunt to expose, but that simple possibility did not occur to the conspiracy theorists in the Centre. Philby's accurate report that 'at the present time the HOTEL [SIS] is not engaged in active work against the Soviet Union' was also, in the Centre's view, obvious disinformation.[52]

To try to discover the exact nature of the British intelligence conspiracy, the Centre sent, for the first time ever, a special eight-man surveillance team to the London residency to trail the Five and other supposedly bogus Soviet agents in the hope of discovering their contacts with their non-existent British controllers. The same team also investigated visitors to the Soviet embassy, some of whom were suspected of being MI5 provocateurs. The new surveillance system was hilariously unsuccessful. None of the eight-man team spoke English. All wore conspicuously Russian clothes, were visibly ill at ease in English surroundings, and must frequently have disconcerted those they followed. The Five were not officially absolved of the charge of being British deception agents until after the D-Day landings.[53]

Stalin remained suspicious, however, that his Western allies were involved in a plot to replace Hitler with a conservative German government with which they could negotiate. His suspicions were strengthened by the bomb plot of 20 July 1944, which almost succeeded in killing Hitler. A week later, one of the plotters, Joachim Kuhn, an officer on the German General Staff, succeeded in crossing Red Army lines on the Eastern Front and gave himself up. His account of the bomb plot, which was passed to Stalin, immediately aroused suspicion that he was a plant sent by the pro-Western plotters, possibly with the connivance of Western intelligence, to conceal the anti-Soviet conspiracy being hatched between the plotters and Russia's Western allies. A report by Beria's protégé, Viktor Abakumov, concluded on 23 September:

> Bearing in mind that in Germany Kuhn has been declared a traitor and an active participant of a plot and moreover in his

testimony somewhat talks up his own role in the plot, the possibility is not ruled out that under the pretext of all this he has been planted on our side with some kind of special aims. The above has been reported to comrade Stalin.[54]

Stalin's continued belief in the anti-Soviet machinations of British intelligence were evident when he met Churchill in Moscow in October. At dinner in the Kremlin, Stalin proposed a toast to 'the British Intelligence Service which had inveigled Hess into coming to England', adding, 'He could not have landed without being given signals. The Intelligence Service must have been behind it all'.[55] Kuhn also continued to be viewed with suspicion, despite the fact that he was able to reveal the hiding place of secret documents related to the bomb plot. He eventually lost his reason, probably as a result of attempts to force him to admit to his part in a non-existent anti-Soviet conspiracy.[56]

Stalin was undoubtedly able to extract bargaining advantage at Yalta from his advance knowledge of the British and American bargaining positions provided by Soviet agents (among them Alger Hiss, who was a member of the US delegation), but his conspiratorial mindset prevented him from gaining a serious insight into the far less conspiratorial mindsets of Churchill and Roosevelt. The successes of Soviet intelligence collection during the early Cold War continued to be offset by Stalin's continued role as his own chief intelligence analyst and the tailoring of intelligence reports to his own distorted view of the West. In the spring of 1949, for example, he misinterpreted reports on the imminent withdrawal of US forces from Korea as a move designed to give the South the freedom of action to attack the North. Though the Soviet ambassador in Pyongyang, Terentii Shtykov, had access to North Korean intelligence disproving Stalin's assessment, he dared not report it to him. Instead he selectively reported intelligence which appeared to support Stalin's conclusions. A year later, in the spring of 1950, Stalin made an even more important error in concluding that the United States would not intervene if the North invaded the South. Intelligence from the United States, following its failure to intervene to prevent the Communist victory in China, indicated, he declared, that 'the prevailing mood is not to interfere' in Korea. That erroneous conclusion seems to have been based on his misinterpretation of NSC-48 (probably supplied by Donald

Maclean), which excluded the Asian mainland from the US defence perimeter. Having thus misinterpreted US policy, Stalin was prepared for the first time to allow Kim Il-Sung to attack the South and begin the Korean War.[57]

The Centre's ability to collect intelligence from the West always comfortably exceeded its capacity to interpret what it collected. Moscow was to find it easier to replicate the first atomic bomb than to understand policy-making in Washington and London – for the plans of the bomb provided by Soviet agents in the Los Alamos nuclear laboratories did not have to be adjusted to fit Stalin's distorted understanding of the West. Stalin attached enormous importance to atomic intelligence. After Hiroshima, he summoned Boris Vannikov, the Commissar of Munitions, his deputies, and Igor Kurchatov, the scientist in charge of the atomic programme, to the Kremlin. 'A single demand of you, comrades!', announced Stalin. 'Provide us with atomic weapons in the shortest possible time! You know that Hiroshima has shaken the whole world. The balance [of power] has been destroyed'. To give greater urgency to the project, Stalin transferred control of the project from Molotov to Beria. According to Kurchatov's assistant, Igor Golovin, 'Beria's administrative abilities were obvious to us all ... He was unusually energetic'. All the labour for the project came from the Gulag. Both Stalin and Beria insisted that the Soviet atomic bomb should be an exact copy of the American. Until the successful explosion of the first bomb at the Kazakhstan test site in September 1949, however, they were frequently fearful that some vital American nuclear secret remained undiscovered by their agents in the West.[58]

Stalin's use of his foreign intelligence agencies was not limited to intelligence collection. There were moments both before and after the Great Patriotic War when pursuit of 'enemies of the people' abroad was an even greater priority than discovering the secrets of Western governments. OGPU penetration and surveillance of Russian émigré circles was extensive. Stalin's former assistant Bazhanov, who fled the Soviet Union in 1928, later told French intelligence: 'I often heard Politburo members and major OGPU functionaries say that the émigré organisations were so saturated with [OGPU] agents that at times it was difficult to make out where émigré activities began and [INO's] provocational work ended'.[59] The OGPU also created the 'Union for Return to the Motherland' movement, aimed at encouraging the repatriation of White émigrés to the Soviet Union by exploiting their homesickness and poverty in the West.[60] Stalin's conspiracy theories about the plots being hatched by émigré groups were compounded by fears for his own security.[61] These fears were exacerbated by an OGPU report of a failed attempt to assassinate Stalin in November 1931, in which a ROVS (White Guard) member alleged to have been 'sent by the English intelligence service onto [Soviet] territory', happened to pass Stalin on Il'inka Street in Moscow and tried to draw his revolver, before being restrained by the OGPU agents tailing him.[62]

At the beginning of the 1930s the chief target was the ROVS in Paris, whose leader, General Aleksandr Kutepov, was kidnapped in January 1930 by the OGPU and died while on his way to interrogation and execution in Moscow. Though the ROVS remained a target, and Kutepov's successor, General Evgenii Miller was exfiltrated to Moscow and shot seven years later, Stalin's main target by the mid-1930s was Leon Trotsky. As Isaac Deutscher wrote without great exaggeration in his biography of Trotsky:

> The frenzy with which [Stalin] pursued the feud, making it the paramount preoccupation of international communism as well as of the Soviet Union and subordinating to it all political, tactical, intellectual and other interests, beggars description; there is in the whole of history hardly another case in which such immense resources of power and propaganda were employed against a single individual.[63]

From the spring of 1937 the Centre was increasingly diverted from the war against Franco by what became known as the Civil War within the Civil War. The destruction of Trotskyists became a higher priority than the liquidation of Franco. By the end of 1937 the hunt for 'enemies of the people' abroad took precedence over intelligence collection. INO was in turmoil, caught up in the paranoia of the Great Terror, with most of its officers abroad suspected of plotting with the enemy. During the same period, the ranks of the Comintern were also decimated by a campaign to purge the organisation of mostly non-existent spies. In November 1937, Stalin told Dimitrov that, 'The Trotsk[y]ists [in the Comintern] should be persecuted, shot, destroyed. These are worldwide provocateurs, the most vicious agents of fascism'.[64] The chief European organiser of the Trotskyist movement for most of the 1930s was not Trotsky himself (who left for Mexico in 1937,

having failed to find a secure European base), but his elder son, Lev
Sedov, who from 1933 was based in Paris. It was Sedov who
organised publication of his father's *Bulletin of the Opposition* and
maintained contact with Trotsky's scattered supporters. Sedov's
entourage, like his father's, was penetrated by the OGPU and
NKVD. From 1934 onwards, his closest confidant and collaborator
in Paris was an NKVD agent, the Russian-born Polish Communist
Mark Zborowski, known to Sedov as Étienne. Sedov died in
February 1938 – though it remains unclear whether he was
assassinated by the NKVD or died from natural causes before the
assassins reached him. The NKVD's euphemistically named
Administration for Special Tasks was, however, certainly
responsible for the death of Rudolf Klement, chief organiser of the
founding conference of the Trotskyist Fourth International. Yet the
names Kutepov, Miller, Sedov and Klement are conspicuous by
their absence from many histories of the Stalin era. Such was the
obsession with 'enemies of the people abroad' that in 1938 an
NKVD file was opened on the former head of the 1917 Provisional
Government, Alexander Kerensky, and a considerable range of
intelligence assets – legal and illegal residencies, foreign agents and
Comintern – mobilised to keep track of him.[65]

Studies of Stalin's foreign policy tend to concentrate on what
constituted foreign policy in the West and to omit the more
unorthodox and less wholesome activities of the Administration for
Special Tasks. For Stalin, however, the killing of the leading
Trotskyists was a major foreign policy objective which could be
accomplished only by the NKVD. At the beginning of 1940 he
appears to have been more preoccupied by Trotsky than by Hitler.
Yet Trotsky's assassination in August 1940 is not even mentioned in
the 400 pages of Gabriel Gorodetsky's magisterial study of Stalin's
policy towards Germany from 1939 to 1941.[66]

In the aftermath of the Second World War, covert action to
influence events was once again a greater priority of Soviet foreign
intelligence than intelligence collection. The MGB (post-war
predecessor of the KGB) played a crucial part in the creation of the
post-war Soviet Bloc. Throughout Eastern Europe, Communist-
controlled security services, set up in the image of the MGB and
overseen – except in Yugoslavia and Albania – by Soviet 'advisors',
supervised the transition to so-called 'people's democracies'.
Political development in most East European states followed the

same basic pattern. Coalition governments with significant numbers of non-communist ministers, but with the newly founded security services and the other main levers of power in communist hands, were established immediately after German forces had been driven out. Following intervals ranging from a few months to three years, these governments were replaced by bogus, communist-run coalitions which paved the way for Stalinist one-party states taking their lead from Moscow.

The German communist leader and former NKVD agent, Walter Ulbricht, announced to his inner circle on his return to Berlin from exile in Moscow on 30 April 1945, 'It's got to look democratic, but we must have everything under our control'. Because a democratic façade had to be preserved throughout Eastern Europe, the open use of force to exclude non-communist parties from power had, so far as possible, to be avoided. Instead, the new security services took the lead in intimidation behind the scenes, using what became known in Hungary as 'salami tactics' to slice off one layer of opposition after another. Finally, the one-party people's democracies, purged of all visible dissent, were legitimised by huge and fraudulent communist majorities in elections rigged by the security services. During the early years of the Soviet Bloc, Soviet advisors kept the new security services on a tight rein. The witch-hunts and show trials designed to eliminate from the leadership of the ruling communist parties of Eastern Europe the mostly imaginary supporters of Tito and Zionism with whom Stalin was obsessed were orchestrated from Moscow. Their most celebrated victims were the Hungarian Interior Minister, Laszlo Rajk, and seven 'accomplices' who confessed at a carefully-rehearsed show trial in Budapest to taking part in a vast non-existent plot hatched by Tito and the CIA, and the Secretary-General of the Czechoslovak Communist Party, Rudolf Slánský, and 13 accomplices who confessed at a similar trial in Prague to involvement in an equally imaginary Zionist conspiracy to overthrow the 'popular democratic regime'.[67]

The final act of Stalin's foreign policy before he died in 1953 was a plan to assassinate Josip Tito (then codenamed 'Stervyatnik', 'Carrion Crow'), who had succeeded Trotsky as the leading heretic of the Soviet Bloc. The chosen assassin was one of the most remarkable of all Soviet illegals, Iosif Grigulevich (then codenamed 'Maks'), who had taken a leading part in the first, narrowly unsuccessful, attempt on Trotsky's life in Mexico City in May 1940,

later acquired a false identity as the Costa Rican citizen Teodoro
Castro, and in 1951 became Costa Rican *chargé d'affaires* (later
Minister Plenipotentiary) in Rome.[68] Since Costa Rica had no
diplomatic mission in Belgrade, Grigulevich was also able to obtain
the post of non-resident envoy to Yugoslavia. The MGB reported to
Stalin in February 1953:

> While fulfilling his diplomatic duties in the second half of the
> year 1952, ['Maks'] twice visited Yugoslavia, where he was
> well received. He had access to the social group close to Tito's
> staff and was given the promise of a personal audience with
> Tito. The post held by MAKS at the present time makes it
> possible to use his capabilities for active measures against
> Tito.[69]

Grigulevich volunteered for the role of assassin. At a secret meeting
with senior MGB officers in Vienna early in February 1953
Grigulevich suggested four possible ways to eliminate 'Carrion
Crow' when he finally met him. The Centre asked him to submit
more detailed proposals. In the meantime it assured Stalin that
there was no doubt that 'MAKS, because of his personal qualities
and experience in intelligence work, is capable of accomplishing a
mission of this kind'.[70]

The use of an accredited Central American diplomat as Tito's
assassin was intended to conceal as effectively as possible the hand
of the MGB. Using his Costa Rican alias, Grigulevich composed a
farewell letter addressed to his Mexican wife to be made public and
used to reinforce his Latin American cover if he were captured or
killed during the assassination attempt. On 1 March 1953, the
MGB reported to Stalin that 'Maks''s attempt to 'rub out' Tito had,
unfortunately, not yet succeeded. This disappointing report, which
Stalin read at about midnight, may well have been the last
intelligence document he saw before suffering a fatal stroke in the
early hours of 2 March.[71]

Much further research is still required on Stalin's use of
intelligence and his intelligence services. Though no biographer of
Churchill nowadays fails to mention his passion for Ultra, Stalin's
biographers invariably ignore his own interest in Sigint (signals
intelligence) altogether – partly (but by no means wholly) because
of the continued classification of the Soviet inter-war and wartime
Sigint archive. Historians of Soviet foreign policy during the Cold

War continue to show a similar lack of curiosity about the role of Sigint, despite the availability of intelligence documents which show, for example, that in 1960 alone the KGB forwarded no less than 133,000 diplomatic decrypts to the Central Committee.[72] The failure to give due weight to the role of intelligence in studies of Stalin is thus merely one example of a more general failure to take adequate account of the operations of the KGB and its predecessors in histories of Soviet foreign policy.

NOTES

1. T.R. Samolis (ed.), *Veterany vneshnei razvedki Rossii: kratkii biograficheskii spravochnik* (Moscow: SVR Press, 1995). The editor, Tat'yana Samolis, was spokeswoman for the SVR. One striking example of this volume's reverential attitude towards the pious myths created by the KGB is its highly sanitised account of the frequently unsavoury career of Hero of the Soviet Union Stanislav Alekseevich Vaupshasov; cf. Christopher Andrew and Vasili Mitrokhin, *The Mitrokhin Archive*, vol.1, *The KGB in Europe and the West* (London: Penguin, 1999), p.97.
2. Evgenii Primakov *et al.* (eds.), *Ocherki istorii rossiiskoi vneshnei razvedki* (Moscow: Mezhdunarodnye otnosheniya, 1995–).
3. 'The Bomb' (1996) celebrates the heroic achievements of the KGB's 'Big Atomic Five' – Leonid Kvasnikov, Anatoli Yatskov, Vladimir Barkovskii, Semen Semenov and Aleksandr Feklisov – in using their Anglo-Soviet agents to acquire the plans of the first atomic bomb and so end the US monopoly of nuclear weapons. 'The Cambridge Five' (2000) eulogises what the SVR describes as an 'a unique agent network' – Kim Philby, Donald Maclean, Guy Burgess, Anthony Blunt and John Cairncross: 'The contribution of this group to informing the USSR leadership during the pre-war period and the victory over fascist Germany, to the creation of a just post-war world order and to the liquidation of the USA's nuclear monopoly, is incalculable'. 'The Red Orchestra' (2001) similarly celebrates 'the activities and struggle of the most important anti-fascist organisation and simultaneously the most important agent network of USSR foreign political intelligence in Germany on the eve of and during the Great Patriotic War'. For details of these and other SVR historical videos, see http://www.svr.gov.ru/material/video.html.
4. There is no space in this article for a detailed analysis of the controversial and complex question of whether Stalin had been an agent of the Tsarist *Okhrana*. Most of the contents of Stalin's *Okhrana* file were later destroyed – doubtless, on Stalin's orders, to remove compromising material. Stalin also went to great pains to falsify both the day and the year of his birth. Though most of his biographers give his date of birth as 9 December 1879 (in the Tsarist calendar), recent research has established that he was born on 6 December 1878. Stalin may have been prompted to make this change by fear that, even if all reference to himself by name as an *Okhrana* agent had been eradicated from the files, there might still exist somewhere in the Tsarist archive a reference to an agent identified only by codename whose date of birth was 6 December 1878, Andrew and Mitrokhin (note 1), vol.1, p.36. The most detailed English-language analysis of the evidence linking Stalin to the *Okhrana* is Roman Brackman, *The Secret File of Joseph Stalin* (London: Frank Cass,

2001). However, the only surviving documents in the State Archive of the Russian Federation which clearly identify Stalin as an *Okhrana* agent, cited by Brackman, are of dubious authenticity; Z.I. Peregudova, *Politicheskii sysk Rossii. 1880–1917* (Moscow: ROSSPEN, 2000).

5. Svetlana Lokhova, 'The Evolution of the Cheka, 1917–1926', unpublished M.Phil. thesis, Cambridge University, 2002, pp.43–5.

6. Aleksandr Plekhanov, 'Dzerzhinskii khotel posadit' Beriya', *Vek* 31 (2002), available at: http://www.fsb.ru/history/autors/plehanov.html.

7. Brackman (note 4), p.192. We are not convinced by Brackman's argument that Stalin had Dzerzhinskii poisoned.

8. See, for example, Stalin's detailed response to a report from Menzhinskii of 2 October 1930 with his proposals/instructions for redrafting the 'script' for the Promparty trial, reproduced in Diane P. Koenker and Ronald D. Bachman (eds.), *Revelations from the Russian Archives: Documents in English Translation* (Washington, DC: Library of Congress, 1997), p.240.

9. Nikolai Sidorov, 'Kak Stalin Feliksa zarubil', *Ogonek*, no.50, 14 December 1998.

10. Christopher Andrew and Oleg Gordievsky, *KGB: The Inside Story of its Foreign Operations from Lenin to Gorbachev*, paperback edn. (London: Sceptre, 1991), pp.125–6.

11. Sergei Konstantinov, 'Malen'kii chelovek?', *Nezavisimaya gazeta*, 13 April 2000, available at: http://ng.ru/style/2000-04-13/16_ezhov.html.

12. Marc Jansen and Nikita Petrov, *Stalin's Loyal Executioner: People's Commissar Nikolai Ezhov, 1895–1940* (Stanford, CA: Hoover Institution Press, 2002), p.207.

13. Svetlana Alliluyeva, *Only One Year* (London: Hutchinson, 1969).

14. Amy W. Knight, *Beria: Stalin's First Lieutenant* (Princeton: Princeton University Press, 1993).

15. Plekhanov (note 6).

16. See V.M. Chebrikov *et al.* (eds.), *Istoriya sovetskikh organov gosudarstvennoi bezopasnosti* (Moscow: 1977), p.215, available at: http://www.fas.harvard.edu/~hpcws/KGBhistory.htm, for an account of similar measures undertaken by OGPU in the late 1920s.

17. Andrew and Gordievsky (note 10), ch.4.

18. V.N. Khaustov, 'Nekotorye problemy deyatel'nosti organov gosbezopasnosti v 1920–1930-e gody', *Istoricheskie chteniya na Lubyanke 1999 god. Otechestvennye spetssluzhby v 20–30-e gody*, available at the FSB's official website: http://www.fsb.ru/history/read/1999/haustov.html.

19. There had, however, been an SIS presence in the British trade delegation in Moscow in the early 1920s.

20. Christopher Andrew, *Secret Service: The Making of the British Intelligence Community*, 3rd edn. (London: Sceptre, 1992), p.573. Though inter-war SIS files remain closed, the most important SIS attempt to penetrate the Soviet Union during the 1930s appears to have been run by the head of its Prague station, Harold 'Gibby' Gibson. Archival material released by the SVR to celebrate what it regarded as its 80th birthday on 20 December 2000 plausibly indicates that Gibson's supposedly reliable agent network in Moscow, which he believed included Party officials, was in reality the fictitious creation of Soviet intelligence. Claims that this network was used as a major instrument of deception which had 'London's ruling circles dancing to Moscow's tunes' are, however, wildly exaggerated. Petr Sukhanov, 'Lubyanskaya "Tarantella"', *Nezavisimoe voennoe obozrenie*, 22 December 2000.

21. A top secret 1977 KGB-produced textbook on the history of the Soviet state security organs shows the extent to which Britain's intelligence presence in the

USSR during this period was exaggerated. The authors claim that,

> Several autonomous English secret services carried out subversive work against the Soviet state [in the late 1920s] ... The SIS had a special Russian section, engaged in the organisation of subversive work against the USSR directly from London and via its residencies in countries bordering on the Soviet Union (in Finland, Estonia, Latvia, Poland, Romania, Persia, Afghanistan, China and Japan), and also in states with Soviet diplomatic representation or ... significant numbers of White Guards (in Germany, France, Austria, Bulgaria, Yugoslavia, Czechoslovakia, Iraq, Palestine). In addition to the SIS, subversive work against the USSR was conducted by Scotland Yard, Indian secret service, and also the intelligence sections of a series of ministries (military, naval, aviation, foreign affairs and trade). Military, naval and aviation attachés, staff of diplomatic institutions, the crews of commercial vessels visiting Soviet ports, and agents recruited on USSR territory, were used to gather espionage information about the Soviet Union. From 1926 English intelligence also used the intelligence organs of Finland, Latvia, Lithuania, Poland and Romania to carry out subversion actions, pushing their French allies out of the intelligence services of these countries.

Chebrikov *et al.* (note 16), pp.184–5. In a similar vein, a recently published Russian history asserts that Western special services 'continued to step up intelligence activities against the USSR' in the 1930s; that the British created a special centre in Vienna for the recruitment of Austrians who were then sent on missions to the USSR undercover as 'specialists', and that the Americans set up a residency in Latvia for work with 'local White Guard youth organisations', A.I. Kolpakidi and M.L. Seryakov, *Shchit i mech. Rukovoditeli organov gosudarstvennoi bezopasnosti Moskovskoi Rusi, Rossiiskoi imperii, Sovetskogo Soyuza i Rossiiskoi Federatsii* (St Petersburg and Moscow: Neva and OLMA-PRESS Obrazovanie, 2002), p.394.

22. Christopher Andrew, *For The President's Eyes Only: Secret Intelligence and the American Presidency from Washington to Bush* (New York and London: HarperCollins, 1995), pp.212–13.

23. After Francesco Constantini was sacked for dishonesty in 1935 by the British embassy (which failed, however, to realise that he was a Soviet agent), his brother, Secondo, continued supplying British diplomatic documents to Soviet intelligence until 1937, when the Centre wrongly suspected that he was part of an elaborate British or Italian deception. Andrew and Mitrokhin (note 1), vol.1, pp.46–7, 64–5, 67–9.

24. Ibid., vol.1, chs.3–4.

25. Primakov *et al.* (note 2), vol.3, ch.13. The original text of the Foreign Office records of the talks with Hitler, Litvinov, Beck, Beneš and Mussolini are published in W.N. Medlicott *et al.* (eds.), *Documents on British Foreign Policy* (London: HMSO), 2nd series, vol.12 (1972), pp.703–46, 771–91, 803–10, 812–17; vol.13 (1973), pp.477–84; vol.14 (1976), pp.329–33. The version of the record of Simon's and Eden's talks with Hitler given to Stalin consisted of translated extracts rather than the full Foreign Office document (see below, n.33, p.92). The same probably applies to the records given to Stalin of Eden's talks with Litvinov, Beck, Beneš and Mussolini, which are not yet accessible.

26. Constantini may well not have been the only source for the document. The Foreign Office record of Simon's and Eden's talks with Hitler, also in March 1935, was provided by both King and Constantini.

27. Eden's meeting with Stalin took place in the Kremlin on 30 March 1935, following his talks with Litvinov during the previous two days. His telegram on the talks to the Foreign Office records that a copy was sent to the Rome Embassy. Medlicott *et al.* (note 25), 2nd series, vol.12, pp.766–9.

28. Wellington A. Samouce, 'I Do Understand The Russians', pp.52–3, Samouce papers, US Army Military Institute, Carlisle Barracks, PA. Andrew and Gordievsky (note 10), pp.237–40. As of the late 1930s, bugging devices were also used as a matter of course in places frequented by foreigners, such as restaurants; see Chebrikov *et al.* (note 16), p.309.
29. George Kennan, *Memoirs 1950–1963* (New York: Pantheon Books, 1983), pp.154–7. Andrew and Gordievsky (note 10), pp.454–6. A replica of the bugged seal is on display in the International Spy Museum, Washington, DC. Kennan was declared *persona non grata* in October 1952, though chiefly for reasons unconnected with the bugging incident.
30. Aleksandr Orlov, *Handbook of Intelligence and Guerilla Warfare* (Ann Arbor: University of Michigan Press, 1963), p.10; John Costello and Oleg Tsarev, *Deadly Illusions* (London: Century, 1993), p.90; Alexander Fursenko and Timothy Naftali, 'Soviet Intelligence and the Cuban Missile Crisis', *Intelligence and National Security* 13/3 (1998), p.66.
31. Gabriel Gorodetsky, *Grand Delusion: Stalin and the German Invasion of Russia* (New Haven: Yale University Press, 1999), p.53. Towards the end of Ezhov's leadership of the NKVD, Stalin came to suspect Ezhov of collecting compromising materials against him; see Jansen and Petrov (note 12), p.176.
32. Primakov *et al.* (note 2), vol.3, pp.6, 161, 245.
33. The Foreign Office record of the meeting, held on 25–26 March 1935, is printed in Medlicott *et al.* (note 25), 2nd series, vol.12, pp.703–45. In the course of the meeting, Hitler suggested an Anglo-German naval agreement with a 100:35 ratio in favour of the Royal Navy. This formed the basis of an agreement concluded in London on 18 June 1935.
34. The abbreviated Russian translation of the Foreign Office record of the talks is published as an appendix to Primakov *et al.* (note 2), vol.3, pp.461–7. An editorial note (appendix, n.11) asserts that, by his statement on Austria, Simon 'opened the path to the *Anschluss*'.
35. Primakov *et al.* (note 2), vol.3, p.6.
36. Ibid., vol.3, p.155.
37. Minute by R.A. Sykes, 23 Oct. 1952, FO 371/100826, NS 1023/29/G, Public Record Office (PRO).
38. Samolis (note 1), p.64.
39. Ibid., p.154. Some of the intelligence warnings of the preparations for 'Barbarossa' are printed as appendices to Primakov *et al.* (note 2), vol.3.
40. The report and Stalin's comment on it were published in *Izvestia of the Central Committee of the CPSU*, April 1990; cf. Costello and Tsarev (note 30), p.86.
41. Andrew and Gordievsky (note 10), pp.275, 282. Gordon W. Prange *et al.*, *Target Tokyo: The Story of the Sorge Spy Ring* (New York: McGraw Hill, 1985), chs.42–7.
42. JIC(41)218(Final), CAB 81/102, PRO. On Churchill's warnings to Stalin, see Gabriel Gorodetsky, *Stafford Cripps' Mission to Moscow 1940–42* (Cambridge: Cambridge University Press, 1984) chs.2–4. Exactly which JIC reports reached Stalin, and in what form, cannot be determined at present. But, given both the volume of highly classified intelligence from London and the numerous JIC assessments which contradicted Churchill's belief that Hitler was planning an invasion of Russia, Stalin must surely have been aware of the JIC view. The files noted by Mitrokhin show that Stalin had access to at least some of the telegrams exchanged between the Foreign Office and the British ambassador in Moscow, Sir Stafford Cripps.
43. Andrew and Gordievsky (note 10), p.274.
44. Andrew and Mitrokhin (note 1), vol.1, p.123.

45. Barton Whaley, *Codeword Barbarossa* (Cambridge, MA: MIT Press, 1974), pp.223–4, 241–3.

46. Arkady Vaksberg, *The Prosecutor and the Prey: Vyshinsky and the 1930s Moscow Show Trials* (London: Weidenfeld and Nicolson, 1990), p.220.

47. Samolis (note 1), p.154.

48. V.V. Sokolov, 'I. M. Maiskii mezhdu I.V. Stalinym i U. Cherchillem v pervye mesyatsy voiny', *Novaya i noveishaya istoriya* 6 (November–December 2001), pp.27–8.

49. As recalled by Maiskii's successor, Gusev, cited M. Yu. Myagkov, 'I.V. Stalin i U. Cherchill' v gody voiny. Po materialam seminara v Londone', *Novaya i noveishaya istoriya* 4 (July–August 2002), pp.90–1.

50. Jonathan Haslam, 'Stalin's Fears of a Separate Peace 1942', *Intelligence and National Security* 8 (1993), pp.97–9.

51. Andrew and Gordievsky (note 10), pp.273–4, 305; Rainer F. Schmidt, 'Der Hess-Flug und das Kabinet Churchill. Hitlers Stellvertreter im Kalkül der Britischen Kriegsdiplomatie', *Vierteljahreshefte für Zeitgeschichte* 42 (1993).

52. Genrikh Borovik, *The Philby Files* (London: Little Brown, 1994), pp.216–18.

53. Andrew and Mitrokhin (note 1), vol.1, pp.157–60, 165–6.

54. Boris Khavkin, 'Gitler i Stalin protiv mayora Kuna', *Novoe vremya*, no.12, 17 March 2002. For a more detailed account of the Kuhn case, see 'Novyi istochnik po istorii zagovora protiv Gitlera 20 iyulya 1944 g. iz Tsentral'nogo arkhiva FSB Rossii', *Novaya i noveishaya istoriya* 3 (May–June 2002), pp.148–79.

55. British record of dinner at the Kremlin, 18 Oct. 1944, FO 800/414, PRO.

56. Khavkin (note 54).

57. Kathryn Weathersby, '"Should We Fear This?" Stalin and the Danger of War with America', Cold War International History Project, Working Paper no.40 (July 2002), accessible on www.cwhip.si.edu.

58. Andrew and Gordievsky (note 10), pp.383–6; Andrew and Mitrokhin (note 1), vol.1, pp.173–5; David Holloway, *Stalin and the Bomb* (New Haven: Yale University Press, 1994).

59. '"Unichtozhit' vragov, predvaritel'no ikh obmanuv"', *Istochnik* 6 (2001), p.38. Bazhanov also stated that the movement to repatriate Soviet émigrés – 'to destroy enemies, having first deceived them' – was an OGPU initiative based on the argument that 'any enemy of the regime was much more dangerous abroad than in Russia', an idea which was then taken up by the Politburo.

60. See further B.G. Strukov, 'Bor'ba OGPU protiv rossiiskoi politicheskoi emigratsii', *Istoricheskie chteniya na Lubyanke 1999 g. Otechestvennye spetssluzhby v 20–30-e gody*, available at: http://www.fsb.ru/history/read/1999/strukov.html.

61. Ibid., p.65.

62. Molotov circulated the report to Politburo members, noting that Stalin should no longer go around Moscow on foot; '"Agent angliiskoi razvedki sluchaino vstretil Vas"', *Vestnik Arkhiva Prezidenta Rossiiskoi Federatsii* 3 (1996), pp.161–2. The incident is also mentioned in A.I. Kolpakidi and D.P. Prokhorov, *KGB: Spetsoperatsii sovetskoi razvedki* (Moscow: Olimp, Astrel' and AST, 2000), p.21.

63. Isaac Deutscher, *Trotsky*, vol.3, *The Prophet Outcast, 1929–1940*, paperback edn. (Oxford: Oxford University Press, 1970), pp.125–6.

64. Jansen and Petrov (note 12), p.101.

65. Kerensky continued to be kept under surveillance even during the Second World War. There is uncorroborated testimony by Pavel Sudoplatov that there were plans to assassinate him as late as 1952. V.V. Gurzhiya, 'Razvedka NKVD protiv A.F. Kerenskogo', *Novaya i noveishaya istoriya* 6 (November–December 2001).

66. Gorodetsky (note 31).

67. Andrew and Gordievsky (note 10), ch.9.
68. Andrew and Mitrokhin (note 1), vol.1, pp.114–15, 130–2, 212–13, 464–6.
69. MGB report to Stalin, first published by Dmitri Volkogonov in *Izvestiya*, 11 June 1993; reprinted in 'Stalin's Plan to Assassinate Tito', *Cold War International History Project Bulletin* 10 (1998), p.137.
70. MGB report to Stalin, first published by Dmitri Volkogonov in *Izvestiya*, 11 June 1993.
71. After Stalin's death three days later, plans for the assassination were suspended. Two months later Grigulevich was hurriedly withdrawn to Moscow when the pre-war Soviet defector, Aleksandr Orlov, began publishing reminiscences of Stalin and the NKVD in *Life* magazine. The Centre feared that Orlov, who knew of Grigulevich's sabotage missions before and during the Spanish Civil War, might blow his cover – though, in the event, he did not do so. So far as the puzzled Costa Rican Foreign Ministry and Rome diplomatic corps were concerned, Grigulevich and his wife simply disappeared into thin air. Andrew and Mitrokhin (note 1), vol.1, p.466.
72. Andrew and Mitrokhin (note 1), vol.1, ch.21.

6

Stalin's Martyrs:
The Tragic Romance of the
Russian Revolution

MICHAEL G. SMITH

Ludwig: My question is this. You have been repeatedly exposed to risks and dangers. You have been persecuted. You have participated in battles. Several of your closest friends have been killed. Yet you remain alive. How do you explain this? Do you believe in fate?
Stalin: No, I do not. Bolsheviks, Marxists, do not believe in 'fate'. The whole concept of 'fate', of Schicksal, is a prejudice, nonsense, a vestige of mythology, like the mythology of the ancient Greeks, whose heavenly gods steered human fates.
Ludwig: So the fact that you were not killed is coincidence?
Stalin: There are both external and internal reasons, the totality of which has resulted in my not being killed. But regardless of this, someone else might have taken my place, for someone surely *had to* sit here. 'Fate' is something strange, something mystical. I do not believe in mysticism. There were of course reasons that danger passed me by. But there could have been a whole series of other coincidences that could have led to an altogether opposite result. These had nothing to do with so-called fate.[1]

I offer this brief passage from Emil Ludwig's 1931 interview with I.V. Stalin (Dzhugashvili) more for the significance of the question than the answer. Dzhugashvili, whose given name I am using in an effort to demythologise and historicise the person, was circumspect. His life was something less than fate (*sud'ba*); but something more than mere coincidence (*sluchainost'*). He only cited a modest 'totality' of reasons for his survival. It is not a very revealing answer given the kinds of hubris we find in his biographies and writings. He could have easily referred to the certainty of the Marxian dialectic, or to the beneficence of the Party will, or to the strength of his own character. But as for the question, it was as provocative and 'startling' as Ludwig had promised. And if Dzhugashvili did not answer it so completely, then we need to explore other possible answers in his world: namely in the cult of martyrdom and redemption, founded upon Karl Marx's tragic reading of history, that governed Bolshevik ideology and Dzhugashvili's place within it.

Marxist socialism was a political movement haunted by several kinds of tragedies: in the bourgeoisie, the class that had given so much to history but was imperilled by the fatal flaw of its own inner contradictions; or in the proletariat, which was fated to suffer through humiliating but redemptive traumas of violence like the Paris Commune of 1871. Marx raised a benevolent mortality for these tragic villains and heroes of revolutionary struggle. Some revolutionaries were more valuable to the cause dead than alive. His was a 'Tragic account of history', one both 'heroic and militant in tone'.[2] 'Tragedy' carries a variety of meanings. It can express the whole structure of a plot, spiralling downward from possibility and nobility into dejection and defeat. Or it can represent one moment in the upward, salvation trajectory of a romance. I will examine Soviet representations of 'tragedy' in this second sense.[3]

Tragedy was a crucial element in the tortured ethic of Socialist Realism that wound its way through literature, history-writing, the popular media and daily life. In formal terms, Socialist Realism was a 'revolutionary romanticism'.[4] It displayed Marxism's faith in the future 'realm of freedom', a soundly romantic myth about the progressive course of history. Its stories verged on the melodramatic in their stylised, often flat portrayals of villains and heroes, protagonists struggling through actual experience toward ideal utopia. The plot always led to ultimate victory. But these stories also required eternal vigilance against enemies within and without, even within the deepest recesses of the best communist. There was always some anguish or pathos, that moment of death or disaster urging the hero on to victory.[5] The romance of Marxist communism demanded the existential contemplation of this tragic moment. It gave the stories of Socialist Realism their traction and depth, their bounce.[6] It even made these stories, in literature and through history, more tragic than melodramatic, more tragic than romantic.[7]

The Russian Bolsheviks enshrined Marx's general philosophy of violence, class struggle, into their own particular culture of violence: as both the objects of Tsarist oppression and the subjects of their own kinds of class terror in turn. Looking ahead to the gathering dangers of the twentieth century, Semen Frank recognised this dynamic at work in the false 'asceticism' of Russian populists and terrorists, 'the strength of self-sacrifice and the resolve to sacrifice others'.[8] Looking backward upon its remains, Katerina Clark recognised that 'the increasing emphasis on revolutionary sacrifice in Stalinist hagiography more or less coincides with the increasing "sacrifice" in Soviet political practice, i.e., with the intensification of the purges'.[9] There was a raw honesty in this practical law of the revolutionary. The Bolsheviks were only willing to dispense that which they were also willing to suffer. The pain that the Bolsheviks received from their enemies became the pain they returned, acts of revolutionary violence to redeem them and the world.[10]

For some historians, this compulsion to violence has been endemic to Russian history at large. For others, it has been one aspect of Russia's experiences in modern war and revolution.[11] I will explore this culture of violence as a context within which Dzhugashvili worked and ruled. So many of his critical biographies get too personal. We see the vengeful Georgian, rooted in the literary personage of 'Koba the Avenger', acting out the age-old blood vendetta against personal slights and professional disagreements. Or we see the scheming Orthodox seminarian, five years of religious schooling leaving him with a 'liturgical' style: catechistic, declamatory, dogmatic and literal.[12] But the Bolshevik discourse of suffering and redemption played its part in his professional conduct, too. There was a narrative fold in Dzhugashvili's life, bound to the larger history of Leninism and the longer history of Bolshevism, stitched together by the threads of tragic memory.[13] At significant moments in his life and once in his own death, he appealed to the deaths of fellow comrades to promote his professional career and his own historical legacy. With compatriots in the party, he contributed to the revolutionary martyrologies of these victims, calling forth religious sensibilities to heighten the public awareness of immediate loss and to validate class struggle.[14] For them, tragedy expressed enduring values about the certainty of human mortality and the promises of social immortality; about the falsehoods of personal identity and the truths of ideological representation; about the vulnerability of the individual and the power of the collective. Tragedy represented a moment of renovation, a point of genesis.

These terms offer us entries into the proto-religious and totalitarian pretensions of the Soviet regime. Bolshevism as a 'political religion' has been one of the most enduring of investigative methods in the scholarship.[15] The study of 'totalitarian subjectivity' is more recent, as scholars of varying approaches have investigated the writings of Stalinism's speaking 'subjects' for their surface and deep meanings, for values imparted and to some degree believed.[16] Dzhugashvili has been placed under a similar microscope, Alfred Reiber's 'politics of personal identity'.[17] This makes perfect sense. If the ordinary subjects of Stalinism are valid objects of study, then its leading subject is, too. He must have believed some if not all of the propaganda written about him. There must be traces of his self-perceptions in the words he and others left to posterity.

There is nothing especially unique in these patterns. State dynasties, national movements and political parties pretended to a totalising religious legitimacy long before the Bolsheviks ever did. The nation, not so much the church, was their model of inspiration. When the Bolsheviks constructed a cult of violent sacrifice and veneration of martyrs, they were adapting to a European model. They were also, I would argue, transforming their class values into national vales. Their rituals of mourning and commemoration delineated a circle of beliefs and behaviours that was already becoming national, already creating the 'horizontal comradeship' of the nation.[18] The Bolshevik cause, like any good king or flag or nation before it, was worth dying for.

The Revolutionary Underground: Martyrs and Ritual

For the Bolsheviks, from the seemingly losing side of history, from the depths of the underground, class struggle was a fact of life. Russian revolutionaries transformed their plight into a crystalline culture of violence. In their political trials after 1870, they perfected a theatricality and performance ethic, inverting the procedure and setting of the legal stage to highlight the drama of class struggle. They developed a 'secularised religious sensibility' in the working class and intelligentsia, an ethic of asceticism and moralism highlighting their self-sacrifices and collective immortality, their pursuit of the common good and conceit of purpose.[19] Like Marx, but perhaps with more devotion than sarcasm, they borrowed the words and images of Christianity, the sacrificial person of Jesus Christ and the redemptive symbol of the 'cross', to give vent to their suffering.[20] In each of these cases, the 'language' of Bolshevism was beholden to the wealth of meanings from modern standard Russian and from Old Church Slavonic. It was not a language at all, but an idiom, often a sacred vocabulary turned profane, infused with new political meanings and purposes, but consistently applying older verbal forms. Depending on the source and the moment, it could be either a mark of sincere religious fervour or a simple act of subversive translation. This is an insight worth remembering. The Bolsheviks, no matter how hard they tried to make things anew, consistently inhabited a world of older forms: in their physical spaces, in their values and customs, in their very persons and in their language.

'Red funerals', as Thomas Trice has canvassed the phenomenon after 1870, fused the best of revolutionary theatricality and proto-religiosity. These were public commemorations for the 'victims of capital', those killed from industrial accidents or political murders. They offered a release for the earnest and zealous members of the revolutionary movement; served as reservoirs of their intense emotion. The red funeral was the perfect ritual; a 'revolution in ritual form', in Trice's words. It joined vertical and horizontal space in a web of sensations and impressions: the raised banners and wreaths; the dead body and catafalque; the marchers, police escort and onlookers; the choirs and their hymns; the fiery speeches at the grave. These funerals were reverent. They plumbed a universal emotional depth: certain death. Everyone, regardless of political sympathy, identified. They were, like similar rituals throughout Europe, a delicate balance of the 'sacred and secular'.[21] But they also turned the dead body into a prop: flaunting revolutionary resistance along the boulevards of power and wealth, affirming revolutionary ideals through the subversion and 'desacralisation' of the values of the Orthodox state.[22]

How did Dzhugashvili fit within this culture? The historical record, and his own revisions and falsifications of it, reveals that he mastered the art of performance, the idiom of proto-religiosity, and the cult of violence and martyrdom. The official biographies of the personality cult recounted his exploits in Tiflis, Batum and Baku, junctions along the young man's path to consciousness and leadership, where as 'pupil' and 'apprentice' (not yet a 'master') he was 'baptised in revolutionary combat'.[23] This baptism included organising the first May Day and similar demonstrations in Tiflis after 1901, which Dzhugashvili claimed created a kind of sacrificial 'democracy' of the knout. The violent 'street demonstration', he argued, strategically joined political rebels and 'curious onlookers', people attracted to the scandal and spectacle, to 'the lash of the Cossack's whips'. As they drew closer to the scene of savagery, they came to share blows with the rebels, joining them. 'Every militant who falls in the struggle, or who is torn out of our ranks, rouses hundreds of new fighters'.[24] The ultimate victory of the proletariat was ensured by such temporary defeats. The life of the Party was born in this violent clash, this moment of possible death.

Dzhugashvili and his biographers cultivated his standing as a comrade of martyrs, especially Vladimir Z. Ketskhoveli and Aleksandr G. Tsulukidze, who together were said to have forged Georgian Bolshevism. He appeared as faithful friend to them while they were alive, their humble successor after their deaths.[25] Among his earliest achievements were several funeral speeches, including those for his lost friends, framed within the rhetoric of class violence and comradely pathos, two of his hallmark themes as a young agitator and propagandist.[26] He came to see the red funeral as a potent kind of street demonstration. During a 9 March 1902 workers' protest in Batum, at which some 15 were killed and over 50 wounded, Dzhugashvili was said to have stoically 'stood in the midst of the turbulent sea of workers' orchestrating the action, even nursing one of the casualties with his own hands. He also apparently helped to organise the funerals, which 'turned into a grand political demonstration against Tsarism', a common refrain of the literature. In words later assigned to him, he called the victims sanctified, regal 'martyrs' for the cause, ghosts whose 'pale and faltering lips' cried for justice. He repeated these images in coming years, tapping into the street politics of 'fallen victims' and class 'vengeance'.[27] A painting of the protest from the 1930s shows him baring his chest and clenching his fists before the bullets. In retrospect, but perhaps also at the moment, he fancied himself a living martyr, a martyr survivor.[28] As he intimated in his interview with Ludwig, he could have been killed at any time.

Dzhugashvili never spoke over Ketskhoveli's grave.[29] But he did participate in the 1905 funeral for Tsulukidze. With other Bolsheviks, he marched in the procession and spoke over the body. A later painting of the scene showed him raising a solemn oath in Tsulukidze's memory. His 'big speech' promised that the crowds would someday return to the grave proclaiming, 'We have won!'[30] One of his Menshevik rivals, R. Arsenidze, remembered the events with a twist. He described how Dzhugashvili, after supposedly losing a debate with a Menshevik opponent after the funeral, tried to hide the loss by having his comrades carry him out of the debate as if he were the champion. Aghast at the indiscretion, Arsenidze recounted the 'triumphal procession of eight men bearing upon their arms one man, the ninth', implying that Dzhugashvili presumed to inherit the very authority of the just-buried corpse. What a stunning example of his appreciation for the authority of the dead. Having just proceeded along the path of the funeral with the corpse, he now traversed it, as if he were returning from the dead, like a modern-day Lazarus, or perhaps simply as the 'new' Tsulukidze.[31]

In Dzhugashvili's recorded memory, as in the ledger of historical facts, his days in oil-rich Baku were perhaps the most formative: where he became 'Stalin', where 'the oil workers had served to steel me as a practical fighter', where the 'acute and stormy conflicts' had 'taught me for the first time to know what leading large masses of workers meant'.[32] He proudly claimed that 'he literally won Baku for Bolshevism', this in the context of the widening Stolypin reaction and a waning Bolshevik Party elsewhere in Russia. As he once wrote nostalgically, 'If you ain't seen the forest of oil drills', referring to the inspiring industrial wasteland, 'you ain't seen nothin' yet'.[33]

The city had witnessed its share of red funerals. One of the most memorable was the commemoration for the worker activist, Petr Montin, murdered in December 1905 in suspicious circumstances. Demonstrators and onlookers filled the streets of Baku to bid farewell. 'All life in the city of Baku was frozen still on that day', wrote one memoirist. Most moving was the sermon of an Orthodox priest who compared Montin to Jesus Christ: he was the 'dead comrade who also brought truth to the people and was also killed'.[34] A Russian Social Democratic Labour Party (RSDLP) pamphlet of the time, dedicated to several other worker-victims, recalled Dzhugashvili's own rhetoric: these men 'had not fallen in vain', for their sacrifice had revealed the utter decay of Tsarism and had called forth new workers to the cause 'by the tenfold'.[35] Orchestrating red funerals like Montin's, so one of Dzhugashvili's biographers claimed, proved his charisma and leadership. The pathos of the red funeral was the ground upon which his voice resounded for class struggle, to 'incite hatred in the masses' for their oppressors, and for the arming of the proletariat into fighting squads for their self-defence.[36]

Among Baku's red funerals, Khanlar Säfäräliyev's was unique. He had been a member of the RSDLP and a leader of its Muslim faction, shot on 19 September 1907 during a labour protest. It was a typical affair: a 'mass army of thousands' was said to 'bear its chest' in his belated defence.[37] But as a Muslim, Khanlar was buried according to the rites of Shi'a Islam, reflecting the yearly Mühärräm rituals, commemorations of the martyrdom of the Imam Huseyn, filled with graphic public renderings of the sad story and colourful processions of flagellants and mourners. With Bolshevik collusion, so I have argued elsewhere, Khanlar's funeral and gravesite, like other funerals and cemeteries in the Shi'ite tradition, exploited even these sacred rituals to help join the Muslim masses to the class struggle.[38] Like his other non-Muslim comrades, Dzhugashvili was a bit uncomfortable with these developments. In a newspaper article published on the day of Khanlar's funeral, he noted that the Muslim 'oil workers' were 'appearing on the scene' in 'clumsy' and 'comical' ways.[39] But in later years, Dzhugashvili and his official biographies remembered Khanlar's funeral with care and pride: how he directed the choirs and factory whistles to mourn for Khanlar; how he celebrated him as Azerbaijan's 'first victim' for the Russian Revolution; how he gently told Khanlar's elderly father, 'Do not cry, old man, we will have our own holidays someday, and you for your most noble son'.[40]

Dzhugashvili paid his own personal sacrifices to the Bolshevik cause. His biographies elevated him as a living martyr, one who endured privation, persecution and the gauntlet, but who survived to mourn the dead and govern the living.[41] Wrote one biographer, 'Between 1902 and 1913, Stalin was arrested seven times, exiled six times, and escaped from exile five times'. Wrote another, 'First he is here, then he is there, then arrest, exile, escape, and once again he is among us'.[42] What mystery! He bore the terrors of the Tsarist police to live another day. He was the great invisible man, the disappearing and reappearing man, but always at just the right moment and for the true cause.

Nor did Dzhugashvili fail to honour violent clashes and martyrdoms beyond those of his personal experiences. Through his exile, on his way to St Petersburg and becoming a 'master of the revolution', he consistently reminded the proletariat to take heed of its terrifying sacrifices during Bloody Sunday (1905) and the Lena Massacre (1912). Death was a ground for rebirth. The 'bloody drama' of the Lena fields was a mark of 'real life in all its inexorable contradictions'. It had helped the proletariat 'be born again'.[43] He reduced the lessons to a quote from Walt Whitman (the consummate poet of equality and camaraderie, of martyrdom and death). It was, he later claimed, the 'perfect' summary of the philosophy of Bolshevism: 'We are the living, our scarlet blood seethes by the fire of boundless energies'.[44] This sentiment was not simply a matter of personality. As for other young Bolsheviks like him, so for Dzhugashvili, it was a matter of common conviction.

The Russian Civil War: Villainy and Terror

The proto-religious casts of underground Bolshevism only fortified as the revolutionary movement transformed into a state. 'The Russian Revolution, if it becomes isolated', proclaimed one editorial in early 1918, 'threatens to be crucified upon the cross of world imperialism'.[45] But the Bolsheviks now acquired the means to defend their gains and defeat their enemies in the context of the Civil War and its 'Red Terror'. Scholars have recently explained their recourse to violence as part of a pattern of European state policies during the First World War, or as a more peculiar element of the regime's fixation on ideological purity.[46] The Bolshevik culture of violence and martyrdom offers another perspective. Perhaps the romance of the Russian revolution, in the mentality of Party members, was simply following its proper course; the tragedy of martyrdom transforming into the release of 'revenge-terror', the 'furies', the 'righting of the balance'.[47] The Bolsheviks entertained this righteousness. They also faced increasingly diverse and violent threats from their opponents. Righteousness and threat married in the content of the terror, which accelerated in 1918 with the assassinations of M. Volodarskii (June) and M.N. Uritskii (August), the attempt on V.I. Lenin's life (August), and other atrocities of the 'White Terror'.[48] The victims were properly honoured as 'martyrs' for the revolution: as 'sacred victims' who would live on in the 'memory of undying humanity' where they would 'meet with the heroes of the Paris Commune, with Comrades Uritskii and Volodarskii, and with the great ghosts of Marx and

Engels'. But the call to vengeance was also deliberate, a fight 'to the death', to the very last 'drop of blood'.[49]

Among the fallen comrades were the famous Twenty-six Commissars, Bolshevik leaders of the 'Baku Commune', including the Armenian S.K. Shaumyan and the Georgian Alesha Dzhaparidze. Their short-lived Commune had risen and fallen under troubling circumstances in 1918: the anti-Muslim violence of March and the anti-Armenian violence of September. The commissars were murdered in the deserts of Turkmenistan by anti-Bolshevik forces on 20 September, after their retreat from the city and their surprise capture. The myth of the Commune and the Twenty-six was one of the most prolific and enduring in Soviet political culture. It predated the Lenin death cult. It helped reinvent the red funeral of underground days with newly innocent, noble victims, now honoured in a formal, stylised literature of state commemoration. It reinforced the consciousness of the USSR as global commune, represented in the ideological precept of 'capitalist encirclement'. It echoed the pathos of the Paris Commune of old – surrounded by French reactionaries and German imperialists and betrayed by internal class enemies – one of the most venerated of historical moments during the Civil War (and beyond).[50]

The myth of the Twenty-six also contained all the mysteries of a good crime scandal, with conniving Mensheviks and Socialist Revolutionaries (SRs) within, secret British agents and vicious White terrorists without, escapes by boat, arrests and evacuation by railroad, cold-blooded executions and anonymous burials in the desert sands. But perhaps best of all, it had the earmarks of a tragic romance. The condemned were said to have welcomed the bullets with stirring words. 'We are dying for Communism. Long Live Communism', as if they were about to enter the gates of a promised heavenly paradise. These themes of scandal and vindication carried over in the cult of the Twenty-six, which first peaked during the fifth anniversary of the murders in 1923. In the logic of suffering and redemption, the Commissars had to die so that the USSR might live. 'The Baku Commune fell only so as to rise again'.[51] Avel Enukidze offered an especially poignant remembrance of the Twenty-six, namely Dzhaparidze and Shaumyan (the 'Caucasus Lenin'). They were the 'most' any Bolshevik could hope for, the most 'knowledgeable', the most 'beloved', the most 'energetic'. 'Torn from the ranks of our party', he wrote, their deaths had been an 'irreplaceable loss' for the party.[52]

The history of the Baku Commune did have a muted, alternate reading. Several official commentators implicitly admitted that the Commune was so unstable and short-lived because of its own complicity in the sectarian violence surrounding it, especially the anti-Muslim pogroms of March 1918. Its 'very tragedy was its failure to win over the native masses'.[53] But the most interesting of all the alternate readings was Dzhugashvili's. He effectively launched the official interpretation, representing the Commune as that cautionary tale about enemies without (British imperialism) and within (Mensheviks and SRs). But in his view the Twenty-six were also their own worst enemies, a rather uncharacteristic disrespect for the recent and honourable dead. They had become false martyrs out of their own failures to defend the Commune properly from its enemies. True martyrdom would have meant shedding their blood in Baku, dying at the gates. Instead, they 'cleared out' and 'slipped away' from the 'field of battle', allowing the city to fall without a fight.[54]

The cult of the Twenty-six diminished as Dzhugashvili consolidated power. He was powerless to defeat it completely, so he emphasised his own role as precursor and successor.[55] A 1931 editorial in *Izvestiya* repeated the cult's main values. But now Dzhugashvili was positioned standing 'upon their bones', like them in many ways except that he was the living twenty-seventh who would ensure their visions came true.[56] E.N. Burdzhalov's historical study of the Twenty-six followed this approach, offering a detailed account of the mysterious encounters and events, painting their noble and romantic values, but in the end holding Dzhugashvili as the one who survived, the one who compensated for failure.[57] The Paris Commune 'took the first blow' in the history of the world revolution for communism. The Baku Commune took a second. Dzhugashvili was to return them with a last, fatal blow to capitalism.[58] This was all part of the new personality cult that stressed his courage and tenacity during the Civil War, not without some exaggerated truth. He was the one sent away to the 'most decisive and dangerous fronts', where 'confusion and panic' reigned and where the regime was in its 'death throes'.[59] He showed only calm resolve, the martyr who survived, defended 'the USSR on all its fronts with his own breast'.[60] He was 'that man who is always standing between what has been done and what is to be done'.[61] He was that man who, as before the Civil War and so afterward, occupied a strange middle ground between death and life.

The Lenin Cult: Leader and Succession

The Lenin cult was at the centre of Soviet life, broadcast over space and time. It raised at least three generations of children on its half-real, half-mythic founder. But Lenin's death was unique. Yes, he had suffered as a living martyr to the cause after the assassination attempt in 1918. He was one who, like Jesus 'had sacrificed themselves for the masses'.[62] In the tradition of class struggle, he cradled a 'sacred hatred, a hatred of slavery and oppression unto death'; he enjoyed that 'revolutionary passion that moves mountains, that boundless faith in the creative forces of the masses'.[63] But he died a natural death in 1924, a death brought on by several illnesses and a gradual eclipse from the affairs of state. He had become the old man of the revolution. His passing lacked a certain tension. The best it could summon was a mournful respect and sad nostalgia. 'Lenin has died' (umer Lenin), was the refrain. His heart simply 'stopped beating'. He 'passed away'. Like some cataclysmic act of nature, so one commemorative poem had it, his death stirred up melancholy and longing in the vast tracts of the USSR, from the snowy tundra of the north to the sandy deserts of Central Asia.[64] All this was very touching, but it was hardly the perfect martyrdom. The pattern in Bolshevik political culture was to venerate the broken and corrupted body of the martyr. The assassins of 1881, the victims of Lena, Uritskii and Volodarskii, all were memorialised within the 'marble columns' and evergreen wreaths of mourning.[65] Dead martyrs were the rule. Lenin's corpse was the odd exception. His was more like the holy and uncorrupted body of the saint.[66] In iconic terms, Maxim Gorky hailed him as the 'mother of mankind', a man who was 'a flame of almost feminine tenderness towards humanity'.[67]

Lenin's mummified corpse came to lie in a conflicted pose. What did he represent? Death or life? Mortality or immortality? Or what degrees of both? Victoria Bonnell's discussion of 'Lenin's two bodies' offers an insight: the mortal body as corpse presupposed the immortal body politic of the USSR.[68] Lenin represented death. But his death represented life for others. He died so that the USSR might live. Official annual remembrances followed this logic. The country marked his death on 20 January in the middle of winter with the utmost seriousness and devotion. But his birthday soon followed on 22 April, just as spring was upon Russia, and which the country celebrated in more joyful tones. As one of Lenin's more fawning of commentators wrote, 'it seems as though the man who lies in the tomb, in the centre of that nocturnal, deserted square, is the only person in the world who is not asleep, and who watches over everything around him'. But it only seemed so. 'The dead do not survive except on earth. Wherever there are revolutionaries, there is Lenin'.[69] This was certainly true for the succession struggles that followed so quickly upon his illness and death, turning his corpse into a political weapon and emblem of legitimacy. Before 1924 was out, as the first 'mourning' busts went on sale, Party leaders united together under Dzhugashvili's lead against the 'oppositions', now increasingly subject to vilification. Lenin took on the persona of posthumous martyr victim, despoiled by a series of villains who threatened to undermine the truth and rightness of his legacy.[70] The full martyrdom denied him in life was granted to him in death, a fitting *post mortem*.

Dzhugashvili venerated the dead Lenin in his saintly and martyred poses. But he also gradually teased at the limits of proper subservience. During the anniversary celebrations of his 50th birthday in December 1929, the slogan 'Stalin is the Lenin of today' highlighted a modest equality. He was Lenin's successor. But he was also very much alive. He was the model of a true Bolshevik, 'to the credit of the great Party of the working class which bore me and reared me in its own image and likeness'. He began to embody the Party will: his policies always came from its core and its core always agreed with his policies. To attenuate the conceit, he vowed that he was ready to give 'all my blood, drop by drop', to defend the revolution. He was alive, but was ready to die, to assume martyrdom for the cause.[71]

In coming years, Dzhugashvili took on a variety of titles. He was the 'best pupil', or 'father of peoples', or 'warrior knight'. In Socialist Realist paintings he was sometimes the new Messiah, enveloped in halos of light and taking on a Christ-like pose.[72] But one mantle we tend to forget, perhaps because it is so obvious, is that of martyr survivor. He was the one who succeeded, who held the party standard as its central dynamic figure. He was also the one who mourned, who suffered with the sadness of loss. In all humility and respect for the dead, he was the one who literally carried the remains of his fallen comrades to their premature graves. It was an image expressed in elegant prose. 'He stands in for the Lenin wounded by the gangsterous shot fired by the SR Kaplan', wrote Emilian Yaroslavskii. 'He stands in for the Lenin felled by sickness'.[73] It was an image expressed in Dzhugashvili's own funeral lament, the 'Oath to Lenin' (1924); and in later Stalinist folklore, the poetic lamentations of the dead Lenin that presupposed the praises for the living Dzhugashvili.[74] It was an image reflected in the brief biographical account of his life (during the hours between 9am on 23 January and 4pm on 27 January), as he accompanied Lenin's body from place to place, stood as honour guard over it, and helped to deliver it to the crypt.[75] It was an image captured in the photographs of Dzhugashvili as honour guard and pallbearer. There is a haunting, almost surreal photograph of him watching over Lenin's body, his face bathed in muted light and dark shadows.[76] Then we see Dzhugashvili, his head bowed and his eyes drawn, carrying Lenin's body to the mausoleum. This became a familiar image in the public sphere as he helped to bury M. Frunze and F.E. Dzerzhinskii. Here he was an honour guard at S.M. Kirov's coffin (1934). There he was a pallbearer for Maxim Gorky's ashes (1936). In time, the image was captured in formal painting as well, as in P. Kotov's, 'At Lenin's Death-Bed' (c.1944); or in N.Kh. Rutovskii's 'Stalin at the Bier of S.M. Kirov' (c.1935); or in Aleksandr Gerasimov's, 'I.V. Stalin by A.A. Zhdanov's Coffin' (1948).

All of these words and scenes spotlighted Dzhugashvili as guardian of that middle ground between life and death. Not as some ghastly, sinister figure stalking the corridors of politics. On the contrary, he had both a light and a hard touch in his public demeanour, often entertaining and stirring. He certainly knew how to connect with his audiences. He could regale them with wit and sarcasm, as he did in a 1930 speech lambasting the recent opposition groups.[77] Or he could inspire with fear and pathos, as he did in a 1933 speech filled with warnings about the real dangers of capitalism, even its 'dying' elements in the USSR, and about the looming tragedies of strife and war. The success of collectivisation and industrialisation was in peril, depending on the 'enthusiasm' and 'passion' (*pafos*), the 'courage' and 'faith', of all Party members. They were to draw from a wellspring of passion – part hatred and vengeance, part sympathy and compassion – to drive them to right purpose and action.[78] A short list of 'exemplary' and 'outstanding' dead Bolsheviks, in Dzhugashvili's view, had this emotion, what he termed (reminiscent of his favorite Whitman quote) the 'burning passion' of an 'ebullient life'. Ya.M. Sverdlov had it. So did the old Bolshevik I.F. Dubrovinskii (who perished in Turakhansk exile). The military men, Kotovskii and Frunze had it. F.E. Dzerzhinskii had it most of all. The trouble was, with so many good old Bolsheviks going to their graves in 1925 and 1926, how to replace them with younger comrades made of the same spirit?[79]

Dzhugashvili was on trusted ground here. His words connected with a Russian cultural attraction to the tragic and pathetic. The new holidays of Soviet culture, wrote one editorialist in 1928, demanded one overriding emotion: 'the pathos of class struggle, the poignant desire for the self-defence and the self-affirmation of class'. This was not some 'theatrical pathos' but the living pathos of proletarian will and action.[80] Yet theatrical pathos still enjoyed prominence in other venues. Sergei Eisenstein's montage style adapted it in the wrenching scene of the Odessa steps massacre (*Battleship Potemkin*); or in scenes of slaughtered cattle and workers (*Strike*). Aleksandr Dovzhenko's lyrical romanticism represented it through the immortal proletarian, baring his chest against bullets, impervious to their force (*Arsenal*); or in the burial of the murdered collective farm activist, set amid wonderful images of birth and rebirth (*Earth*).[81] Isaak Brodskii, one of the founders of the 'historical-revolutionary style' in painting, memorialised suffering and sacrifice in his 'Red Funeral' (1905), a moving study of popular melancholy and resolve;[82] and his 'Execution of the Twenty-six Baku Commissars' (1925), a stirring portrait reminiscent of Francisco Goya's 'The Shootings of May Third 1808' and the many drawings of the Paris Commune executions.[83]

The whole ethic of Socialist Realism was founded upon *pafos*. It was that 'great passion', the product of 'profound and serious life experiences, thoughts, and feelings', the heartbeat of a 'great people, living the mighty pathos of socialism'.[84] The classic text, Nikolai Ostrovskii's *How the Steel was Tempered*, exemplified this truth. In a pivotal scene, while experiencing an 'immense sadness' at 'the little cemetery where his comrades lay in their communal graves', Pavel Korchagin comes to the crucial insight: 'Man's most precious possession is life itself ... And one should make haste to use every moment of life' so as to live well and die well. He was both the tragic figure and the dutiful Bolshevik par excellence.[85] Fyodor Gladkov's

Cement exemplified this truth, too, perhaps even more to Dzhugashvili's liking. Mitka, the accordion player, has just died in a needless industrial accident. Mourned by his co-workers, as 'silently and gravely, their faces filled with suffering and pain, the workmen stood shoulder to shoulder, gazing down at the dead comrade lying at their feet'. But Gleb breaks the mood. 'Comrades, this man is a sacrifice to conflict and toil! But we should not mourn or weep for him. No – instead we should be filled with the joy of new triumphs'.[86]

The Great Terror: Politics and History

'Terror is the blood relative of socialism', wrote Barrington Moore for his generation, a product of the mentality to force immediate change and the central means to enforce command socialism. Soviet terror was external force, an 'instrument of control', of fear and obedience.[87] But terror also had its persuasive functions, its mythic role in a culture of violence that predated the Bolshevik assumption of state power and Dzhugashvili's eventual dictatorship. The 'Great Terror' (peaking in 1937–38) had a long history. It told a compelling story about the nasty villains and tragic victims of class struggle.[88] By no means was it a singular, uniform event. Recent studies have successfully argued that it was governed by all kinds of starts and stops, lulls and spikes. But the narrative of violence that ran through the Terror offers us one possible thread of continuity. For the Party and those literate in its idioms of class struggle, this narrative took shape in the 'omnipresent conspiracy' and web of 'fear and belief'. The Party line dictated that the dawn of socialism triumphant was the most dangerous moment yet. Communists were told to believe that enemies were everywhere, that they should question their very selves. This was the perfect tragic moment. Enemies had to be destroyed; zealots had to examine their consciences. People probably believed in these plots and conspiracies as either a rational way to make sense of the political administration or as an article of political faith. Dzhugashvili most likely believed them too, although he enjoyed the privilege of manipulating the police state and political culture to promote his own preferred versions.[89] Others manipulated the labels and categories ('enemies of the people', for example) in their own interests.[90]

The murder of Kirov in December 1934 was the focal point of a new round of conspiracies and a revived cult of violence. Its mysteries continue to fascinate us. Robert Conquest's and Amy Knight's studies remain compelling indictments of Dzhugashvili as criminal. New studies out of Russia and the US question these accounts with equally compelling evidence and argument.[91] Several have even offered that 'it does not matter whether Stalin was behind the killing or not', such were the contradictory material facts and Dzhugashvili's obvious complicity in so many other crimes.[92] There has always been contextual evidence exculpating Dzhugashvili of the crime. After all, the 'Stalin' personality cult was already in place since 1929, reaching a new peak just before Kirov's death with all the heroes of Stakhanovites, pilots, polar explorers and Party-State leaders. In the last months of his life, Kirov himself participated in the personality cult and in the writing of new, statist histories.[93] As Sarah Davies has written, his 'unexpected death was a severe interruption' to the regime's cult of the leader. Adam Ulam's argument, which has gained more currency of late, also makes perfect sense: Dzhugashvili did not necessarily need a new and risky venture into assassination in late 1934. Or as Robert McNeal has persuasively argued, the 'murder' of close comrades was not his standard *modus operandi*.[94]

The Party's first reactions to the assassination seem heartfelt and true. Kirov was termed the 'perfect image of the Bolshevik' and martyr victim: calm and fearless in adversity, kind and good-hearted in victory.[95] Dzhugashvili was genuinely moved and disturbed by the death.[96] We already know that the sentimental commemoration of the dead, the weaving of dramatic stories about them, was part of his revolutionary portfolio. We can see this in the photographs of Dzhugashvili at Kirov's coffin; in the way he accompanied the body at nearly every step toward interment; and in the cult of martyrdom accorded to his dead friend. Or consider the scene of the last viewing of Kirov's body. Amid an air of absolute 'silence' and 'sorrow', Dzhugashvili stoically approached the body, bowed to it, gently kissing the forehead, at which point the coffin was dramatically closed. And then, as if out of a Walt Whitman poem or Socialist Realist novel, 'a sense of eternal, invincible life replaced the very face of death'.[97] The bow was significant, recalling Dzhugashvili's 'oaths' to Tsulukidze and Lenin; the kiss on the forehead, a mark not only of a beloved friend but also of a successor, of a martyr survivor.[98] This role was made all the more dramatic since Kirov had been one of the original patrons of the cult to the martyred Twenty-six, and now Dzhugashvili was crafting a cult of martyrdom for him.[99] The torch had been passed.

Perhaps we have been distracted all these years by the fascination of the murder and the urge to spotlight Dzhugashvili as the villain. The real story was the way in which Kirov was remembered, in what the Party leaders did with the murder once it was committed, and in the cult of the dead Kirov that now partially eclipsed even the Lenin and Stalin cults. The real meaning of the murder was not to be found in the forensics of the crime, but in the discourse of martyrdom and tragedy applied to its victim. The pattern of tragic remembrance manifest in Bolshevik culture and in Dzhugashvili's political life proves neither his guilt nor innocence in the murder of Kirov. It only proves complicity after the fact. For the Kirov murder was the great tragic myth that informed all future Stalinist patterns of vilification, confession and leadership. This is the truth of the Kirov murder on which all must agree.[100]

The dominant storyline held that Kirov was but the 'first victim' in a planned wave of assassinations. Menzhinskii, Peshkov, Kuibyshev and Gorky were targeted and killed. Molotov, Kaganovich, Voroshilov and Dzhugashvili were targeted but survived. It was a vicious act, a moment of agony and pathos that set 'a wave of wrath and deep sorrow through the country'. Over the next four years, the murder encompassed a conspiracy of astonishing breadth and scope: from the Leningrad Centre to the Moscow Centre, from the Zinoviev-Kamenev to the Trotskii-Bukharin oppositions, indeed eventually to 'all Party members'.[101] The rhetoric of Bolshevik martyrology now became the apologetics for the terror. The pathos of the first act of violence, the tragic beauty of the first martyr, became the pathology of many acts of violence. The death of one (Lenin) had once meant the immortality of all (the USSR). The death of another (Kirov) now meant the possible death of all (the Great Terror's victims). Not 'all' perished in the terrors of the 1930s. But everyone was suspect, everyone was susceptible, everyone was culpable. No one was safe from the dragnet. Not even Dzhugashvili himself, whose political body was so often portrayed as the target of assassins and so occupied a central place in the overlapping circles of opposition and vilification.[102]

The coincidence in the famous *Short Course* between these murderous conspiracies and the imperative to rewrite history is remarkable. Kirov's dead body became the incubus for a new regime and a new history, the essential subtext for the cult of personality. Dzhugashvili was now portrayed ever more graphically as the living sacrifice, the avenging angel, whose renewed message was that death gave purpose to the living; the victim gave meaning to those who survived.[103] The regime now just as easily wrote the old Bolsheviks out of the historical record as it wrote Dzhugashvili and his coterie in. The Bolshevik ideal of collective immortality, the immortality of memory, was reduced to nonsense. History became a blank slate. The living could either remember or forget the dead, just as the regime wished. It thereby joined what Philippe Aries has called the nineteenth century's 'beautiful death' of public display and commemoration; and the twentieth century's 'invisible death' of anonymity and denial.[104] One death was highlighted as origin. But millions of deaths flowing from it were hidden in night-time arrests, transport trucks, unmarked prisons, the 'Gulag archipelago'. All this proceeded against a backdrop of film comedies and élite consumerism, a whole system of entitlements to mask the violence and reward loyalty.[105] For those who had survived Russia's recent wars and famines, the contrasts must have been stark. No victims of the Great Terror lay in the streets as before. Instead, the regime universalised and institutionalised death in the complexity and anonymity of bureaucratic procedure and consumerist culture. These patterns of state policy finally confirm, at least in a provisional and broadly interpretive way, a quote widely attributed to Dzhugashvili: 'one death is a tragedy, a million are a statistic'. He may have never actually said it, but his policies embodied its truths as to the powerful dramatic license of violence set against, in Hannah Arendt's words, the twentieth century's 'banality of evil'.

Dzhugashvili's regime did not enjoy a monopoly hold on the cult of violence and discourse on martyrdom. Tragic heroism was a role that nearly anyone could play. M.N. Ryutin appealed to it in his opposition 'platform' of 1932. In expressive revolutionary terms, reminiscent of the nihilists and terrorists of old, he called for a 'struggle to destroy' the regime; 'a struggle gives birth to leaders and heroes'. An act of violence, of tragic 'sacrifice', was necessary to renew the country. Here were echoes of Mikhail Bakunin's anarchism: the urge to destroy as a creative urge. Popular rumours of the day entertained the urge, too. One 'story' made Kirov's assassin out to be a brave and 'noble terrorist' who killed for a true cause, sanctifying death like the Russian populists of old.[106] Leading members of the Central Committee took on tragic roles in the ritual of 'self-confession' (*samokritika*) that J. Arch Getty has studied with special attention. The ritual confession, like the 'show trial', was a scripting of tragic flaws among Party members. It was recognition of personal failings in the context of grand struggles and mass solidarity.[107] N. Bukharin assumed the most conventional tragic role of all, scripting himself as 'the representative of a martyred Bolshevik movement'.[108]

Conflicting patterns of tragic remembrance appeared within the regime itself. Literary and cinematic 'tragedies' survived the 1930s, although not without criticism and dispute. Stalinist censors had a mild tolerance for the Shakespearean style, one that explored the shadows of evil and the good in our conflicted human natures. Such classically tragic novels were published; similarly tragic films, like Eisenstein's *Ivan the Terrible*, were made. But in the end party élites preferred not the ironic 'tragedies' but the purer 'romances'.[109] The one painted only a canvas of stark foreboding, of pity and fear; the other delivered the real tension of history, of zeal and passion (*pafos*). Ironic tragedy was the true art of creative contradiction and revelation; tragic romance the more potent political art of false resolution. By 1939, the regime no longer needed to make tragic heroes. It was already ascending to the sure romance of communism, no longer descending to agony or suffering. The terror had climaxed. So Dzhugashvili proclaimed, 'we shall have no further need of resorting to the method of mass purges'.[110]

'The phases of tragedy move from the heroic to the ironic'[111]

Dzhugashvili's death in 1953 both completed the cycle of tragic remembrance and ruptured it. His death completed it in the technique of commemoration. After Lenin, he was given a magnificent funeral, embalming and volumes of praise. His successors found themselves in familiar poses: mourning at the bier, quietly carrying the remains, bidding their last farewells. For a few years, the country recognised his death (5 March), along with his birth (21 December), following its earlier remembrances of Lenin. The two mummified remains now occupied a single place in the mausoleum at Red Square. Plans were even made for a grander 'Revolutionary Pantheon' for both bodies, along with other martyrs and heroes of the Bolshevik cause.[112] The discourse was complete. Dzhugashvili was not like Kirov because he had lived to avenge the murder. But Dzhugashvili was like Lenin because he had died to be remembered. He reached from beyond the grave just as Tsulukidze, or the Twenty-six, or Kirov had before him. With one exception. Dzhugashvili knew he would be memorialised and mummified. He was, unlike any of the others, the architect of his own entombment and glorification.

Yet his death also ruptured the historical cycle. For most of Stalinism, as Jorg Baberowski has argued, died with him.[113] If the early Bolshevik martyrs and the dead Lenin graced history for the first time as 'tragedy', then the Kirov murder and Stalin cult repeated history a second time as 'farce'.[114] This was the view, at least, of the Khrushchev reformers who set out to investigate the murder as a sordid conspiracy and soon displaced Dzhugashvili from his vaunted state. Khrushchev eventually buried him. But he and his successors could not bury the 'tragic'. They tried to reinvent Kirov as a tragic hero, only now a victim of Dzhugashvili himself. They succeeded in rehabilitating scores of tragic old Bolsheviks unjustly executed in the Stalinist purges.[115] The Brezhnev regime muted these reform tendencies. But it, too, could not dispense with tragic heroes and martyr victims all its own. These years saw state patronage of the tragic arts, as in Tatyana Nazarenko's 'historical-revolutionary' painting, 'Execution of the People's Will Activists' (1969), and the continued publication of novels in the Socialist Realist style.[116] They saw state-sponsored revivals of the imagery of the red funeral (namely for the victims of the 1917 Revolution), of the Lenin personality cult, and of the cult of the Twenty-six Baku Commissars.[117] The paradigm of tragic remembrance was highly adaptive.

The historiography is implicated in this paradigm, too, the result in part of how we have come to understand modern revolutions. By their very nature, so we have been led to believe by those who have survived them and by those who have studied them most, revolutions are ironic, conflicted events. They are cycles bounded by peaks of excess and slopes of reaction, by high hopes and contradictory results.[118] They are essentially tragic. This perspective translated into Leon Trotskii's 'revolution betrayed', his Stalinist 'Thermidor'. It informs the scholarship of the 'revisionist' school too, in its appreciations for the worthy social achievements of the Russian Revolution under Lenin, always betrayed and undone by Stalin, the maker of a national tragedy of epic scale.[119] Such tragic irony is more sophisticated, more penetrating than tragic romance. It breaks through the culture of violence, the bind of victim and vengeance. It places evil not in the dangerous present or expectant future but in the distant past, in an ill-fated Tsarism or corrupt Stalinism. Still, these evils only draw the truth and justice of the Russian Revolution into sharper, romantic relief.[120]

No one seems immune from the pull of tragic memory. The violence so pervasive through the long Russian Revolution haunts the historiography. 'Tragedy' has become one of its most universal themes and enduring clichés. It has been the voice of Dzhugashvili's youth, at the very origins of the Soviet experience. It has been the judgement delivered upon the USSR just before its demise.[121] It has been the lament of all varieties of critics and commentators upon the Russian Revolution.[122] The history of the Soviet experiment in Marxist communism has become a battleground of competing tragedies. They unite the present to the past, drawing lines of political sympathy between the actual participants of the Revolution and its later chroniclers. As once for A.S. Izgoev the Russian Revolution marked a tragic descent into unrivalled violence and destruction, so also for Richard Pipes the revolution created mostly 'agony', 'catastrophe' and 'sorrow'.[123] As once the SRs and Mensheviks decried the Bolshevik defilement of its leftist rivals as a 'great tragedy', so also has Ettore Cinella represented the 'promise and default' of the Left SRs as one of the very 'tragedies' of the Russian Revolution.[124]

Judging Dzhugashvili as a tragic figure seems unavoidable too. Shakespearean imagery comes easy with a tyrant like him.[125] But we should guard against colouring our narratives too dramatically with the spectacles of violence that raise tyrants and count victims. Because in doing so, we participate in the culture of violence too.[126] It is just as dangerous, as some writers are inclined, to remember and honour only Stalin's victims as truly righteous.[127] This turns the Bolshevik martyrologies into Stalinist victimologies. It is selective justice, really no justice at all, as if only those victims mattered. Aleksander Solzhenitsyn's condemnation of the Soviet regime, from Lenin to Brezhnev and nearly everything in between, has its fault lines. *The Gulag Archipelago* is not academic history, keen to distinctions and complications and contradictions. But at least it does not commit the blunder of honouring select victims of the Russian Revolution. It maintains the higher code of honouring them all.[128] It repudiates the central tenet of the Bolshevik narrative of violence and martyrdom: that some deaths, like some lives, were more valuable and meaningful than others. This narrative endured over the course of the twentieth century with a plural and reciprocal force. It influenced the life and thought of the young Dzhugashvili as a typical conspirator and propagandist. It governed the ideologies and policies of the fully formed dictator. It defined the official values and public practices into the 1930s. Beginning with Khrushchev's denunciations and continuing with our own, we can mark the narrative's mutations. We can begin to recognise it as morbid or imperious. Yet the narrative was also quite compelling and persuasive. It made sense of individual suffering and legitimised the dispensing of corporal justice in turn. It elevated a regime of state power as fearsome as any in the twentieth century. It provided that regime and its subjects with a system of values and beliefs couched in the idiom of religion, presuming to a totalitarian reach into their lives, centred on the certainty and mystery of death. These, perhaps, were the signal achievements and contradictions of the Soviet experiment: that it confused the sacred with the profane, life with politics, what was still living from what was already dead.

NOTES

1. 'Beseda s nemetskim pisatelem Emilem Lyudvigom', 30 April 1932, in I.V. Stalin, *Sochineniya* (Moscow: Gosudarstvennoe izdatel'stvo politicheskoi literatury OGIZ, 1946–51), tom 13, pp.119–20.
2. The essential texts are 'The Communist Manifesto', 'The Eighteenth Brumaire of Louis Bonaparte', and 'The Civil War in France'. Cited from Hayden White, *Metahistory: The Historical Imagination in Nineteenth-Century Europe* (Baltimore, MD and London: Johns Hopkins University Press, 1973), pp.27, 310–13.
3. See Northrop Frye, *Anatomy of Criticism: Four Essays* (Princeton, NJ: Princeton University Press, 1973), pp.158–220, on how the genres of 'romance, tragedy, irony and comedy are all episodes in a total quest-myth'. They consistently blend and mix.
4. A.A. Zhdanov advanced this definition at the First Congress of Soviet Writers (1934). Igor Golomstock, 'Problems in the Study of Stalinist Culture', in Hans Günther (ed.), *The Culture of the Stalin Period* (New York: St Martins Press, 1990), p.116, calls Socialist Realism a 'creative method', a 'worldview', a 'secular religion'. Jeffrey Brooks, 'Socialist Realism in *Pravda*: Read All About It!', *Slavic Review* 53/4 (Winter 1994), pp.973–91, offers an innovative approach grounded in complexities and contradictions.
5. Katerina Clark, *The Soviet Novel: History as Ritual* (Chicago: University of Chicago Press, 1981), p.258, defines the climax of the Socialist Realist novel as 'an actual, symbolic or near death'.
6. See Vladislav Todorov, *Red Square, Black Square: Organon for Revolutionary Imagination* (Albany, NY: State University of New York Press, 1995), p.122.
7. On the appeal of literary tragedy in early Soviet Russia, see Leon Trotskii, *Literature and Revolution* (Ann Arbor, MI: University of Michigan Press, 1968), pp.240–5;

Katerina Clark, *Petersburg: Crucible of Cultural Revolution* (Cambridge, MA: Harvard University Press, 1995), p.110; and Julie A. Cassiday, *The Enemy on Trial: Early Soviet Courts on Stage and Screen* (DeKalb, IL: Northern Illinois University Press, 2000), pp.84–6.

8. Semen Frank, 'The Ethic of Nihilism: A Characterization of the Russian Intelligentsia's Moral Outlook', in Boris Schragin and Albert Todd (eds.), *Landmarks: A Collection of Essays on the Russian Intelligentsia, 1909*, trans. Marian Schwartz (New York: Karz Howard, 1977), p.80. For similar conclusions, see Sergei Bulgakov, 'Heroism and Asceticism: Reflections on the Religious Nature of the Russian Intelligentsia', in ibid., p.35; and Nicolas Berdyaev, *The Origins of Russian Communism* (New York: Charles Scribner's Sons, 1937), p.86. For context, see James H. Billington, *Fire in the Minds of Men: Origins of the Revolutionary Faith* (New York: Basic Books, 1980); and Arthur P. Mendel, *Vision and Violence* (Ann Arbor, MI: University of Michigan Press, 1992), p.181.

9. Clark (note 5), p.177. See also Rene Fuelop-Miller, *The Mind and Face of Bolshevism* (New York: Harper and Row, 1965), p.277.

10. On this 'dual aspect of ritual sacrifice – the legitimate and the illegitimate', or 'sacrifice' as 'sacred obligation' and sacrifice as 'criminal activity', as 'murder', see Rene Girard, *Violence and the Sacred*, trans. Patrick Gregory (Baltimore, MD and London: Johns Hopkins University Press, 1972).

11. For two rather sweeping surveys, see Daniel Rancour-Laferriere, *The Slave Soul of Russia: Masochism and the Cult of Suffering* (New York: New York University Press, 1995); and Helene Carrerre d'Encausse, *The Russian Syndrome: One Thousand Years of Political Murder*, trans. Caroline Higgitt (New York and London: Holmes and Meier, 1992). On the 'tragic' contradictions in Russian culture and identity, see Tim McDaniel, *The Agony of the Russian Idea* (Princeton, NJ: Princeton University Press, 1996). For more focused studies on revolution and war, note Nina Tumarkin, *The Living and the Dead: The Rise and Fall of the Cult of World War II in Russia* (New York: Basic Books, 1994); and Catherine Merridale, *Night of Stone: Death and Memory in Twentieth-Century Russia* (New York: Viking, 2001).

12. Three classic studies along these lines are Robert C. Tucker, *Stalin as Revolutionary, 1879–1929: A Study in History and Personality* (New York and London: W.W. Norton, 1973), pp.80–1; Edward Ellis Smith, *The Young Stalin: The Early Years of an Elusive Revolutionary* (New York: Farrar, Straus and Giroux, 1967), p.97; and Alan Bullock, *Hitler and Stalin: Parallel Lives* (New York: Alfred Knopf, 1992), p.13.

13. Stalin's personal life was not without its own moments of intense grief, especially the premature deaths of both his first and second wives. But he seems to have compartmentalised these sad turns of event, and it would be purely speculative to find reflections in his professional life or ideological system. This did not stop Leon Trotskii from trying. He cited Dzhugashvili's 'theatrically pathetic and unnatural' words upon the death of his first wife as a reflection of 'his first heartfelt sorrow' and a lifelong 'penchant for strained pathos'. Leon Trotsky, *Stalin: An Appraisal of the Man and His Influence*, trans. and ed. Charles Malamuth (New York: Stein and Day, 1967), p.87.

14. Tucker (note 12), p.284, notes that Dzhugashvili's 'religious cast' and love for 'ceremony and ritual' were typical among Bolsheviks.

15. I need only refer to the work of Nicolas Berdyaev (note 8), Hans Günther (note 4), Rene Fuelop-Miller (note 9), Nina Tumarkin (note 11), Stephen Kotkin (note 89), among others. Igal Halfin, *From Darkness to Light: Class Consciousness and Salvation in Revolutionary Russia* (Pittsburgh: University of Pittsburgh Press, 2000), pp.2–3, is the most recent and comprehensive study of Marxism and Bolshevism as types of 'eschatological messianism'. See also Richard L. Hernandez, 'The Confessions of Semen Kanatchikov: A Bolshevik Memoir as Spiritual Autobiography', *Russian Review* 60 (January 2001), pp.13–35.

16. Cited from Jochen Hellbeck, 'Self-Realization in the Stalinist System: Two Soviet Diaries of the 1930s', in David L. Hoffman and Yanni Kotsonis (eds.), *Russian*

Modernity: Politics, Knowledge, Practices (New York: St Martin's Press, 2000), p.235. See also Igal Halfin, 'Looking into the Oppositionists' Souls: Inquisition Communist Style', Russian Review 60 (July 2001), pp.316–39; and Veronique Garros, Natalia Korenevskaya and Thomas Lahusen (eds.), Intimacy and Terror: Soviet Diaries of the 1930s (New York: New Press, 1995).

17. Alfred Rieber, 'Stalin, Man of the Borderlands', American Historical Review (December 2001), p.1653; I am indebted to this essay for influencing my approaches toward Dzhugashvili. See also Ronald Grigor Suny, 'Beyond Psychohistory: The Young Stalin in Georgia', Slavic Review 50/1 (Spring 1991).

18. I have borrowed this insight on the transformative power of the nation from the influential philosopher of the 1920s, G.G. Shpet, who argued in his Vvedenie v etnicheskuyu psikhologiyu (1927) that class collectives were essentially new nations in formation. See Gustav Shpet, Sochineniya, ed. E.V. Pasternak (Moscow: Pravda, 1989), p.574. The quote is from Benedict Anderson, Imagined Communities (London and New York: Verso, 1991), p.7. Studies of Bolshevism's 'national' forms in later years include Robert C. Williams, 'The Nationalization of Early Soviet Culture', Russian History/Histoire Russe 9/2–3 (1982), pp.157–172 (who also mentions its related 'culture of self-sacrifice and martyrdom'); and David Brandenberger, National Bolshevism: Stalinist Mass Culture and the Formation of Modern Russian National Identity, 1931–1956 (Cambridge, MA: Harvard University Press, 2002). For a relevant European comparison, see Jay W. Baird, To Die For Germany: Heroes in the Nazi Pantheon (Bloomington and Indianapolis, IN: Indiana University Press, 1990).

19. Cassiday (note 7). The quote is from Laurie Manchester, 'Harbingers of Modernity, Bearers of Tradition: Popovichi as a Model Intelligentsia Self in Revolutionary Russia', Jahrbücher für Geschichte Osteuropas 50/3 (2002), pp.323–43. See also Robert C. Williams, 'Collective Immortality: The Syndicalist Origins of Proletarian Culture, 1905–1910', Slavic Review 3 (September 1980), pp.391–3; and idem, The Other Bolsheviks: Lenin and His Critics, 1904–1914 (Bloomington and Indianapolis, IN: Indiana University Press, 1986), pp.3–4, 120.

20. Jay Bergman, 'The Image of Jesus in the Russian Revolutionary Movement: The Case of Russian Marxism', International Review of Social History XXXV (1990), pp.220–3; and Mark D. Steinberg, 'Workers on the Cross: Religious Imagination in the Writings of Russian Workers, 1910–1924', Russian Review 53 (April 1994), pp.213–39. See also Hernandez (note 15), pp.32–3; and Dave Pretty, 'The Saints of the Revolution: Political Activists in 1890s Ivanovo-Voznesensk and the Path of Most Resistance', Slavic Review 54/2 (Summer 1995), p.303. On the proletariat as 'class messiah' destined to suffer as part of its 'sacred mission', see Halfin (note 15), pp.96–103.

21. Thomas Reed Trice, 'The 'Body Politic': Russian Funerals and the Politics of Representation, 1814–1921, Ph.D. Dissertation, University of Illinois, 1998, pp.262, 273–5, 285. Merridale (note 11), pp.83–5, 93, discusses red funerals too, along with the 'languages of martyrdom' and 'the search for meaning, for pathos'. Also see Orlando Figes and Boris Kolonitskii, Interpreting the Russian Revolution: The Language and Symbols of 1917 (New Haven and London: Yale University Press, 1999).

22. Trice (note 21), pp.134, 186, 264.

23. 'Otvet na privetstviya rabochikh zh.-d. masterskikh v Tiflise', 10 June 1926, in Stalin (note 1), tom 8, pp.174–5. Also cited in Ronald G. Suny, 'A Journeyman for the Revolution: Stalin and the Labour Movement in Baku, June 1907–May 1908', Soviet Studies 23/3 (January 1972), p.373.

24. 'Rossiiskaya sotsial-demokraticheskaya partiya i ee blizhaishie zadachi', November–December 1901, in Stalin (note 1), tom 1, p.27.

25. E. Yaroslavsky, Landmarks in the Life of Stalin (Moscow: Foreign Languages Publishing House, 1940), pp.86–90. 'Biograficheskaya khronika', in Stalin (note 1), tom 1, pp.416–17. The discussion (with accompanying images) in D. Rodionovich,

'Stalin v proizvodeniyakh khudozhnikov Gruzii', *Molodaya gvardiya* 1 (1937), pp.210–11.

26. See Tucker (note 12), p.119, on the 'class war' theme. My reading of Dzhugashvili's published writings confirms Tucker's conclusion. They are filled with battlefield and graveyard imagery: 'wartime readiness', 'army of proletarians', 'our bloody duty', 'death attack', 'grave of the popular revolution' – all summarised in the popular slogan of 1905, 'Death or Revolution', and in Dzhugashvili's consistent attraction to armed uprisings. Stalin (note 1), tom 1, pp.137, 67, 79, 178, 185–95, 266.

27. The quotes are from Yaroslavsky (note 25) pp.23, 27; Smith (note 12), p.97; and A.M. Pankratova (ed.), *Istoriya SSSR: Uchebnik dlya X klassa srednei shkoly* (Moscow: Gosuchpedizd, 1946), pp.12–13. Similar descriptions are offered in *Stalin i Khashim (1901–1902 gody): Nekotorye epizody iz batumskogo podpolya* (Sukhum: Abkhazskoe Partiinoe Izdatel'stvo, 1934), pp.22–3; and V. Golubovich, 'Molodoi Stalin', *Istorik marksist* 1/77 (1940), p.125.

28. Note the description and painting in Henri Barbusse, *Stalin: A New World Seen Through One Man*, trans. Vyvyan Holland (New York: Macmillan, 1935). Trotsky (note 13), p.32, also took note of this imagery. This ideal of living martyr, martyr survivor, has some folkloric references in the literature of the personality cult. Georgii Leonidze, 'Arsen (Iz poemy 'Detstvo vozhdya')', *Molodaya gvardiya* 12 (1939), pp.102–5, fancied Dzhugashvili in the guise of the immortal Georgian rebel, Arsen Odzelashvili, the 'hope of the hopeless', the man who comes back from the dead to right wrongs and seek justice. Adam B. Ulam, *Stalin: The Man and His Era* (New York: Viking Press, 1973), p.389, also referred to Dzhugashvili's 'aura of martyrdom' after S.M. Kirov's murder.

29. After Ketskhoveli was shot by prison guards on 17 August 1903, his body was hastily buried without ceremony. But Dzhugashvili did take credit for a memorial on the first anniversary of his death, and Ketskhoveli's brother made the poignant testimony (seemingly on Dzhugashvili's behalf and in a defiance worthy of him) that some of his last words (referring to Tsarist authorities) were, 'They will pay dearly for my death'. G. Lelashvili, 'Besstrashnyi revolyutsioner Lado Ketskhoveli', pp.87–90; and V. Ketskhoveli, 'Druzi'ya i soratniki tovarishcha Stalina', pp.75–86, both in *Rasskazy o velikom Staline*, 2nd edn. (Tbilisi: Zarya Vostoka, 1941).

30. Yaroslavsky (note 25), pp.65, 72–4; Rodionovich (note 25), p.210 (with accompanying painting). N. Aladzhalova, 'Vstrechi c Aleksandrom Tsulukidze', pp.72–4; and 'Rasskazy o proshlom', p.65, both in *Rasskazy o velikom Staline* (note 29). Smith (note 12), p.140, said perceptively of this funeral: 'Koba had attempted for the first time to utilize the death or funeral of a revolutionary comrade to advance his personal political position'.

31. R. Arsenidze, 'Iz vospominanii o Staline', *Novyi zhurnal* (New York) 72 (1963), pp.229–30. Ulam (note 28), p.36, offers another reading of this event.

32. Cited from Yaroslavsky (note 25), p.52. Isaac Deutscher, *Stalin: A Political Biography* (New York: Oxford University Press, 1978), pp.99–101, framed Dzhugashvili's transformation into 'Stalin' within the Baku context. Dzhugashvili once claimed that his comrades gave him the title sometime in 1910–11, perhaps during his last free days in Baku, or during his stay in its Bailov prison (March–September 1910). 'Imya eto ko mne podkhodit. I.V. Stalin o svoem psevdonime', *Istochnik* 5 (1999), p.79.

33. The quote is from 'Pis'mo t. Dem'yanu Bednomu', 15 July 1924, in Stalin (note 1), tom 6, p.273.

34. K. Norinskii, 'O Petre Montin', *Proletarskaya revolyutsiya* 6 (1922), pp.28–31.

35. Cited from Institut Istorii Partii, TsKKP Azerbaidzhana, *Ocherki istorii kommunisticheskoi partii Azerbaidzhana* (Baku: Azerbaidzhanskoe gosudarstvennoe izdatel'stvo, 1963), pp.98–9.

36. I. Vatsek, 'Stalinskaya shkola revolyutsionnoi bor'by', in *Rasskazy o velikom Staline* (note 29), pp.24–5.

37. Cited from a protest pamphlet in Institut Istorii Partii (note 35), pp.132–3.

38. Michael G. Smith, 'The Russian Revolution as a National Revolution: Tragic Deaths

and Rituals of Remembrance in Muslim Azerbaijan (1907–1920)', *Jahrbücher für geschichte Osteuropas* 49/3 (2001), pp.363–88. For context, see Yurii Larin, *Rabochie neftyanogo dela (Iz byta i dvizheniya 1903–1908 gg)* (Moscow: n.p., 1909), pp.18–26.

39. 'Nado boikotirovat' soveshchanie!', 29 September 1907, in Stalin (note 1), tom 2, pp.81–6.

40. The quotes are from Pankratova (note 27), p.85; and M. Moskalev, 'I.V. Stalin vo glave Bakinskikh Bol'shevikov i rabochikh v 1907–1908 godakh', *Istorik marksist* 1/77 (1940), pp.84–5, 94. Also see Barbusse (note 28), p.27; Golubovich (note 27), p.127; and A.N. Guliev, *I.P. Vatsek v revolyutsionnom dvizhenii v Baku* (Baku: Azebaidzhanskoe gosudarstvennoe izdatel'stvo, 1965), pp.96–8.

41. See G.F. Aleksandrov *et al.*, *Iosif Vissarionovich Stalin: Kratkaya biografiya*, 2nd edn. (Moscow: Gosudarstvennoe izdatel'stvo politicheskoi literatury, 1947), p.11; and Yaroslavsky (note 25), pp.167, 81, 66.

42. Aleksandrov *et al.* (note 41), p.44. Vatsek (note 36), p.25.

43. 'Zhizn' pobezhdaet!', 15 April 1912, and 'Novaya polosa', 15 April 1912, both in Stalin (note 1), tom 2, pp.232–3 and 225 respectively. He repeated these points in a series of articles: Stalin (note 1), tom 2, pp.223–4, 238, 244, 266–7, 373–6.

44. I have not been able to locate the original line in Whitman; the translation is mine. The Russian reads: *My zhivy, kipit nasha alaya krov' ognem neistrannykh sil.* 'Novaya polosa', 15 April 1912, in ibid., tom 2, p.225. For the later use of the quote, see 'Pis'mo t. Dem'yanu Bednomu', 15 July 1924, in ibid., tom 6, p.273.

45. 'Mirovaya revolyutsiya stala faktom', *Izvestiya* 15, 20 January 1918.

46. Peter Holquist, *Making War, Forging Revolution: Russia's Continuum of Crisis, 1914–1921* (Cambridge, MA: Harvard University Press, 2002); Amir Weiner, 'Nature, Nurture, and Memory in a Socialist Utopia: Delineating the Soviet Socio-Ethnic Body in the Age of Socialism', *American Historical Review* (October 1999), pp.1114–55; and Eric Naiman, *Sex in Public: The Incarnation of Early Soviet Ideology* (Princeton, NJ: Princeton University Press, 1997).

47. The terms are from Frye (note 3), p.209. See also Arno J. Mayer, *The Furies: Violence and Terror in the French and Russian Revolutions* (Princeton, NJ: Princeton University Press, 2000), p.xvi.

48. For the imagery of the 'Red Terror' as an answer to the 'White Terror', see Vladimir Bonch-Bruevich, 'Pokushenie na V.I. Lenina', *Molodaya gvardiya* 9–10 (1923), pp.95–105; Roman Neiman, 'Cherty bortsa (k desyatoi godovshchine smerti M.S. Uritskogo)', *Krasnaya panorama* 38, 21 September 1928, p.5. On the assassination attempt, see Nina Tumarkin, *Lenin Lives! The Lenin Cult in Soviet Russia* (Cambridge, MA: Harvard University Press, 1983), pp.80–5.

49. The quotes are from 'Pamyati pogibshikh', *Pravda* 216, 28 September 1919, referring to victims of a Moscow bomb blast; and 'K ubiistvu tov. Uritskago', *Izvestiya* 189, 3 September 1918, p.5.

50. For context, see Ronald G. Suny, *The Baku Commune, 1917–1918: Class and Nationality in the Russian Revolution* (Princeton, NJ: Princeton University Press, 1972). On the Paris Commune in Bolshevik ideology, see G.I. Il'ina, 'Obraz evropeiskikh revolyutsii i russkaya kul'tura (mart 1917 g. – noyabr' 1918 g.)', in V.Yu. Chernyaev (ed.), *Anatomiya revolyutsii. 1917 god v Rossii. Massy, partii, vlast'* (St Petersburg: Glagol, 1994), pp.383–93.

51. Cited from G. Chernomora, 'Tragediya dvadtsati shesti', *Krasnaya panorama* 40 (1929), pp.2–3; and 'Bakinskaya kommuna', *Izvestiya* 212, 20 September 1923, p.1. On the 'romantic pathos' of the cult in poetry, see V. Devitt, *Dvadtsat' shest' bakinskikh komissarov v sovetskoi poezii (russkoi i azerbaidzhanskoi)* (Baku: Izdatel'stvo Akademii nauk ASSR, 1965), p.9.

52. A. Enukidze, 'Pyataya godovshchina', *Izvestiya* 212, 20 September 1923, p.1.

53. 'Natsional'nyi vopros', *Izvestiya* 267, 22 November 1923, p.5, counted the losses during the events of March 1918 as 'up to thirty thousand Muslim' dead, far higher than the usual Soviet estimate of only 3,000 dead on all sides. Cited from Ya. Ratgauzer, *Revolyutsiya i grazhdanskaya voina v Baku (1917–1918)* (Baku: Istpart, 1927), p.177.

54. Iosif Stalin, 'K rasstrelu 26-ti bakinskikh tovarishchei agentami angliiskogo imperializma', *Izvestiya* 85, 23 April 1919, p.2. Ulam (note 28), p.56, cites this article as 'singularly unsentimental'.

55. See Iv. Tovstukha (ed.), *Iosif Vissarionovich Stalin: Kratkaya biografiya* (Moscow and Leningrad: Gosizdat, 1927), p.9; *The Life of Stalin: A Symposium* (New York: Workers' Library, 1930), p.6; and Aleksandrov *et al.* (note 41), p.46.

56. 'Na ikh kostyakh', *Izvestiya* 90, 1 April 1931, p.1.

57. E.N. Burdzhalov, *Dvadtsat' shest' bakinskikh komissarov* (Moscow: Gosudarstvennoe izdatel'stvo politicheskoi literatury, 1938), pp.79–81, 108–12.

58. Em. Yaroslavskii, 'Stalin – eto Lenin segodnya', *Istorik marksist* 1/77 (1940), p.12.

59. Aleksandrov *et al.* (note 41), p.81; Yaroslavsky (note 25), pp.107, 121, 167.

60. Yaroslavskii (note 58), p.10.

61. Barbusse (note 28), p.275.

62. Bergman (note 20), pp.226, 244–6.

63. Tsentral'nyi komitet RKP, 'Umer Lenin', *Molodaya gvardiya* 2–3 (1924), p.5.

64. The memorial in *Izvestiya* 21, 21 January 1931, p.1; Aleksandr Flit, 'Pyat' minut', *Krasnaya panorama* 3 (1924), p.4.

65. I share this appreciation for the imagery of 'marble columns' with Cassiday (note 7), p.110. The popular photo-magazine, *Krasnaya panorama*, was especially adept at marketing images and sentiments about these varied 'tragedies' in the history of class struggle; and about the victims whose names were inscribed 'in the golden book of socialist heroes, in the martyrology of socialist martyrs'. From 'Vpered za kommunu!', *Krasnaya panorama* 6 (1924), p.5.

66. On the 'contrast between the abused body of the martyr and the glorified body of the saint', see John R. Knott, *Discourses on Martyrdom in English Literature, 1563–1694* (New York: Cambridge University Press, 1993), pp.9–10.

67. Cited in A. Garin, 'Lenin-Chelovek', *Krasnaya panorama* 3, 18 January 1929, p.2.

68. Victoria E. Bonnell, *Iconography of Power: Soviet Political Posters Under Lenin and Stalin* (Berkeley, CA: University of California Press, 1997), p.149. Boris Groys, *The Total Art of Stalinism: Avant-garde, Aesthetic Dictatorship, and Beyond*, trans. Charles Rougle (Princeton, NJ: Princeton University Press, 1992), p.67, notes that the corpse is both 'simultaneously buried and displayed', dressed as if still alive, as if Lenin had just come back from the office.

69. Barbusse (note 28), pp.275, 282. Similar sentiments were expressed in the poem by V. Bugaevskii, 'V mavzolee', *Krasnaya panorama* 3, 18 January 1929, p.2.

70. For context, see Tumarkin (note 48), p.110, on the two ideological pillars of 'hagiography' and 'demonology'. Matthew E. Lenoe, 'Reader Response to the Soviet Press Campaign Against the Trotskii-Zinoviev Opposition, 1926–1928', *Russian History/Histoire Russe* 24/1–2 (Spring–Summer 1997), pp.93–5, 114–5.

71. 'Vsem organizatsiyam i tovarishcham, prislavshim privetstviya v svyazi s 50-letiem t. Stalina', 22 December 1929, Stalin (note 1), tom 12, p.140; also cited in Yaroslavsky (note 25), p.169. B. Legran, 'Put' vozhdya', *Krasnaya panorama* 2 (1930), p.3. For context and insight, see also D. Furman, 'Stalin i my s religiovedcheskoi tochki zreniya', in Kh. Kobo (ed.), *Osmyslit' kul't Stalina* (Moscow: Progress, 1989), pp.416–17.

72. Bonnell (note 68), p.168; Golomstock (note 4), p.117.

73. Yaroslavskii (note 58), p.10.

74. See Frank J. Miller, *Folklore for Stalin: Russian Folklore and Psuedofolklore of the Stalin Era* (Armonk and London: M.E. Sharpe, 1990), pp.62–70, 156–65.

75. 'Biograficheskaya khronika', Stalin (note 1), tom 6, pp.418–19. This was one of the few times, besides the night of 9 November 1932, when Dzhugashvili's second wife died, that the 'Biographical Chronicles' recounted (by the hour or minute) the course of his days.

76. Reproduced in Barbusse (note 28), p.147.

77. See 'Zaklyuchitel'noe slovo po politicheskomu otchetu TsK XVI S'yezdu VKP(b) (2 iyulya 1930g)', Stalin (note 1), tom 13, pp.1–16. For a discussion of Dzhugashvili's

formidable dramatic acting talents, ranging from the 'comic' to the 'tragic', see A. Antonov-Ovseenko, 'Teatr Iosifa Stalina', in Kobo (note 71), p.103.

78. 'Itogi pervoi pyatiletki (Doklad 7 Yanvarya 1933g)', Stalin (note 1), tom 13, pp.178, 186. I have translated *pafos* as 'passion' to stress the double meaning of both agony and enthusiasm. '*Pathos* or catastrophe, whether in triumph or in defeat, is the archetypical theme of tragedy', Frye (note 3), p.192.

79. Obituaries and reminiscences in Stalin (note 1), tom 6, pp.278–9; tom 7, pp.250–1; tom 8, pp.99, 192–3.

80. A. Kurella, 'Kakimi dolzhny byt' nashi proletarskie prazdniki!', *Revolyutsiya i kultura* 17 (1928), pp.47–9.

81. 'Passion'(*Pafos*) was a recurrent theme in the films of the 1920s and 1930s. For context, see Robert C. Williams, *Artists in Revolution: Portraits of the Russian Avant-garde, 1905–1925* (Bloomington, IN: Indiana University Press, 1977).

82. I.I. Brodskii and S.M. Ivanitskii, *Brodskii* (Moscow: Izobrazitel'noe iskusstvo, 1986), pp.1–2, defined this style as the 'pathos of historical optimism and humanist life-affirmation'; and described 'Red Funeral' as a 'portrayal of the people as the driving force of history'. Trice (note 21), pp.275–9, discusses the painting as well.

83. Both paintings are reproduced in I. Brodskii, *Moi tvorcheskii put'* (Leningrad and Moscow: Gosizdat Iskusstvo, 1940), pp.23 and 94–5.

84. G. Brovman, 'Pafos i tema', *Molodaya gvardiya* 7 (1936), pp.187–91.

85. See the 'Introduction', and Nikolai Ostrovsky, 'How the Steel was Tempered', in Nicholas Luker (ed.), *From Furmanov to Sholokhov: An Anthology of the Classics of Socialist Realism* (Ann Arbor, MI: Ardis, 1988), pp.29, 432–3. On Korchagin as 'ascetic "heroic vanquisher" (*podvizhnik*)', a prototype for the 'steeliness' in Stalin, see Hans Günther, 'Education and Conversion: The Road to the New Man in the Totalitarian *Bildungsroman*', in Günther (note 4), pp.202–5. For one testimony on the influence of Ostrovskii's novel, see Mariya Demchenko, 'Ego kniga dala mne uverennost' v pobede', *Molodaya gvardiya* 1 (1937), pp.196–7.

86. Fyodor Gladkov, 'Cement', in Luker (note 85), pp.276–7.

87. Barrington Moore, *Terror and Progress – USSR* (Cambridge, MA: Harvard University Press, 1966), pp.170–2.

88. For the rhetoric of evil enemies and class struggle as a kind of preface to the terror, see A. Vyshinskii, 'Zavershim delo, nachatoe parizhskim kommunaram', *Izvestiya* 76, 13 March 1931, p.5; and 'A Conversation Between Stalin and Wells', *New Statesman and Nation*, 27 October 1934, p.604 of the 'Supplement'.

89. The quotes are from Gabor Tamas Rittersporn, 'The Omnipresent Conspiracy: On Soviet Imagery of Politics and Social Relations in the 1930s', in J. Arch Getty and Roberta T. Manning (eds.), *Stalinist Terror: New Perspectives* (Cambridge and New York: Cambridge University Press, 1993), pp.99–115; and Robert W. Thurston, *Life and Terror in Stalin's Russia, 1934–1941* (New Haven and London: Yale University Press, 1996), pp.81–3, 138, 151–5, 229. On these modes of belief, see also the essential new source, J. Arch Getty and Oleg V. Naumov (eds.), *The Road to Terror: Stalin and the Self-Destruction of the Bolsheviks, 1932–1939*, trans. Benjamin Sher (New Haven and London: Yale University Press, 1999), pp.259, 455, 488; Robert Conquest, *The Great Terror: A Reassessment* (New York and Oxford: Oxford University Press, 1990), pp.110–19; Stephen Kotkin, *Magnetic Mountain: Stalinism as a Civilisation* (Berkeley, CA: University of California Press, 1995), pp.280–344; and Moshe Lewin, 'Stalin in the Mirror of the Other', in Ian Kershaw and Moshe Lewin (eds.), *Stalinism and Nazism: Dictatorships in Comparison* (Cambridge: Cambridge University Press, 1997), p.132.

90. See Sarah Davies, *Popular Opinion in Stalin's Russia: Terror, Propaganda and Dissent, 1934–1941* (Cambridge: Cambridge University Press, 1997), pp.1–7, 124–62, 179–84; Sheila Fitzpatrick, 'Readers' Letters to *Krestyanskaya Gazeta*, 1938', *Russian History/Histoire Russe* 24/1–2 (Spring–Summer 1997), p.161; and Golfo Alexopoulos, 'Victim Talk: Defense Testimony and Denunciation under Stalin', in Hoffman and Kotsonis (note 16), pp.205, 213.

91. Compare Robert Conquest, *Stalin and the Kirov Murder* (New York: Oxford University Press, 1989); and Amy Knight, *Who Killed Kirov? The Kremlin's Greatest Mystery* (New York: Hill and Wang, 1999); with Lesley Ann Rimmel, *The Kirov Murder and Soviet Society: Propaganda and Popular Opinion in Leningrad, 1934–1935*, Ph.D. Dissertation, University of Pennsylvania, 1995; Alla A. Kirilina, *Rikoshet, ili, skol'ko chelovek bylo ubito vystrelom v Smol'nom* (St Petersburg: Znanie, 1993); and Yu.N. Zhukov, 'Sledstvie i sudebnye protsessy po delu ob ubiistve Kirova', *Voprosy istorii* 2 (2000), pp.41–7.

92. Quoted from Thurston (note 89), p.22. This suggestion has received comprehensive treatment in Matt Lenoe, 'Did Stalin Kill Kirov and Does it Matter?', *Journal of Modern History* 74 (June 2002), pp.352–80.

93. Tumarkin (note 48), p.250, notes that the Lenin cult was at its 'low ebb' by 1933, while Dzhugashvili's was 'blossoming'. Kirilina (note 91), discusses Kirov's work in detail.

94. Davies (note 90), p.154. The argument in Ulam (note 28), p.385, is one confirmed in Reiber (note 17), Lenoe (note 92), and Kirilina (note 91). Robert H. McNeal, *Stalin: Man and Ruler* (New York: New York University Press, 1988), pp.169–74.

95. Kirov's obituary in *Istorik marksist* 1/41 (1935), p.3.

96. Rieber (note 17), pp.1662–3, makes a strong case that the combined grievous effect of his second wife's death (likely by suicide) and Kirov's murder made Dzhugashvili see 'himself as the victim', prompting a 'form of vengeance in the code of blood revenge'. He has Dzhugashvili singing laments and mourning songs for his dead friend. Kirilina (note 91) also discusses the strong bonds between the two men in detail.

97. L. Nikulin, 'Kirov', *Molodaya gvardiya* 6 (1939), p.133.

98. Party loyalists followed suit by raising similar 'oaths' at the coffin and grave, as discussed in 'Sergei Mironovich Kirov', *Nauka i zhizn'* 1 (1935), p.6. The poem by Mikola Bazhan, 'Iz "Povesti o Kirove"', *Molodaya gvardiya* 12 (1937), p.158, had Kirov himself making such a kiss to the forehead of a dead comrade (during the 1905 Revolution) as he took the party standard from his arms.

99. S.M. Kirov, 'Vrag proschitalsya: Iz rechi na zasedanii bakinskogo soveta (20 sentyabrya 1922 g.)', *Bakinskii rabochii*, 20 September 1922, had proclaimed that the spilled blood of the Twenty-six was the 'supreme meaning of the Baku tragedy'. But Kirov's tragic murder now overshadowed the Twenty-six. Semen Kirsanov's poem, 'Dvadtsat' shest'' (1938), had the dead Kirov laying a memorial wreath at their monument as an oath of sorts, as a taking up of their sacrifice. Dzhambul's poem, 'Pesnya o Baku', *Molodaya gvardiya* 4 (1938), pp.28–9, did not even mention the Twenty-six but only Kirov and Dzhugashvili as Baku's premier Bolsheviks and dispensers of justice.

100. Every major and relevant study I have read supports this point, most of them emphatically.

101. Central Committee of the CPSU (b), *History of the Communist Party of the Soviet Union (Bolsheviks): Short Course* (New York: International Publishers, 1939), pp.326–7. On the naming of 'enemies', see Conquest (note 89), p.375; and Rimmel (note 91), p.128. Also see Conquest (note 91), on Dzhugashvili's 'four stories'; and L. Trotskii, 'Stalinskaya byurokratiya i ubiistvo Kirova', *Byulleten' oppozitsii* 41, January 1935, p.1, on his 'grandiose amalgamation'. On the 'fiction of popular wrath', see Roman Redlikh, *Stalinshchina kak dukhovnyi fenomen* (Frankfurt/Main: Posev, 1971), pp.98–9.

102. Davies (note 90), pp.117, 177, recounts the rumours that Dzhugashvili would soon be assassinated, too. In the world of intentions before Kirov's murder, Dzhugashvili may very well have never even conceived the possibility of an artificial assassination, as Ulam suggested. But he clearly did not fear the model of assassination after the fact. He fortified his authority on it. Once the deed had been committed, the image of the positive martyr victim was only meaningful when weighed against the negative image of the assassin. They became inseparable. The original and most meaningful 'terror'

of the 1930s, in this sense, was the terror aimed against the Stalin regime. For the rhetoric, see Vyshinskii's 'Speech for the Prosecution', 22 August 1936, in *The Case of the Trotskyite-Zinovievite Terrorist Centre: Heard Before the Military Collegium of the Supreme Court of the USSR (Moscow, August 19–24, 1936)* (New York: Howard Fertig, 1967), pp.117–64.

103. Central Committee of the CPSU (b) (note 101), pp.327–8. Yaroslavsky (note 25), pp.160–1. George Enteen, 'The Stalinist Conception of Communist Party History', *Studies in Soviet Thought* 37/4 (May 1989), pp.267–73, discusses the Stalinist paradigms.

104. Philippe Aries, *The Hour of Our Death*, trans. Helen Weaver (New York and Oxford: Oxford University Press, 1991).

105. For the contexts, see Merridale (note 11), pp.197–9; and James van Geldern, 'The Centre and the Periphery: Cultural and Social Geography in the Mass Culture of the 1930s', in Stephen White (ed.), *New Directions in Soviet History* (Cambridge: Cambridge University Press, 1992), pp.62–77. In the later 1930s, *Molodaya gvardiya* depicted all of this in simple form: positioning propaganda photos of a smiling Kirov (recently dead) in its pages with new advertisements for ladies perfume and toilet soap.

106. Cited from the 'The Ryutin Platform', in Getty and Naumov (note 89), p.58. Cited from Davies (note 90), pp.114–16.

107. J. Arch Getty, 'Samokritika Rituals in the Stalinist Central Committee, 1933–1938', *The Russian Review* 58 (January 1999), pp.49–70. Cassiday (note 7), pp.6, 108–9, 114–15, offers the historical context of the 'show trial's totalizing legal discourse' and 'totalizing script', based on 'overlapping models of confession, repentance, and reintegration'.

108. Stephen F. Cohen, 'The Afterlife of Nikolai Bukharin', in Anna Larina, *This I Cannot Forget: The Memoirs of Nikolai Bukharin's Widow*, trans. Gary Kern (New York: Norton, 1993), pp.12–22. It is no wonder, then, that Stephen Cohen, Bukharin's able biographer, saw Dzhugashvili's hand in Kirov's death. This completed the role of Bukharin as positive martyr, along with such references to Dzhugashvili's terror as Bolshevism's 'death agony', Bukharin's 'letter-testament' a 'prayer', his death a 'tragedy'.

109. Kevin M.F. Platt and David Brandenberger, 'Terribly Romantic, Terribly Progressive, or Terribly Tragic: Rehabilitating Ivan IV under I.V. Stalin', *Russian Review* 58/4 (January–October 1999), pp.635–54; Bernd Uhlenbruch, 'The Annexation of History: Eisenstein and the Ivan Grozny Cult of the 1940s', in Günther (note 4), pp.274–7. On an appreciation for Shakespeare's 'tragic' characters, crushed by the weight of 'tragic' class contradictions and world-historical conflicts, see G. Boyadzhiev, 'Vil'yam Shekspir', *Molodaya gvardiya* 7 (1936), pp.152–6.

110. Cited in Conquest (note 89), p.440 (from Dzhugashvili's *Problems of Leninism*).

111. Frye (note 3), pp.219–21.

112. The circumstances of Stalin's death and funeral are vividly described, based on new materials, in Merridale (note 11), pp.257–63. See also Ulam (note 28), pp.5–6.

113. Jorg Baberowski, 'Wandel und Terror: die Sowetunionen unter Stalin, 1928–1941: Ein Literaturbericht', *Jahrbücher für Geschichte Osteuropas* 43/1 (1995), pp.96–129.

114. Or, in Andrei Sinyavskii's phrase, they were a study in Dzhugashvili's own 'black humour'. A. Sinyavskii, 'Stalin – geroi i khudozhnik stalinskoi epokhi', in Kobo (note 71), p.121.

115. For Khrushchev's references to tragedy, see the drafts of his Secret Speech at the 20th Congress of the Party (1956), 'O kul'te lichnost i ego posledstviyakh', in *Istochnik* 6 (2000), pp.98, 101.

116. Luker, 'Introduction' (note 85), pp.29–35.

117. E.N. Burdzhalov, who had written the classic work on the Twenty-six as a Stalinist history, now applied his literary and ideological skills to the mythic memory of the February revolution: *Vtoraya russkaya revolyutsiya: Vosstanie v Petrograde* (Moscow; Nauka, 1967); *Russia's Second Revolution: The February 1917 Uprising in Petrograd*,

ed. and trans. Donald J. Raleigh. (Bloomington and Indianapolis, IN: Indiana University Press, 1987), pp.337–40; Tumarkin (note 48), p.259; Suny (note 50), pp.363–95, offers citations to a variety of works dedicated to the Twenty-six, many published after 1953.
118. Crane Brinton, *The Anatomy of Revolution* (New York: Vintage, 1965); and Sheila Fitzpatrick, *The Russian Revolution, 1917–1932* (Oxford and New York: Oxford University Press, 1982), based partly on his model.
119. See the categories in Stephen Cohen, *Rethinking the Soviet Experience: Politics and History Since 1917* (New York: Oxford University Press, 1985), pp.27–70.
120. The Soviet style of tragic romance and the revisionist style of ironic tragedy joined in the English-language edition of Burdzhalov's *Russia's Second Revolution* (note 117), celebrated as an 'exceptional book' by an 'exceptional man', largely for its innovative and quality scholarship. Donald T. Raleigh, 'Translator's Introduction', pp.ix–x, found the author's Stalinist passion for the Twenty-six and his revisionist passion for the victims of February 1917 fully irreconcilable. Yet one could argue that Burdzhalov showed a remarkable consistency in the two studies: an abiding loyalty to the power of the Soviet style of tragic commemoration and romance.
121. Joseph Iremaschwili, *Stalin und die Tragedie Georgiens* (Berlin: Verfasser, 1984 [1932]). Dmitrii Volkogonov, *Triumph and Tragedy*, ed. and trans. Harold Shukman (New York: Grove Weidenfeld, 1991).
122. Compare Martin Malia, *The Soviet Tragedy: A History of Socialism in Russia, 1917–1991* (New York: Free Press, 1994); with Orlando Figes, *A People's Tragedy: A History of the Russian Revolution* (New York: Viking, 1997).
123. Compare A.S. Izgoev, 'Tragedii i vina', *Nash vek*, 23 March/5 April 1918; and Richard Pipes, *The Russian Revolution* (New York: Alfred Knopf, 1990), pp.xxi–xxii.
124. Compare the discussion in Trice (note 21), pp.302–4; and Ettore Cinella, 'The Tragedy of the Russian Revolution: Promise and Default of the Left Socialist Revolutionaries in 1918', *Cahiers du Monde Russe* 38/1–2 (January–June 1997), pp.45–82.
125. Ian Grey, *Stalin, Man of History* (Garden City: Doubleday, 1979), paints him as a Julius Caesar. More often, we see him as tragic perpetrator of a 'Witches Sabbath', as in Ulam (note 28), p.741; or dark 'Walpurgis Night', as in Moshe Lewin, *The Making of the Soviet System: Essays in the Social History of Interwar Russia* (New York: Pantheon Books, 1985), pp.207–10. L. Batkin, 'Son razuma. O sotsio-kul'turnykh masshtabakh lichnosti Stalina', in Kobo (note 71), pp.27–42, argues convincingly that Dzhugashvili and his cohort are not fit for Shakespearian imagery.
126. 'In tragedies of tyrants, the theatrical power of evil and the appeal of violence are as much exploited as they are condemned', Rebecca W. Bushnell, *Tragedies of Tyrants: Political Thought and Theater in the English Renaissance* (Ithaca, NY and London: Cornell University Press, 1990), p.187.
127. Kathleen E. Smith, *Remembering Stalin's Victims: Popular Memory and the End of the USSR* (Ithaca, NY: Cornell University Press, 1996); Merridale (note 11), p.vi, for example, is dedicated to 'Stalin's victims', as is Kobo (note 71), p.4.
128. Aleksandr Solzhenitsyn, *The Gulag Archipelago, 1918–1956* (New York: Harper and Row, 1974). For similar approaches, see Stephane Courtois (ed.), *The Black Book of Communism: Crimes, Terror, Repression* (Cambridge, MA: Harvard University Press, 1999); and Alexander N. Yakovlev, *A Century of Violence in Soviet Russia*, trans. Anthony Austin (New Haven and London: Yale University Press, 2002).

7

From Stalinism to Post-Stalinism: De-Mythologising Stalin, 1953–56

POLLY JONES

In October 1955, nearly three years after Stalin's death, the Central Committee received a letter from a retired lawyer in Moscow, bearing the title, 'The Revision of the Stalinist Era of the Party's History'.[1] The author, a certain Aladzhalov, urged the leadership to proclaim a clean break with Stalinism at the 20th Party Congress, the first such gathering in the post-Stalinist era, due to be held in February 1956. Like many domestic and foreign observers, he had understood the reforms that had taken place in the months and years after Stalin's death in March 1953 as an attempt to renounce certain parts of the late leader's legacy, especially in the criminal justice system and the Soviet economy. Whilst this impression was strengthened by the disappearance from much public discourse of the epithets and canonical narratives of the Stalin cult, and indeed of Stalin's name itself, the author, as one of this discourse's intended recipients, argued that its messages remained unclear. It left even sophisticated 'readers' disorientated and it exposed an apparent lack of commitment within the Soviet leadership to 're-write' the history of the Stalin era in any substantive sense. In short, it exposed a disjuncture between post-Stalinism, understood strictly chronologically (Soviet society after the death of Stalin), and post-Stalinism in a broader sense (the completion of the transition from the system charismatically embodied by Stalin).

In what follows, I examine the post-Stalinist leadership's attempts to negotiate this transition, which has often been loosely termed 'de-

Stalinisation', within the specific realm to which de-Stalinisation properly refers, namely the public imagery of Stalin. I show that the Soviet élite's repeated failure to provide a consistent image of Stalin and a coherent narrative of Stalinism to replace the tropes of Stalin's personality cult made complaints and calls for clarity 'from below', such as Aladzhalov's letter, a consistent feature of the first wave of de-Stalinisation (1953–56). The leadership's failure to manage the transition from Stalinism to post-Stalinism, then, left *its* discourse of de-Stalinisation vulnerable to other interpretations and narratives about Stalin and Stalinism. Ultimately, this would be resolved, at the end of 1956, by a partial reversion to Stalinism and by the partial preservation of the cult's symbolism, rather than the principled and explicit confrontation of the Stalin question which Aladzhalov had desired.

Before looking in greater detail at the course that the leadership in fact took at the 1956 Congress, let me first return briefly to the actions taken before that year, which, after nearly three years, had finally prompted Aladzhalov to complain. The Soviet leadership plotted a paradoxical course between renunciation and reverence after Stalin's death in March 1953. Although the death itself prompted an outpouring of the language and rituals of the cult, especially from a grief-stricken population apparently unable to conceive of a future not governed by the *vozhd'* (leader/*führer*), it was precisely this hysterical sense of the impossibility of life without Stalin that the post-Stalinist Central Committee had to contain and, at least implicitly, attack.[2] The very fact of Stalin's death, of course, as with so many personality cults, did much to dissipate the centripetal force of the cult.[3] The edifice of the cult was further weakened by the refusal to reinforce it by perpetuating its language (the epithets of the cult began to be censored), or by creating any new symbols to perpetuate Stalin's memory (other than the placement of Stalin in the Kremlin Mausoleum and the promise to build a pantheon, no other commemorative sites or symbols were created to honour Stalin, despite a wealth of suggestions sent to the authorities).[4] Stalin was further displaced from his central position in Soviet culture when policies associated with him began to be adjusted or implicitly renounced (an example of the latter was the decision to grant amnesty to large numbers of people imprisoned in the Gulag under Stalin, from April 1953 onwards, whilst numerous shifts in economic and foreign policies, which were most radical under Beria, but continued until 1956, typified the former approach).[5] For all that these developments represented a significant departure from the Stalin cult, and an effective means of dismantling some of its constructs, they nonetheless steered clear of explicit criticism, both by shielding Stalin from direct attack, and by periodically asserting his merits.[6]

Therefore, although many elements of the cult *were* irreparably damaged by developments between 1953 and the end of 1955, the full de-mythologisation of Stalin would require more than ignoring or sideswiping the late leader, and a more consistent approach to the totalitarian culture of the cult.[7] Although the death of Stalin, and this early, limited confrontation of the Stalinist past had already rendered a return to Stalinism unlikely, it was still possible, before the 20th Congress, to look to Stalin and the Stalin era at least nostalgically, and often worshipfully. Indeed, such an attitude was seemingly encouraged by the continued saturation of public space with Stalin imagery (portraits, monuments), and the enduring dominance of 'Stalin' as totemic figure in the history books, and therefore within the historical narratives used in the education system – notably the *Kratkii kurs* (Short Course) – museums and public rituals.[8]

Even within the Central Committee, the beginnings of a more comprehensive and principled approach to this discomfiting situation can be dated only from the end of 1955, when the Central Committee ordered a commission to be formed, under adjunct member Pospelov, to research Stalin's part in the Great Terror.[9] The commission's findings were incorporated, over the course of January and February 1956, into a wide-ranging report on Stalin and Stalinism, which, after much wrangling, it was agreed to read out at the forthcoming 20th Party Congress, at a closed session after the end of official proceedings.[10] The 'Secret Speech', as it became known, combined the commission's findings on repressions between 1934 and 1938 with Khrushchev's own, more impressionistic, but nonetheless highly critical, account of other episodes in the Stalin era, notably Stalin's incompetence during the war and post-war period, and his involvement in the creation of his own cult of personality. The speech's combination of Marxist-Leninist theorising (its critique of the '*kul't lichnosti*'), serious historical narrative, scandalous revelations and savage satire seemed calculated to debunk the entire interlocking system of myths that had surrounded and sacralised Stalin throughout his leadership, including the myth of his military expertise (Stalin as *Generalissimo*), his 'modesty' (*skromnost'*) and his benevolent concern for his own citizens (which had justified the 'gratitude' constantly offered to Stalin in public discourse).[11]

The version of the speech that it was decided to circulate around Party organisations (according to a Central Committee decision of 5 March) preserved many of the most shocking revelations of the Secret Speech intact, and strict limits were placed on the nature and extent of its dissemination.[12] Although, for propaganda purposes, the regional authorities were acquainted very rapidly with the speech itself, the lower ranks of the Party were first presented with general statements about the cult during discussions of the 20th Congress as a whole. These meetings, which began at the *aktiv* level in early March, and proceeded to be held at various levels down to the primary Party organisations and general enterprise meetings, were, however, dominated by speeches and written questions about the cult. The speech itself was read out at meetings (*chitki doklada*) with no public discussion whatsoever, although questions submitted and surveillance of listener reactions also permit us to gain some sense of its impact at these gatherings.

The Secret Speech was not only unusual because of the semi-public way in which it was read out, but also because it proved exceptionally difficult to 'read', that is, it lacked the clarity and dogmatic tone of most Soviet propaganda. For some listeners, perhaps the majority, the difficulties were interpretive, since the speech's unprecedented mixture of styles and its insistence on Stalin's merits, within an otherwise swingeing attack on him, did not fit into standard Soviet discourse. As such, it also gave few easily readable instructions to guide the enactment of de-Stalinisation (for example, the degree of censorship required). For others, the speech was more obviously a condemnation or campaign against Stalin, of the type that had been conducted against 'enemies of the people' under Stalin himself (*kampaniya*), but this message was often resisted rather than accepted, and the cult's narratives about Stalin were defiantly repeated to protect him from his successors' verbal assault. For others still, the discourse of de-Stalinisation seemed faulty, illogical or inconsistent in its exclusive focus on Stalin rather than the systemic faults of Stalinism or even Soviet power itself. Let me look briefly at each of these challenges to the Party's discursive monopoly, before turning to the methods used by the authorities to re-assert their control.[13]

By far the most common reported reaction, other than 'unanimous approval', were calls for clarification of one or more aspects of the speech, or of its practical consequences. In a broad sense, the speech's half-hearted insistence on Stalin's merits and its self-proclaimed emphasis on moderation sat uneasily with the many elements that it borrowed from Soviet invective, as well as with the damning quantity of evidence indicting Stalin of the most serious crimes. Faced with this, the disorientation of many listeners can best be summed up in such questions as 'After everything we've heard, what kind of person should we now consider Stalin to be?' and 'what memories of Stalin should we now keep?'[14] Ironically, this deference to the Party's discursive monopoly exposed the leadership's inability to provide clear answers or effective propaganda in this, the first major post-Stalinist propaganda initiative. Many flatly expressed their confusion, and their inability to draw a clear lesson from the speech, requesting further guidance in formulating the appropriate attitude toward Stalin.[15] In Ukraine's Volynskaya *oblast'*, one question asked which of the two official texts about Stalin – the one recited over the 30 years of the cult, or the explosive new discourse – should now be believed.[16] Others looked to the leadership to lead the way by showing their own feelings more plainly.[17]

In expressing their confusion, many listeners inadvertently indicated just how distinctive the speech was, compared to the dogmatic tone of Stalinist rhetoric. The ambiguities of the speech made it problematic to analyse using the categories of Stalinist discourse, but it also proved difficult to abandon the labels of the cult. In Sukhumi, a region in the Caucasus where the cult was particularly strong, one anonymous listener in Tkvarcheli asked with frustration, 'I still don't understand, is Stalin to be considered a leader (*vozhd'*) or not?'.[18] In Tuva, one question attested to the difficulty of understanding the degree of necessary change to former beliefs, 'We used to think of Stalin as our leader and teacher (*vozhd' i uchitel'*), can we now think of him that way?'[19] These questions indicated that the language and attitudes of the cult had become so deeply embedded in the minds of many of the population that it was difficult to imagine that Stalin could be *officially* described in any other terminology except the epithets of the cult.

If the term *vozhd'* still loomed large in thinking about Stalin, equally prevalent were the broader outlines of Stalinist thinking, especially the hero–villain dichotomy. Binary thinking surfaced in

many questions, enquiring whether Stalin was still the exemplary
hero of the cult's discourse, or the polar opposite, an enemy of the
people (*vrag naroda, vreditel'*). In Lithuania, one listener presented a
stark choice of labels for Stalin: was he still an exemplary figure
(*uchitel'*) or a disgrace to the Party (*vrag*)?[20] This pairing of terms was
especially common, although some used other terms from the cult's
discourse, such as 'pupil' (*uchenik*) and 'continuer' (*prodolzhatel'*), as
the opposite pole to the enemy classification.[21] This call for more
definitive categorisation shows that Stalinist thinking – specifically,
the Manichaean division between sanctification and demonisation
most strongly expressed in the cult and the purges, respectively – had
left a deep imprint on many minds and still proved to be the standard
interpretive categories brought to bear on the Party's propaganda.

Nonetheless, there was widespread recognition of the gravity of
this potential charge against Stalin, which reflected both the severity
of previous attacks on designated enemies (most recently, Beria) and
also the legacy of long-standing strictures on unauthorised
descriptions, much less criticism, of the person or image of Stalin.[22]
Trepidation and uncertainty about possible retribution certainly
made several listeners cautious: one, in Vologda, enquired about the
possible criminal penalties for calling Stalin an enemy, before
committing to that view publicly, whilst another in Stalingrad
wondered if he would get into trouble if he asked for a clearer
statement on Stalin.[23] Apart from showing an ingrained fear of the
authorities, such questions also exposed, however, the hesitation and
cowardice of the *leadership* in failing to throw its weight behind a full
condemnation of Stalin.

In the absence of clarification, there were innumerable questions
raising the possibility that Stalin was an enemy, in Chita and
Stalingrad, for example.[24] Others were more forthcoming. In
Ukraine's Sumskaya *oblast'*, it was reported that most collective
farmers now considered Stalin an enemy, and in Stalingrad and
Rostov, for example, it was reported that some workers held similar
convictions.[25] Written questions and statements often amplified this
theme. One emphasised that Stalin was guilty of murder, in (literally)
gory terms –'the question arises, is it worth honouring the memory
of a person who was responsible for shedding the blood of so many
innocent people?' – implying a readiness to make independent
judgements on commemoration (or lack of it) if such a commitment
was not forthcoming from the leadership.[26] Another, asserting that

Stalin had transgressed a fundamental moral principle (the sanctity of human life), asked in frustration, 'why is this being so weakly condemned?'.[27] In Chita, one question left little room for manoeuvre – 'can we consider Stalin an enemy of the people? If he's an enemy, then why is he still in authority, and if he's not an enemy, then why did he destroy the best people?'[28] All of these expressed incredulity that the authorities had not explicitly drawn the obvious conclusion from their own data – that Stalin must now be deemed an enemy.[29] Listeners who had already reached that conclusion also occasionally suggested appropriate rituals of punishment, such as posthumous trial or exclusion from the Party, or stripping Stalin of the titles and honorifics of the cult (such as *Generalissimo*).[30]

All of these judgements pressed the leadership to act with consistency, and to recognise the moral equivalence between Stalin's acts and those of other criminals and enemies. Most such calls took refuge in the relative safety of the anonymous note. However, even where outrage about Stalin, or the insistence on his being named an enemy, surfaced in public statements and speeches, the punishment was curiously irresolute, and usually placed more blame on the failure of Party propagandists (in transmitting misleading signals about Stalin's status) than on the individual respondents.[31]

Other 'readings' of the speech were less benign, and exhibited a greater confidence in decoding, and then often criticising, the apparent intent of the campaign. For some listeners, especially those in higher education establishments, the speech was a disingenuously personalised account of Stalinism which, in demonising Stalin, evaded the need for the Party to interrogate its own failings during the Stalin era. The accusation that the Politburo had waited too long, perhaps to their own benefit, before (posthumously) 'correcting' Stalin was particularly widespread, and not merely among the *intelligentsia*.[32] Where this sentiment was spoken aloud, it was usually picked up on by the local authorities, who would report it as 'slander' (*kleveta*) or, occasionally, and depending on the argument within which such statements appeared, as anti-Soviet.[33] Conversely, less personalised and cynical criticism that instead targeted the underlying systemic faults and occasionally provided cogent visions of the political reforms necessary fully to 'overcome the cult of personality' (pluralist elections, free speech) was both more narrowly confined to intellectual circles and more consistently and ruthlessly punished. Several such serious incidents in Moscow laboratories and academic institutions – among them, famously, the Thermo-Technical Laboratory – were investigated, and their perpetrators punished (and shamed on the pages of *Pravda*) by the central authorities.[34] Similar controversies at less prestigious (and more peripheral) establishments, such as the stormy meetings at the Stalingrad Pedagogical Institute, when many students were severely punished for speaking their mind on the Soviet system and the need for democratisation, were usually dealt with at *oblast'* level, although they were highlighted in *obkom* reports sent to the centre, as examples of the gravest unintended consequences of the anti-Stalin campaign.[35]

Whilst these arguments accepted the speech's representation of Stalin but pushed the authorities to provide an equally coruscating critique of Stalinism and of the flaws of the Soviet system, other critiques of the speech claimed that the regime's demonisation of Stalin was wrong in a narrower sense, since it distorted Stalin's own true identity. The contours of this 'true' identity usually corresponded, in this argument, to the images of the cult. Among the military, for example, the intertwining of the Soviet war myth and the tropes of the Stalin cult often led to a refusal to deconstruct either mythology. A retired colonel from the Moscow garrison responded to the speech, for instance, by saying that:

> Stalin did a great deal for the Soviet state and you cannot belittle his achievements ... thanks to Stalin we triumphed in the years of the patriotic war and were able to rout Hitler's Germany ... I held and will hold Stalin in the highest regard. His merits are great in every domain, our people (*narod*) believed in him like a God and thanks to that we won the war.[36]

An anonymous letter to Molotov from Stalingrad submitted de-Stalinisation to a swingeing attack by referring to this same complex of popular and national tradition, alleging that, '[P]eople fought and triumphed with Stalin's name, why and to whom was it necessary to insult the feelings of our best patriots, those most devoted to communism!'[37] These allegations of popular support for the cult also derived strength in other anonymous letters from references to the working of popular psychology: 'The time has still not come for the leader (*vozhd'*) to be replaced by collective leadership (I'm talking about the popular psyche). The people still needed a leader'; and, contrary to Khrushchev's allegations of Stalin's control over the cult, by alleging popular participation in the creation of the Stalin myth: 'In every family, Stalin's name is linked to happiness. The people continue to love Stalin and create legends about him'.[38]

These references to popular psychology and culture reflected a wider paradox in arguments against the de-mythologisation of Stalin. Where Khrushchev's Secret Speech derived much of its polemical power from the contention that the cult was not only far-removed from reality, but also the antithesis of 'popular' in both content (the preponderant focus on Stalin) and form (pomposity, monumentalism), protests against de-Stalinisation asserted on the contrary the popular support for the traditions 'invented' by the cult. Much protest from the 'people' was thus expressed through the polemical insistence on retaining the formerly canonical images of the old regime; dissent in this instance was expressed in archetypally official discourse, a defiant refusal to reconstruct and reject propaganda received from the party in the past.

At the same time as arguing for the continued validity, and vitality, of the former imagery of Stalin, such complaints also directly attacked the new, negative images of Stalin that were supposed to supplant the cult, often with a viciousness that recalled *Stalin-era* denunciations of enemies. Thus, letters to Soviet leaders and publications in the wake of the speech made allegations such as, 'Everything's been sullied … you'd have to be a real bastard (*podlets*) to stir all this up, dirty everything and throw it out'.[39] Meanwhile, an anonymous letter to Molotov from Stalingrad in the months immediately after the 20th Congress called the basis of the speech 'so-called facts', its author 'a cretin and a moron' (*kretin i nevezhda*), and the end result 'lies from start to finish' whilst, in another, a communist criticised the 'presentation of facts in an exaggerated rather than realistic form'.[40]

All of these responses, for all their surprising diversity, pointed up the same fundamental conclusion – the Secret Speech would not suffice as a definitive new statement on Stalin, whether because it wrongly ignored his merits, or because it was not an effective or conventional propaganda campaign, or because it failed to tackle the issues underpinning the cult. In a broader sense, this explosion of responses indicated that de-Stalinisation had failed because it had been widely misunderstood, and had failed to mobilise the population around its central ideas. Rather, it had mobilised different sectors of the population to adopt and, albeit sometimes warily, to defend a variety of stances on de-Stalinisation that mostly ran counter to the leadership's intentions. Although records of Central Committee Presidium meetings, an invaluable record of the élite decision-making process, remain classified, the consequent evolution of the official position on Stalin and the Stalin cult can be gleaned from a variety of published sources and archival records of other central and local institutions.

Even to contemporary foreign observers, the progress of de-Stalinisation after the initial campaign to disseminate the Secret Speech clearly indicated that the leadership had been compelled, by a number of factors, principally the fear of dissent, to rescind much of its criticism of Stalin; currently available archival materials have not disproved this contention.[41] This retreat from a frontal attack culminated in the official 're-writing' of the Secret Speech in a Central Committee resolution of July 1956, which was openly publicised, unlike the Secret Speech itself, and attacked Stalin's attackers far more than it did Stalin himself.[42] The mild criticism of Stalin, coupled with the strongly worded defence of the Soviet system (not seriously damaged by Stalin) became the standard formula used to negotiate (or evade) the Stalin question within élite discourse, re-surfacing in the final version of the 'Stalin' entry in the much-delayed volume of the *Bol'shaya Sovetskaya Entsiklopediya* eventually sanctioned for publication in summer 1957.[43] Concurrent with this definitive abandonment of the possibility of the Stalinist-type campaign against Stalin was the resumption of quasi-Stalinist methods to deal with dissenters, when arrests for political dissent resumed at the end of the year, preceded by a growing number of public criticisms of such thinking.[44] The combination of these methods left de-Stalinisation itself, and therefore its object, the Stalin cult, in an awkward state.

The halting and anxious process of determining Stalin's status after the Secret Speech was particularly clearly reflected in the vagaries of reforms to the exceptionally 'Stalinised' Soviet education system. Students and teachers at all levels of the educational system who heard the Secret Speech were quick to perceive the practical problems associated with changing Stalin's status, especially given the lack of clear guidelines on the extent of necessary change.[45] In the earliest official responses to these queries about the use of Stalin's works, which had formerly dominated curricula, the texts were described as flawed, but useful in parts.[46] However, the related question of Stalin's canonical status elicited a bewildering variety of assessments. One leading figure thought it instructive that Khrushchev had called Stalin 'one of the strongest Marxists', whilst another claimed, on the contrary, that Stalin as author was to be read as any other, ordinary person.[47] Despite such demotions, however, the greater evil by far was the iconoclastic methods of previous 'campaigns' (*kampanii*).[48] For Stalin to be a 'forbidden' author was, categorically, not an option.[49] That these early local responses derived from an official blueprint, albeit one interpreted by local leaders to yield a variety of nuances, is, furthermore, suggested by the insistent claims in the central press that Stalin remained a worthy theorist.[50]

In response to these indications, universities and other higher education establishments spent some six months after the Secret Speech adjusting their teaching practices and tools to rid them of the cult of personality (*kul't lichnosti*).[51] This largely entailed reducing the hitherto heavy reliance on the *Kratkii kurs* and the study of Stalin quotations, although in practice teachers and students alike found the transition fraught and confusing.[52] As in the meetings examined above, the central signals on Stalin's status exacerbated the perplexity, since Stalin's own works, including those on economics, linguistics and materialism, *were* included on the Education Ministry's reformed university curricula issued over the spring and summer of 1956, although their theoretical and practical dominance of the fields of Marxism-Leninism, social sciences and history was much reduced, and their presence smacked of tokenism.[53] Stalin's scholarly standing, then, was improvised by both the authorities and by individual teachers over the course of 1956. In practice, this perpetuated early attitudes to de-Stalinisation – teachers remained confused, and some still resorted to total censorship as a way of negotiating Stalin and Stalinism in the classroom.[54]

Although corresponding changes to the still more 'Stalinised' school programme had been requested in the immediate aftermath of the Secret Speech, the cult's widespread influence was also only addressed haltingly in this domain. Some guidelines were issued before the end of the school year, to ensure that the worst aspects of the cult, which had been strongly criticised for its influence on children, were no longer allowed to warp young minds.[55] However, it was not until the weeks preceding the start of the new academic year that detailed guidelines and some new teaching materials were made available, and even then, these moves still resembled the improvisatory measures taken earlier, in the middle of the school year. The Russian Education Ministry guidelines, developed during the summer and issued just before the start of the school year, were categorical in their criticism of the 'old' (pre-Secret Speech) textbooks.[56] At the same time, they were largely designed to aid teachers in using these same books in the interim before new textbooks were available.[57] Teachers were instructed, for example, to be more selective in their choice of classwork material (to exclude texts praising Stalin from literary and historical material currently in use) and to censor sections of the texts that mentioned the leader.[58]

As a result, the *Kratkii kurs* and other textbooks issued before the Secret Speech, for all that they had been openly vilified, continued to be used for much of 1956.[59] The de-Stalinisation of education continued, throughout 1956, to operate on the basis of guidelines published in the educational press, and crash-courses in how to de-Stalinise the old programmes.[60] Again, the onus was placed on teachers, who were expected to improvise a new historiography of the Stalin period (and many other 'Stalinised' periods of Russian history) based on guidelines that were both opaquely theoretical and vague. The result, as described by the American journalist Louis Fischer, was a situation where:

> The teaching of history in Soviet schools and its presentation in Soviet journals are in a state of utter confusion ... the poor schoolchildren don't know what to think; their teachers are bewildered; and authors of textbooks are afraid to put pen to paper.[61]

In this sense, the 'progress' of de-Stalinisation did little to move educational reform forward, or to alleviate the pressures that teachers had experienced immediately after the Secret Speech.

The de-Stalinisation of education demonstrates both the initial uncertainties of the campaign, and the problems that endured even after the campaign had been brought under control, since the new moderate and ambiguous stance on Stalin proved difficult to translate into coherent practice. The same paradoxes attended the treatment of the Stalin cult's iconography. The early stages of de-Stalinisation saw all kinds of 'experiments' as listeners to the Secret Speech tried to gauge the new rules of conduct and to ritualise the changes to Stalin's official image.[62] Within certain behavioural and hierarchical limits, removal of Stalinist images was acceptable, and proceeded rapidly during the period when the Secret Speech was the dominant official discourse about Stalin. Moscow would have looked dramatically different to its inhabitants, as would many other places, such as the Golden Ring towns, Saratov, Kazan', Gorkii (Nizhnii Novgorod) and Arkhangel'sk, which had formerly been dominated by the visual culture of the cult, but Stalin had by no means disappeared from view.[63] The number of possible variations on this balance between destruction and preservation, which were often juxtaposed in one city, district or even street, only served to exacerbate the disorientation of Soviet citizens who *saw* de-Stalinisation (removal of iconography) before *hearing* about it (through the long process of disseminating the Secret Speech).[64]

Doubtless the disorientation that such moves were liable to cause had some effect on the leadership, as was indicated in vague caveats issued by *obkom* secretaries to enquiries about iconography submitted to *aktiv* meetings in March.[65] However, it was not until late April, after the position on de-Stalinisation had hardened as a result of radical dissent, that iconoclasm started to decelerate. By the end of the month, the US Embassy in Moscow reported to the State Department that there appeared to be a 'let up in campaign to remove physical memorials [to] Stalin'.[66] Although currently de-classified records do not allow us to verify this rumour of an official command to slow down de-Stalinisation, the (literally) on-the-ground evidence suggests that it was understood from this time onwards that de-Stalinisation would slow down, if not stop entirely.[67]

To compound the impression that very little had changed, requests for authorisation of changes to iconography increasingly went unheeded. The colossal Stalin statue on Stalingrad's Volga-Don canal had been one of the city's most auspicious monuments until right before the Secret Speech; in January 1956, the *obkom* had proposed to the Central Committee that the 'magnificent' Volga-Don monument be moved from the canal to the centre of the town, since this would allow the canal to have a Lenin monument (fitting, given its name), and the city (centre) to have a suitably grand Stalin monument, essential for the 'city that bears the name of Iosif Vissarionovich Stalin'.[68] In a second letter written on 10 March, in the early aftermath of the Secret Speech, however, the *obkom* had had a complete change of heart, and the monument was transformed into an

embarrassment, which ought to be removed, and replaced with a
Lenin statue.[69] The two letters demonstrated well the abrupt switch in
the semiotics of the cult. Whilst the letter preceding the Secret Speech
legitimised its request to alter the symbols of the cult through
reference to the close connection between Stalingrad and Stalin and
between Stalin and Lenin, the letter written in the wake of the speech
legitimised its request to remove the Stalin monument by alluding to
the ideological incongruity between the preserved icon (the
monument) and the destroyed image (that of Stalin). Regardless of this
request's logic, however, the Volga-Don statue remained in place, its
endurance another sign of the failed de-Stalinisation of Stalingrad
(whose name also remained in place until several years later).[70]

An analogous appeal to logic was made in a letter to Bulganin
from a retired teacher, who wrote in April to complain that a vast
Stalin statue had not yet been removed from outside Moscow's
Tret'yakov museum, causing amusement among foreign delegations
taken to the museum.[71] Again, however, despite the appeal to clarify
the 'message' of de-Stalinisation, nothing was done, and the
Tret'yakov statue stayed in place, and under the protection of the
Moscow authorities, throughout 1956 and beyond.[72] Most major
Stalin monuments throughout the Soviet Union likewise survived de-
Stalinisation intact and remained under state or municipal protection,
although mass-produced, minor statues were certainly reduced in
quantity over the same period.[73]

After the infamous resolution of 30 June, there were very few
reports that de-Stalinisation had progressed any further.[74] Most
observers' accounts after this point ceased to mention dramatic
change, and focused instead on the often astonishing degree to which
the cult had *not* changed; now that iconoclasm had stopped, the
quantity of Stalin icons that remained in place became even more
striking. In August, a group of communists from Molotov sent a letter
to the journal *Partiinaya zhizn'* (*Party Life*), to bemoan the fact that,
especially at railway stations, there remained a preposterous number
of Stalin busts, statues and portraits, which no one seemed prepared
to tackle, in order to bring them into line with Stalin's new status.[75]
This picture of inertia, and the absurd incongruities between Stalin's
new image and the irrational excesses of the cult's imagery were not
enough, however, to persuade the authorities to revive its campaign
against the cult. Louis Fischer, visiting a few months later, astutely
observed that:

> There is an incompleteness in the dethronement of Stalin ... neither his image nor his reputation has been 'liquidated' with the customary totalitarian thoroughness ... the fact of his rejection-retention suggests that hesitation governs the minds of Stalin's heirs in dealing with his ugly heritage.[76]

This observation captures well the uniquely hesitant iconoclasm of the campaign.

Although iconoclasm had come to a halt within a year of the Secret Speech, then, this protective attitude toward Stalinist symbolism nonetheless had little to do with the perceived aesthetic worth of these portraits and monuments, or the prestige of the Stalin theme. The art of the cult was officially attacked within weeks of the Secret Speech, and *representations* of Stalin, unlike Stalin himself, never recovered their standing in Soviet culture. Statues and portraits of Stalin were criticised as pompous and aesthetically inferior.[77] Vilified within élite cultural discourse, the visual culture of the cult therefore remained physically present in Soviet life, but disappeared from its aesthetic arsenal and celebratory texts.[78] No new paintings of Stalin were commissioned after the Secret Speech, and, after the first few weeks of the campaign, no substantive moves were undertaken to reverse iconoclasm that had already occurred.[79]

As in education, and in Soviet life more broadly, Stalin therefore remained awkwardly present, in order to avoid the much greater problems that would be caused by his erasure from the Soviet past and present. The preserved symbolism of his cult had by the end of 1956 been deprived of much of its prestige and significance, but its persistence, sometimes at the very heart of Soviet life (as, notoriously, in the preservation of Stalin's body within the mausoleum on Red Square until 1961), reminded the Soviet people and their leaders alike that the transition to post-Stalinism was far from complete.

I have therefore shown that the discourse of de-Stalinisation transformed, with the performance of the Secret Speech, from subtle and irresolute posthumous criticism of Stalin into an explicitly iconoclastic attack on the Stalin myth. However, this discourse was quickly de-stabilised by probing enquiries into its inherent flaws, and plausible, but ultimately impermissible, interpretations of its implications by a wide range of societal actors. The solution to this intolerable disorder was to re-assert the Soviet hierarchy and to develop, then defend, a tense, moderate stance on Stalin. In practical terms, this led to paradoxical and incoherent visual and textual representations of the immediate past (including the figure of Stalin and Stalinism itself) and of the ideals of the post-Stalinist future in public space, discourse and practices alike. These paradoxes would endure until 1961, when the 22nd Congress again returned to the theme of the past in order to clear the way to the 'radiant future', and, finally, as the Secret Speech had promised, to overcome the Stalinist past.

NOTES

Key to abbreviations for archive names:
- GARF – *Gosudarstvennyi arkhiv Rossiiskoi federatsii* – State Archive of the Russian Federation, Moscow.
- GAVO – *Gosudarstvennyi arkhiv Volgogradskoi oblasti* – State Archive of the Volgograd *Oblast'* (region), Volgograd.
- RGALI – *Rossiiskii gosudarstvennyi arkhiv literatury i iskusstva* – Russian State Archive of Literature and Art.
- RGANI – *Rossiiskii gosudarstvennyi arkhiv noveishei istorii* – Russian State Recent History Archive.
- RGASPI – *Rossiiskii gosudarstvennyi arkhiv sotsial'no-politicheskoi istorii* – Russian State Social and Political History Archive.
- TsALIM – *Tsentral'nyi Arkhiv literatury i iskusstva Moskvy* – Central Archive of the Literature and Art of Moscow.
- TsKhDMO – *Tsentral'nyi khranitel' dokumentov molodezhnykh organizatsii* – Central Document Repository of Youth Organisations.
- TsDNIVO – *Tsentr dokumentatsii noveishei istorii Volgogradskoi oblasti* – Document Centre for the Recent History of Volgograd *oblast'*.
- UG – *Uchitel'skaya Gazeta* – a newspaper for teachers.

1. RGANI, f.5, op.34, d.2, ll.47–53.
2. For examples of letters and 'mourning resolutions' sent by individuals and organisations to the Central Committee and Supreme Soviet in March 1953, see *inter alia*, RGASPI, f.82, op.2, dd.1470, 1434; RGASPI, f.558, op.11, d.1487; RGANI, f.5, op.16, dd.593a, 593b; GARF, f.5446, op.54, d.154; and GARF, f.7523, op.52, dd.15, 27, 82.
3. R. Tucker, *The Soviet Political Mind: Stalinism and Post-Stalin Change* (London: Allen and Unwin, 1972), pp.173–205; I. Deutscher, *Russia After Stalin* (London: Jonathan Cape, 1969), p.125. Comparative observations in V. Georgescu, 'Politics, History and Nationalism: The Origins of Romania's Socialist Personality Cult', in J. Held (ed.), *The Cult of Power: Dictators in the Twentieth Century*, East European Monographs, no.140 (Boulder, CO: Columbia University Press, 1983), pp.129–43, esp. p.140.
4. On linguistic censorship of *Literaturnaya Gazeta* in March 1953, see K. Simonov, 'On okazalsya printsipal'nee i energichnee, chem vse ostal'nye', in Iu. Aksyutin (ed.), *Nikita Sergeevich Khrushchev. Materialy k biografii* (Moscow: Izdatel'stvo politicheskoi literatury, 1989), pp.27–31; and RGALI, f.634, op.4, d.424. For a similar incident concerning an official history of the war written for May 1953, see

Yu. Abramova, 'Destalinizatsiya sovetskogo obshchestva i vooruzhennye sily v 1953–1964 gg.', in V.S. Lelchuk and G.Sh. Sagatelyan (eds.), *Sovetskoe obshchestvo: budni kholodnoi voiny. Materialy 'kruglogo stola', Institut Rossiiskoi istorii RAN 29 Marta 2000- g.* (Moscow-Arzamas: Institut Rossiiskoi istorii RAN: Arzamasskii pedagogicheskii institut, 2000), pp.203–20, 203. For some commemorative suggestions that were thus ignored, see RGANI, f.5, op.16, dd.593a, 593b; cf. C. Merridale, *Night of Stone: Death and Memory in Russia* (London: Granta, 2000), pp.332–8.

5. Typical accounts in Yu. Aksyutin and O. Volobuev, *XX s'ezd KPSS: novatsii i dogmy* (Moscow: Izdatel'stvo politicheskoi literatury, 1991), pp.40–65; and M. Geller and A. Nekrich, *Utopiya u vlasti*, new edn. (Moscow: Mik, 2000), pp.530–620.

6. There was some mild direct criticism of Stalin in 1953, especially at the July plenum that condemned Beria, but this was not extensive, R. Conquest, *Power and Policy in the USSR* (London: Macmillan, 1961), p.278; V.S. Avechnikov, G.Sh. Sagatelyan, 'Sovetskoe obshchestvo: politicheskie kampanii 50-kh godov', in Lelchuk and Sagatelyan (note 4), pp.305–35, esp. pp.325–7. M. Rush, *The Rise of Khrushchev* (Washington, DC: Public Affairs Press, 1958), p.38, and Khrushchev's colleague Shepilov, in his memoirs, *Neprimknuvshii* (Moscow: Vagrius, 2001), p.279, contend that Khrushchev derived legitimacy from the Stalin symbol until the start of 1956, using it as a weapon against Malenkov. The ambiguous stance on Stalin was well-reflected in the lack of standard practice for commemorating Stalin's birth and death between 1953 and 1955, procedures for celebrations in RGASPI, f.558, op.11, d.1487, l.110; RGANI, f.5, op.30, d.41, l.1; RGASPI, f.558, op.11, d.1487, ll.120, 121, 125.

7. See J. Brooks, *Thank You, Comrade Stalin! Soviet Public Culture from Revolution to Cold War* (Princeton, NJ: Princeton University Press, 2000), on the dominance of the cult and the constraints that it placed on Soviet discourse through the Stalin era. On the inadequacy of early de-Stalinisation, see A. Pyzhikov, 'XX s'ezd i obshchestvennoe mnenie', *Svobodnaya mysl'* 8 (2000), pp.76–85; and Radio Svoboda, 'Istoriya i sovremennost': XX s'ezd – sorok let spustya', author, convenor, V. Tolz, Broadcast 1, 'Posle Stalina. Gody 1953–1955', available at: http://www. svoboda.org/programs/cicles/XX/xx_01.asp.

8. A typical contemporary account of this paradoxical lack of change to the cult's public symbolism is H. Lazareff and P. Lazareff, *The Soviet Union since Stalin* (London: Odham's Press, 1955).

9. On the Pospelov commission, see, for example, V. Naumov, 'K istorii sekretnogo doklada N.S. Khrushcheva na XX s'ezde KPSS', *Novaya i noveishaya istoriya* 4 (1996), pp.147–68, 156–65.

10. On the creation and authorisation of the Secret Speech, a rapid but politically complex process that has dominated studies of the era, see, for example, F. Barsukov, 'Kak sozdavalsya zakrytyi doklad Khrushcheva', *Literaturnaya Gazeta*, 21 February 1996, pp.1–2; V. Naumov, 'Utverdit' dokladchikom tovarishcha Khrushcheva', *Moskovskie Novosti*, 4–11 February 1996, p.34; idem (note 9); Yu. Aksyutin and A. Pyzhikov, *Poststaliniskoe obshchestvo: problemy liderstva i transformatsiya vlasti* (Moscow: Nauchnaya kniga, 1999), pp.91–111, and their latest article, 'O podgotovke zakrytogo doklada N.S. Khrushcheva XX s'ezdu KPSS v svete novykh dokumentov', *Novaya i noveishaya istoriya* 2 (2002), pp.107–18.

11. Brooks (note 7) sees the trope of gratitude as the cornerstone of the entire edifice of the cult.

12. On the decision to disseminate the speech, see RGANI, f.1, op.2, d.17, ll.89–91; and ibid., d.18, ll.3–90 (the editing process, which added in a few caveats about moderation, more anecdotes, and some 'audience reactions'). Further commentary in Aksyutin and Pyzhikov, 'O podgotovke zakrytogo doklada' (note 10), p.117.

13. Many studies, especially of the last five years, following more extensive de-classification of Khrushchev-era archival material, have been concerned with the balance of public opinion that can be gleaned from these sources: for example, M. Zezina, 'Shokovaya terapiya: ot 1953-goda k 1956 godu', *Otechestvennaya istoriya* 2 (1995), pp.121–35; E. Zubkova, *Russia After the War: Hopes, Illusions and Disappointments, 1945–57* (Armonk: M.E. Sharpe, 1998); Yu. Aksyutin, 'Popular responses to Khrushchev', in A. Gleason, S. Khrushchev and W. Taubman (eds.), *Nikita Khrushchev* (New Haven: Yale University Press, 2000), pp.177–208. However, observations about 'public opinion' were impressionistic before de-classification of these sources – for example, 'Insofar as any pattern … can be discerned, shock at treatment of Stalin seems to be confined to simple people with more sophisticated individuals tending to approve', *Confidential U.S State Department Central Files: The Soviet Union. Internal Affairs 1955–59* (hereafter, *Confidential US Files*), telegram, 17 March 1956, no.2101; 'The overall reaction inside the Soviet Union was one of enormous approval', D. Filtzer, *The Khrushchev Era: De-Stalinisation and the Limits of Reform in the USSR, 1953–1964* (Basingstoke: Macmillan, 1993), p.20 – and, strictly speaking, remain so now. Any attempts to produce a statistical distribution of these tendencies would be fruitless (given the lack of objectivity in local and central reports and the choices made in compiling reports (*svodki*), not to mention the restrictions on free speech); cf. Aksyutin, 'Popular responses', p.178. However, looking at a wide variety of reports allows us to surmise that most regions *did* experience a combination of all these reactions, and to show the unexpected and unprecedented diversity of discourse about Stalin; for example, TsDNIVO, f.113, op.52, d.110, ll.7–10, a microcosm of a typical combination of principled dissent, violence, confusion and penetrating queries from below, in Stalingrad, and, in macrocosm, a compilation of Russian *obkom* secretaries' reports made at an April 1956 meeting, RGANI, f.5, op.34, d.2, ll.6–22.
14. RGANI, f.5, op.32, d.46, l.150; RGANI, f.5, op.32, d.43, l.64.
15. At a major meeting of the intelligentsia in Leningrad, many argued that the Party had been unclear about the cult, and asked for a clear, official statement on Stalin's place in history and theory, RGANI, f.5, op.16, d.747, l.78. Cf. an allegation in Volzhkii that the speech was difficult to interpret, TsDNIVO, f.11606, op.5, d.5, l.27.
16. RGANI, f.5, op.31, d.54, l.76.
17. 'Tell me, after everything that has become clear about Stalin, have you kept love for him in your hearts?', ibid., f.5, op.16, d.747, l.114
18. Ibid., f.5, op.31, d.52, l.38.
19. Ibid., f.5, op.32, d.46, l.182.
20. Ibid., f.5, op.31, d.54, l.128.
21. Ibid., f.5, op.16, d.747, l.114; ibid., f.5, op.31, d.54, l.128; how to 'correctly elucidate Stalin's role', as a leader of world revolution, or as harmful?, ibid., f.5, op.32, d.43, l.93.
22. On enemies, see, for example, A. Knight, *Beria: Stalin's First Lieutenant* (Princeton, NJ: Princeton University Press, 1993), pp.201–29; and, more generally, D. King, *The Commissar Vanishes: The Falsification of Photographs and Art in Stalin's Russia* (New York: Canongate, 1997). On the categorisation of disrespect to Stalin as anti-Soviet conduct, see, for example, V. Kozlov and S. Mironenko (eds.), *58–10. Nadzornye proizvodstva Prokuratury SSSR po delam ob antisovetskoi agitatsii i propagandy. Mart 1953–1991* (Moscow: Mezhdunarodnyi fond 'demokratiya', 1999), pp.18, 21, 26.
23. RGANI, f.5, op.32, d.43, l.133; TsDNIVO, f.113, op.52, d.103, l.20.
24. RGANI, f. 5, op.32, d.45, l.158; TsDNIVO, f.113, op.52, d.103, ll.157, 160.
25. RGANI, f.5, op.31, d.54, l.84; TsDNIVO, f.113, op.52, d.103, l.37; RGANI f.5, op.34, d.2, l.13.

26. RGANI, f.5, op.32, d.46, l.151.
27. Ibid.
28. Ibid., f.5, op.32, d.45, l.188; cf. question in Riga asserting that Stalin was surely now an enemy, ibid., f.5, op.31, d.53, l.8.
29. However, incredulity was also expressed by some listeners who could not believe that Stalin *would* be erased from history, given his historical importance, for example, ibid., f.5, op.16, d.747, l.108.
30. Posthumous trial, ibid., f.5, op.32, d.46, ll.151, 154; exclusion, ibid., d.45, l.124; targeting the titles of *Generalissimo* and Hero, ibid., d.46, l.10; *Generalissimo*, ibid., f.5, op.31, d.54, l.84; and a proposal to call Stalin Dzhugashvili, ibid., f.5, op.32, d.45, l.125.
31. For example, the corrections offered to various angry statements about Stalin as an enemy reported in ibid., f.5, op.32, d.45, l.159; ibid., d.46, l.121; ibid., d.45, l.135.
32. For example, Leningrad intelligentsia, ibid., f.5, op.16, d.747, ll.77–78; a Party secretary of a Tatarstan factory rebuked for responding to such an allegation with the implicitly sympathetic question, 'do you mean to say that it's easier to bash a dead person than a living one?', ibid., f.5, op.32, d.46, l.195.
33. Ibid., f.5, op.32, d.45, l.2; ibid., f.5, op.32, d.46, ll.18, 176.
34. Ibid., f.5, op.32, d.46, ll.82–87; Radio Svoboda (note 7), Broadcast 4, 'XX s'ezd, ekho nesushchestvennogo sekreta', available at: http://www.svoboda.org/programs/cicles/XX/xx_04.asp; *Pravda*, 5 April 1956, pp.2–3.
35. TsDNIVO, f.594, op.1, d.15; Reports such as RGANI, f.5, op.34, d.2, ll.6–22; ibid., f.5, op.32, d.46, ll.2–5, 21–22.
36. RGANI, f.5, op.32, d.46, l.204.
37. RGASPI, f.82, op.2, d.1467, l.2.
38. Ibid., f.82, op.2, d.1467, l.48; ibid., d.1470, l.28.
39. RGANI, f.5, op.30, d.140, l.8.
40. RGASPI, f. 82, op.2 , d.1467, l.1; ibid, l.15.
41. For example, compare G. Boffa, *Inside the Khrushchev Era* (London: Allen and Unwin, 1960); and A. Pyzhikov, *Genezis ofitsial'noi pozitsii KPSS po voprosu o kul'te lichnosti (1953–64 gg.)* (Moscow: 1998).
42. The fullest study of the resolution, which appeared in *Pravda*, 2 July 1956, pp.1–2, is M. Chulanov, 'Postanovlenie TsK KPSS ot 30 Iunya 1956 g. 'o preodolenii kul'ta lichnosti i ego posledstvii' v kontekste svoego vremeni', in T. Islamov and A. Sytalkin (eds.), *Avtoritarnye rezhimy v tsentral'noi i vostochnoi Evrope (1917–1990-e gody)* (Moscow: Institut slavovedeniya RAN, 1999), pp.140–95. This resolution was widely thought at the time to be a concession to pro-Stalinists in the Central Committee; their approval is confirmed in L. Kaganovich, *Pamyatnye zapiski rabochego, kommunista-Bol'shevika, profsoyuznogo, partiinogo i sovetsko-gosudarstvennogo rabotnika* (Moscow: Vagrius, 1996), pp.560–70.
43. Editorial process reflected in RGANI, f.5, op.30, d.140, ll.13–23. Final text in *Bol'shaya Sovetskaya Entsiklopediya*, vol.40 (1957), pp.419–24; cf. the all-but identical text about Stalin in B. Ponomarev (ed.), *Politicheskii slovar'*, 2nd edn. (Moscow: Gosudarstvennoe izdatel'stvo politicheskoi literatury, 1958), pp.555–8.
44. For example, *Pravda*, 5 April 1956, pp.2–3. Circulars were sent round party organisations to crack down on dissent in mid-June, see Chulanov (note 42), p.157, and in late December (on this letter and the resumption of arrests in late 1956 and early 1957 for dissent ('*nedozvolennaya kritika*'); see examples of prosecutions for anti-Soviet reactions to de-Stalinisation in Kozlov and Mironenko (note 22), pp.257, 265, 279; and Naumov's contribution to the round-table discussion, 'Diskussii i obsuzhdeniya – N.S. Khrushchev, lichnost', vremya, reformy', *Svobodnaya mysl'* 10 (1994), pp.27–32, 32. On further circulars in February 1957, see R. Pikhoya, *Sovetskii Soyuz: istoriya vlasti, 1945–91* (Moscow: RAGS, 1998), p.148.

45. Complaints from teachers in RGANI, f.5, op.31, d.54, l.56; TsDNIVO, f.113, op.52, d.103, l.132; students' and academics' consternation at the way Stalin's new status should be, or already was, reflected in changes to university curricula and lectures in, for example, RGANI, f.5, op.16, d.747, l.109; TsKhDMO, f.1, op.32, d.810, ll.5–9; RGANI, f.5, op.30, d.139, ll.5–26.
46. RGASPI f.556, op.1, d.65, l.129; ibid., d.281, l.139.
47. Ibid., d.52, l.108; ibid., d.281, l.139.
48. Ibid., d.752, l.151.
49. Ibid., d.526, l.167; cf. 'Thirteen volumes of Stalin works, can communists really imagine that they'll all be banned? Of course not', ibid., d.705, l.47.
50. For example, *Pravda*, 7 April 1956, pp.2–4; 'Usilit' rukovodstvo partiinoi propagandoi', *Kommunist*, no.14 (1956), pp.3–13.
51. New lectures were attended by local propagandists to ensure that the newly revealed faults of the old system had been eliminated, for example, Party reports in TsDNIVO, f.113, op.52, d.19, d.101 (Stalingrad *partshkola*); ibid., d.132 (including the Mechanical, Pedagogical, Medical, Agricultural institutes, all guilty of major errors in describing Stalin in their lectures and over-use of the *Kratkii kurs*); ibid., d.131, esp. ll.22–5, which describes a lecture where Stalin's works were still implicitly being used, even as the lecturer criticised Stalin and his works. For the process from the teachers' aggrieved point of view, see the discussions at Stalingrad Pedagogical Institute, GAVO, f.6056, op.2, dd.26, 27.
52. In addition to the general de-Stalinisation, some programmes had to be eliminated in the middle of the year and replaced with hastily written lectures about current politics; RGANI, f.5, op.35, ibid., d.25, ll.26–62, shows frantic correspondence between the Central Committee and education ministers trying to formulate a coherent programme for the rest of the academic year).
53. On the process of syllabus formation, see ibid., ll.62–95; and RGANI, f.5, op.35, d.26, where Stalin now appeared only once or twice in each lecture, whilst there were six or seven Lenin texts per class. Also see GARF, f.9396, op.1, dd.734, 744 and esp. d.745. For the official announcement about the new year, see *Pravda*, 23 August 1956, p.2.
54. A number of letters to *Kommunist* in late 1956, for example, came from teachers and propagandists still uncertain about the status of Stalin's works and the possibility of citing and mentioning Stalin, RGASPI, f.599, op.1, d.89, ll.24–42. On censorship, see a report from Moldavia, where students who asked why the Constitution was no longer described as '*Stalinskaya*' were told that it had *never* been named after Stalin, TsKhDMO, f.1, op.46, d.192, l.85.
55. For an official condemnation of the cult's influence in children, at the April 1956 Komsomol plenum, see, for example, TsKhDMO, f.1, op.2, d.347, l.67. The earliest statement on de-Stalinisation in schools came in 'XX s'ezd KPSS i zadachi ideologicheskoi raboty', *Prepodavanie istorii v shkole*, no.3 (1956), pp.3–11, which placed the responsibility on teachers to use the old textbooks with the new doctrine in mind; cf. *Uchitel'skaya Gazeta*, 4 April 1956, p.1.
56. Successive drafts of this document in GARF, f.2306, op.72, d.5628.
57. On the delays to textbooks, worsened by the fact that the new school year's books had been sent to press merely weeks before the 20th Congress, see, for example, GARF, f.2306, op.72, d.5085, l.40; ibid., l.55; RGANI, f.5, op.37, d.4, ll.56, 102–103, 130, 150.
58. Ibid., ll.9, 13, 21, 37.
59. On the complicated instructions on which editions to use with each class, issued a month after the school year had started, see 'Ob uchebnikakh po istorii dlya srednei shkoly', *Prepodavanie istorii v shkole*, no.6 (1956), pp.116–17.
60. For example, A. Pankratova (ed.), *Voprosy prepodavaniya istorii SSSR v svete reshenii*

XX s'ezda KPSS (Moscow: 1956); see also *UG*, 22 September 1956, pp.2–3; and 'Nekotorye voprosy prepodavaniya istorii SSSR v X klasse v pervoi chetverti 1956–7 uchebnogo goda', *Prepodavanie istorii v shkole*, no.4 (1956), pp.12–29.

61. L. Fischer, *Russia Revisited* (London: Jonathan Cape, 1957), p.39.

62. Examples of removals of iconography by local officials (and the rebukes occasionally issued to them) in RGANI, f.5, op.31, d.54, l.7; and ibid., f.5, op.32, d.43, l.8; whilst examples of individual or 'spontaneous' acts of de-Stalinisation, which were more often rebuked, are in TsDNIVO, f.113, op.52, d.110, l.9; RGANI, f.5, op.31, d.53, l.133; and ibid., f.5, op.32, d.46, l.58.

63. Reports of removal in letters to Soviet leaders in, for example, GARF, f.7523, op.75, d.16, l.197; RGASPI, f.82, op.2, d.1467, ll.18, 26; cf. eyewitness accounts of changes in Moscow in *Confidential US Files*, Embassy Telegram, 12 March 1956, no.2045; *New York Times*, 13 March 1956, p.5; *Confidential US Files*, Embassy telegram, 17 March 1956, no.2101; *Confidential US Files*, Embassy telegram, 26 March 1956, no.2177; *Confidential US Files*, Embassy telegram, 28 April 1956, no.2444; *New York Times*, 9 June 1956, p.16.

64. Reports of confusion in *New York Times*, 19 March 1956, pp.1–2; ibid., 22 March 1956, p.1; and ibid., 29 March 1956, p.9. Local authorities' complaints about these discrepancies and the rumours generated by them in RGANI, f.5, op.32, d.45, l.159; ibid., f. 5, op.32, d.46, l.121.

65. For example, the dismissal of suggested changes to portraits and statues as secondary questions in RGASPI, f.556, op.1, d.124, l.156; ibid., d.125, l.93; ibid., d.281, l.64.

66. *Confidential US Files*, Embassy Telegram, 28 April 1956, no.2444.

67. See the report in ibid. of a Moscow metro station statue of Stalin, boarded up in the weeks after the Secret Speech, but then put back on display by the end of April, with no changes.

68. TsDNIVO, f.113, op.52, d.68, l.1.

69. RGANI, f.5, op.30, d.143, l.2. The decision about this letter is in the *obkom* protocol of 7 March, TsDNIVO, f.113, op.52, d.19, l.4.

70. The next time the idea of the Volga-Don Lenin statue re-surfaced in a protocol, it only mentioned the construction of the Lenin statue, without referring to the (presumably shelved) plans to pull down the Stalin monument, ibid., d.20, l.76, protocol dated 12 May 1956. By the end of 1956, it was 'still undecided whether to tear it down or not', according to one visitor, J. Gunther, *Inside Russia Today* (London: Hamish Hamilton, 1958), p.205. A similar lack of commitment led to numerous (and reasonable) requests for the city's re-naming to be ignored; such suggestions are contained in, for example, GARF, f.7523, op.75, d.358, ll.34–111, whilst a specific instruction circulated around the Supreme Soviet in response to one suggestion, in September, deemed the idea inappropriate at that moment, ibid., l.78.

71. RGANI, f.5, op.36, d.26, l.39.

72. TsALIM, f.147, op.1, d.550, l.4, gives details of the numerous Stalin monuments still standing, and under the local council's protection in 1957.

73. R. Medvedev, *Khrushchev*, trans. B. Pearce (Oxford: Basil Blackwell, 1982), p.211. The Stalingrad *obkom* secretary, for example, advertised his intention to remove a portion of Stalingrad's 15 Stalin monuments, although not, as we saw, the most famous one, RGANI, f.5, op.34, d.2, ll.14, 22.

74. Khrushchev himself heralded this, in July 1956, as a return to normality after early expressions of outrage against Stalin, such as portrait removals. This confirms that the party line had by then turned to moderation, 'N.S. Khrushchev: 'U Stalina byli momenty prosvetleniya'. Zapis' besedy s delegatsiei Ital'yanskoi kompartii', *Istochnik* 2 (1994), pp.79–91.

75. RGANI, f.5, op.31, d.51, l.2.

76. Fischer (note 61), p.10.

77. One of the most wide-ranging statements on the harmful effects of the cult on Soviet culture came at the meeting of the Union Ministry of Culture collegium on 9 March 1956, RGALI, f.2329, op.2, d.437, ll.3–60; cf. ibid., d.470, l.24; and the September meeting of the council on monumental sculpture under the Ministry of Culture, RGALI, f.2329, op.4, d.532, ll.1–11.

78. Remaining monuments, for example, were no longer lovingly tended, and, if they fell into disrepair, were allowed to rot or be removed: see the decision to remove, rather than pay for the repair of, a large Stalin *bas-relief* in Chita in June 1956, RGANI, f.5, op.34, d.8, ll.26–33.

79. On the lack of new Stalin images, see M. Cullerne Bown, *Socialist Realist Painting* (New Haven: Yale University Press, 1998), pp.306–13; and Central Committee refusal to issue a commemorative portrait of Stalin, RGANI, f.5, op.36, d.28, ll.113–14. The limits on restoration of the cult are shown in the refusal to grant a request sent to Soviet leaders from some of the inhabitants of Astrakhan' for instructions to restore Stalin monuments and portraits that had all earlier been removed, GARF, f.7523, op.75, d.1585, l.83.

8

Recent Western Views of Stalin's Russia: Social and Cultural Aspects

JOHN KEEP

Fifty years after 'Koba the Dread' passed away the 'Stalin industry' flourishes as never before. There are two principal reasons for this. First, since the Soviet collapse a vast amount of documentary material has become accessible – even though Stalin's personal archive, and that of the security police, is still under wraps. This situation is in stark contrast to that prior to *glasnost'*, when foreign students of the USSR had little more to go on than whatever material the censors permitted to appear in print. It is entirely appropriate that scholars from outside the FSU, often in collaboration with Russian colleagues, should have hastened to exploit these resources with the aim, not just of filling in those once celebrated 'blank spots' in the historical record, but also of drawing a more accurate and hopefully more objective picture of what was really going on in the Soviet Union between 1929 and 1953. The present survey, which can offer no more than a provisional assessment, seeks to give an impression of the range of the vast amount of work done over the last few years, with an emphasis on social and cultural history, and to highlight both the potential and the attendant risks of the new methodological approaches that have been adopted.[1]

The revolution in thought associated with postmodernism and post-structuralism[2] has exercised a particular fascination upon the former sovietological community, particularly the 'new cohort' (Fitzpatrick) of historians keen to dissociate themselves from Cold War bias. They prefer to explore social and cultural issues rather than

the political, intellectual, military or diplomatic history favoured by
their more conventionally minded colleagues or by popular writers.
'Revisionism' in Soviet studies originated in the desire to write
history 'from below', so challenging the stereotyped view of an
'atomised' society wholly in the grip of an omnipotent dictator and
his *apparat*, one in which vertical linkages alone counted. The
revisionists taught us that matters were more complex: people had
divided loyalties; state and society could not be neatly distinguished
since they were linked in a web of intellectual and material inter-
dependencies, existing in symbiosis; grey, not black and white, was
the appropriate colour code. Today most writers on the subject go
along with such reasoning, although they may differ in where they
put the emphasis. Not everyone is willing, for instance, to follow the
pioneers in probing the inner thoughts and secret motives of ordinary
individuals where this involves making speculative inferences and
generalisations, or in focusing on these people's images of reality
rather than the reality itself, which the more traditional historians
still think it is worth while trying to establish.

Our PM-oriented colleagues have tried hard to ascertain Soviet
citizens' 'subjectivities' by examining the diaries they kept, their
letters of complaint to the press or Party leaders, denunciations and
so on, along with such official sources as Party and police reports
(*svodki*).[3] The key assumptions behind this approach, seldom clearly
articulated, would seem to be that (i) individuals construct their own
identities under social pressures of various kinds; (ii) by coalescing
with others in the same group (class, generation and so on) they
acquire a collective *mentalité*;[4] and (iii) such data, if available in
sufficient quantity and correctly processed, could enable one to
establish the degree of support for the regime among various
collectivities at different points in time. This may be regarded as the
'Holy Grail' of much post-sovietology. Whether it is attainable or
not, we are bound to learn much along the way.

It is also taken for granted that ordinary citizens, and more
especially lower-level functionaries, had some input into the political
and social process. Even if the basic decisions were taken at the
centre, people on the 'periphery' (as the provinces are now often
called) had a certain leeway in interpreting and implementing them –
although admittedly they might later be held accountable for any
errors of judgement they made, which were likely to be misconstrued
as inspired by malevolent intent. Hence the purges (a term usually

preferred to 'Terror'), which are seen as resulting from imperfections in the system of bureaucratic control, or from mass psychology, as much as from central direction – but this is an argument we shall not inquire into here. It follows from these assumptions that there was a good deal more opposition, latent or actual, in Soviet society to the regime's policies than earlier historians were willing to recognise, and that even within the authoritarian Stalinist polity there was room for informal 'negotiation'[5] between officialdom and the broader public. This opposition can be broken down by distinguishing between dissidence, deviation, and resistance or open protest.

One last point: most recent work relates to the pre-war decade; as more studies appear on the late Stalin era (1945–53) the evaluation of Soviet internal developments may well take on a darker hue. Let us now turn to some of the principal topics treated.

Peasants

The term resistance is used correctly in regard to the revolts that broke out in the countryside in 1930 in response to the initial measures of collectivisation. This is the subject of a monograph, two documentary volumes and several articles by Lynne Viola (Canada), who has also recently edited a miscellany on resistance in general.[6] The revolts, one quarter of them led by women, and their violent suppression are seen as a virtual civil war between town and country, a 'conflict of cultures' in which villagers of different socio-economic strata stood together against the authorities' efforts to 'colonise' the rural milieu. This perception is not new, but the problem has not previously been treated in such detail or with such authority. The protest wave began with the circulation of apocalyptic rumours, which proved an effective mobilisation device, and continued with acts of 'sabotage', often in a style that 'followed certain socio-political conventions'; finally, aggrieved peasants resorted to desperate assaults on local officials or engaged in riots, 'ritualised displays of rage, ... a specific genre in the peasant culture of resistance'. Though put down by force, they helped to bring about a (temporary) easement of the collectivisation drive.

Likewise the concession of private plots for *kolkhozniki* was a response to peasant disaffection during the 1932–33 famine. This tragic episode has been sensitively examined, on the basis of local archives, in a particular region, namely the Don *oblast'*, by D'Ann

Penner (US), who finds that there was a total collapse of relations between the authorities and the mass of the population.[7] Others have re-examined the lot of collective farmers in the later 1930s and the emergence of new rural élites.[8] Mary Buckley (UK) and her American colleague Lewis Siegelbaum have written several studies on the Stakhanovites that explore their motives, the (largely hostile) reactions evoked by their displays of zeal, and the activists' acquisition of enhanced self-esteem (in PM terminology, 'the importance of labour as self-validation').[9]

Workers

Gone are the days when Western scholars might put together a volume of essays with the title *Making Workers Soviet*.[10] As an analytical tool the concept of 'class consciousness' has fallen into disfavour, to be replaced by investigations into semiotics and symbolic communication, as David Hoffmann has noted.[11] Even so, in 1997 Kenneth Straus (US), after studying factories in one particular district of Moscow during the First Five-Year Plan era, concluded that the most significant sociological development was 'the formation of a relatively homogeneous working class' with shared experiences of recent entry, crash training and employment in brigades; all this produced 'a sense of community' centred on the enterprise, a lasting feature of the Soviet scene.[12] Some critics found Straus's interpretation insufficiently heedful of the conflictual relationships still fermenting beneath the surface calm. The archives also revealed data on previously unsuspected industrial unrest, not least in the textile plants of the Central Industrial region, which have been studied by Jeffrey Rossman (US) and Gabriele Gorzka (Germany). In three articles, Rossman has shown that the demands put forward were wholly economic (poor rations); that they enjoyed public sympathy; and that the authorities, while punishing the ringleaders, also responded positively by increasing food supplies. 'These events contributed to the social pressures that compelled the dictatorship to soften its economic policies'.[13]

Other trouble had to do with gender. Wendy Goldman (US), an authority on Bolshevik policy towards women, has looked at gender conflicts in Leningrad's 'Red Putilovets' factory, where in 1931 male workers in a whole range of jobs were replaced by women; the former are said to have 'frequently expressed their resentment in a sexualized form, regarding women's very presence in the factory ... as a sexual transgression'.[14] Gorzka has conducted research in Yaroslavl', site of one of Russia's oldest factories, founded in 1722 and known in Soviet times as 'Krasnyi Perekop'. After describing graphically the primitive physical conditions that obtained there, wages and prices, disciplinary measures, and social differentiation within the work force, she concludes that 'the political authorities were unable to find the right approach to the masses'; they ignored their everyday concerns and underestimated their intellectual level; only the educational opportunities offered proved successful.[15] A more critical view of workers' cultural level emerges from Laura Phillips's entertaining study of alcoholic indulgence in the 1920s.[16] She notes that the traditional practice of heavy ritual drinking survived, since it constituted a major element in workers' masculine identity. Like most of her fellow researchers, Phillips seeks evidence of social pressure from below, and finds that in this field too, workers did indeed compel the authorities to back down – over temperance policy! Whether this was good for them, or for the state, is not really her concern, presumably because the 'cultural studies' approach does not cover such mundane matters as the physical consequences of drunkenness or the liquor monopoly's contribution to state revenue, which would be of interest to the more conventionally minded.

Where Gorzka and Phillips place the cultural aspects of working-class life in the forefront, the editor of the volume in which Goldman's essay appeared, the British scholar Melanie Ilić, is the author of a study in which she pursues a more traditional topic: measures taken to protect women's health at the workplace and their practical implementation.[17] It is no surprise to learn that, given the emphasis on rapidly increasing physical output, such regulations were frequently by-passed, but Ilić points out that women themselves often flouted these restrictions in order not to lose their jobs, even when they were called on to work night shift. Nevertheless her conclusions are on the whole positive: despite sex segregation, women did receive 'unprecedented economic opportunities' and training that usefully fitted them for active service in wartime.

Gender and Everyday Life

For feminists women's studies ought to reach out far beyond the workplace. Claudia Kraft, an activist in the newly formed Swiss and

German workshop, the 'Basle Initiative for Gender Studies', complains that 'the old discourses about femininity' just trod water and failed to assist in 'the deconstruction of inherited images of gender'.[18] Previous studies of women in employment, she avers, said too much about the fate of their male comrades (although it is hard to see how this blemish could be avoided); one should recognise that the ideas commonly put forward on 'social space' were but constructs, and mostly made up by men anyway. Kraft does have a point: not much has appeared in a Soviet context on the history of women's bodies, say, by comparison with Western countries. However, Frances Bernstein has written two articles on the excesses of biological determinism among Soviet health experts in the 1920s and the shift in official policy towards prostitution once Stalin took over the helm.[19] There are also three recent studies on the post-war period that highlight the deficiencies of Soviet maternity clinics and the prevalence of abortion.[20] Most work in this area, however, stops in 1929–30. Carmen Scheide, who has closely followed the lot of Moscow women workers under NEP, provides new figures for their situation at that latter date.[21]

Especially welcome are the products of two oral history projects that offer a selection of primary sources in English translation.[22] Barbara Engel has the good grace to remark that these often heart-rending testimonies cannot readily be assessed 'within the framework of Western feminism': women interviewees did not feel inferior to men and were proud of their achievements in the face of hardship on a scale that Westerners had never had to bear.[23]

Earlier writers devoted a fair amount of attention to family matters. The 'cultural turn' has built on this by extending the discussion to the entire domestic environment, in the context of studies of everyday life (*Alltagsgeschichte*). The keyword here is *kul'turnost'*. In the later 1930s, at a time of scarcity and terror, the regime launched a remarkable drive to promote more civilised standards of life and behaviour: refined speech, personal cleanliness, a more varied diet and modern household conveniences. Stalin may have disapproved of women using perfume,[24] but he evidently had no objection to women's journals featuring illustrated articles on dresses, carpets, lampshades and the like. In a language reminiscent of old books of etiquette, élite wives were called on to take better care of their appearance and to try to provide decent conditions for their menfolk in the home. On top of this the *obshchestvennitsa* (socially engaged wives) movement set out to introduce higher standards in factory canteens or workers' apartments. A sizeable literature has grown up on these topics, with the enviably productive Catriona Kelly (UK) in the van.[25] Fascinating though these cultural studies often are, with their semiotic approach they risk confusing style with substance, highlighting superficial changes in *byt* while neglecting the horrors lurking in the background. Perhaps to the conventionally minded the most useful aspect is the attention directed towards consumer goods distribution and marketing. Sheila Fitzpatrick, in her widely acclaimed *Everyday Stalinism*, comments on the paradoxical emergence of 'a new (and, in Marxist terms, surprising) appreciation of commodities'; she cites a contemporary newspaper description of a Moscow grocery store that sold 38 types of sausage.[26] Soviet 'consumerism' in the 1930s was limited to people in the most privileged strata and withered as increased appropriations had to be made to defence, followed by wartime scarcities (and worse); yet it revived in new forms after 1953 and in the long run helped to undermine the regime.

Another feature of everyday life under Stalin was the holding of mass parades and other officially sponsored festivities. Such rituals are examined with great skill by Karen Petrone (US), who places the celebrations held of the 20th anniversary of October in the setting of those arranged to acclaim heroic exploits by Arctic explorers or the secular New Year (*elka*) substitute for Christmas.[27] She explores their multiple symbolic meanings and argues that such occasions could be used by the participants to articulate an alternative outlook that was subversive of official myths. In other words, we have here a two-way process in which 'individual actors shape discourse even as it shapes them' and 'Soviet citizens employed the state's mandates for their own ends ... to regain control over their lives'. We may expect much new work in the PM mode on entertainment and popular culture generally,[28] as a follow-up to the profusion of earlier writing on the cinema, which inevitably was seen from the producer's standpoint rather than that of the audience.

Higher Culture

Scholars influenced by PM thinking as a rule take an anthropological (or material) view of culture, and the work being done on the loftier emanations of the human spirit is quite naturally devoted either to the formative NEP years or to the post-1953 era, when intellectual life revived.

The sub-field that is perhaps most in need of consideration, religion and moral values, is dealt with today in two contrasting ways. The more traditionally minded writers explore the range of responses to state-sponsored atheism by believers, from forced accommodation to the tenacity of the underground 'catacomb churches', while another set of researchers, avoiding overt expression of religious commitment, tries to take as far as possible a morally neutral stance. The latter are keener to pinpoint the strengths and weaknesses of the churches' foes, and the more adventurous see the struggle in cultural terms, as part of the worldwide process of modernisation and secularisation. At least three writers have in recent years investigated the affairs of Yaroslavsky's League of (Militant) Godless. Glennys Young, who focuses on the campaign at parish level in the 1920s, finds that rural clergy mounted a counter-offensive against the intruders, using local soviets to promote their parishes' interests – an interpretation that may owe something to a literal reading of complaints on this score in OGPU reports.[29] Daniel Peris's approach is more institutional; he justifiably makes much of the division within the movement between moderates ('culturalists') and radicals ('interventionists').[30] Both writers agree, as does Sandra Dahlke, that the League's failures were due in large part to its activists' ignorance, superficiality and addiction to coercive measures.[31]

William Husband goes furthest, endeavouring to treat the religious–atheist struggle in a broader context of 'the divergent cultural perceptions and aspirations that coexisted within Russian society'.[32] The issue was decided, in his view, by 'the critical mass who stood between the extremes': for instance, youngsters might hold to religious belief within the family circle but deny it when in the company of their peers. Husband has much of interest to report about how ordinary people behaved under stress, but his account intentionally blurs the issue that was being fought over by treating it as a cultural matter. He succeeds in getting away from stereotypes, but there is an underlying ambiguity here that seems to be reflected in the inverted commas placed around the 'Godless Communists' of the book's title.

None of these four authors takes us very far into the 1930s. One who does is the Finnish scholar Arto Luukkanen; in the second of two monographs he focuses on the CEC's 'Cult commission', which served as the Politburo's auxiliary in its 'war ... to implement its strategic objectives in religious policy'.[33] Vacillating between pressure from atheist zealots and the pleas of believers, it was within narrow limits a force for moderation, but lacked a ramified apparatus and so was powerless to stop local officials ignoring its instructions. Its failings are attributed here primarily to administrative factors, much in the spirit of Arch Getty, rather than as deriving logically from its sinister purpose.

As for conventional ecclesiastical history, both the Russian and the Armenian, but not the Georgian, Orthodox churches have each found their historian; there are various estimates of the number of victims among the religious (Catholic as well as Orthodox); an attempt has been made to analyse Stalin's motives in concluding the 1943 'Concordat'; and there is a critical account of the harsh treatment meted out to the Uniates.[34]

Moving back to secular affairs, the fate of the academic intelligentsia has been the subject of several excellent studies. Michael David-Fox, author of a pioneering work on political culture (and more specifically, Party-political education) in the 1920s, points out that state dictation in the social sciences was not just imposed on the learned from above but was to some extent actively self-inflicted.[35] This opens up a proverbial 'can of worms': to what extent, for what reasons, and by whom precisely? Vera Tolz presents a close analysis of 20 members of the prestigious Russian Academy of Sciences who were elected to that body before 1917, with biographical profiles of five men, each of whom stands for a certain attitude and behaviour pattern. After analysing their conduct at the crucial turning-point in 1929, when the institution was 'bolshevised', she points out that subsequently several academicians bravely intervened to defend colleagues threatened with arrest.[36] Even so, accommodation came more easily to natural scientists than to scholars in the humanities (to say nothing of creative artists), as Dietrich Beyrau observes in his foreword to a valuable collection of essays comparing the fate of professionals under Communism and Nazism.[37]

A noted historian of science now resident in the United States, Nikolai Krementsov, begins his vigorously written *Stalinist Science* by remarking on the paradox that 'many of [its] greatest triumphs ... occurred exactly at the time of greatest repression', when 'Gulag camps [were] overflowing'.[38] Identifying with the 'culturologists', he takes issue with earlier writers who advanced explanations 'that relied on ... the totalitarian nature of the Soviet state' and presents a more complex picture of '[an] interaction of institutions, professions, disciplines, interest groups and networks', much as in Western countries. Certainly political control was stricter in the USSR, but the scientific community, he contends, devised more elaborate ways of evading and even exploiting it, adopting the Party's militant rhetoric and 'play[ing] intricate games ... to advance their careers'.[39] One might interject here that it surely matters whether the game being played was ladies' croquet or Russian roulette: alas, under Stalin a successful intrigue against one's rivals might not just hold up scientific progress but entail highly unpleasant consequences for the losers. Krementsov's expertise in biology and access to archival sources enable him to give the fullest picture yet of Lysenko in his 'finest hour', and of course one applauds the civic courage shown by the professionals in resisting his assaults. Yet the picture drawn of these struggles here is rather too benign: after all, despite their colleagues' opposition the Lysenkoites had a remarkably long run, and Soviet biology's sad fate does not bear out the author's thesis convincingly.

In physics, to be sure, it was a different matter: this was simply too important in an atomic age to be allowed to become the plaything of scientific coteries or ideologists. Krementsov's brief remarks on this are enlarged on by Peter Kneen and Paul Josephson.[40] Thanks to Soviet national security interests, and the happy absence of any 'alternative physics' to match Lysenko's aberrant doctrine, in 1948 the Party leadership had to abandon its plan to purge this discipline.

Practitioners in several other specialised branches of knowledge are emerging from the shadows: geologists, engineers, ethnographers, even doctors engaged in forensic medicine.[41] This is highly commendable and suggests that we may one day have a complete picture of the impact of Stalinism on one of its most favoured sectors, science and technology.

We are unlikely to be so lucky for the social sciences, some of which were all but killed off, but good work has been done on Soviet historiography *after* Stalin,[42] and two scholars in particular, Maureen Perrie and Rainer Lindner, have enlarged our appreciation of the turn towards Russian nationalism in historical writing after 1934. That the dictator fancied himself as a latter-day Ivan Groznyi is hardly news, but Perrie examines with scrupulous care the development of this curious cult, which had ramifications in the arts as well as in historiography. It was touched off, it seems, by the Soviet annexation of the Baltic states in 1940 rather than by the Terror, where the analogy with Ivan's *oprichnina* was most obvious.[43] Lindner's theme is the imposition of a Great Russian chauvinist interpretation on historians in Belarus, and the efforts of nationally conscious locals to resist it. They were less successful than Ukrainian historians, whose motives were similar, as is shown by the Canadian scholar Serhy Yekelchyk, who has written a number of articles on efforts to defend Ukrainian culture under Stalin. Lindner gives a very detailed picture of the intrigues among Belarussian historians, which he calls a 'ritual performance' – an interpretation close to Krementsov's for the biologists, although Lindner's view of the academic atmosphere in the late Stalin era is a good deal darker.[44]

Conclusions

This brief survey has hopefully shown that in many fields of inquiry, Western researchers have been successfully beating back the frontiers of our ignorance about social relationships and cultural patterns in Stalin's USSR, generating a host of fascinating new problems that in turn demand investigation. The field is vigorously alive, well informed and often controversial. The ingenuity displayed by PM-oriented scholars deserves respectful admiration, even if on occasion the pioneering spirit leads to over-interpretation of the evidence.[45] Putting ordinary citizens in the spotlight gives us a clearer understanding of the disparate ways in which they responded to pressures from above and of the active role that many of them played in constructing the collectivist order. Quite correctly our attention is now focused on the 'grey' intermediate spaces (*Freiräume*) between the decision-makers at the top and the people at the base of the power pyramid. The political structure over which the dictator presided with such apparent self-assurance has been relativised, its inner tensions revealed to view along with its inefficiency and limited reach. Where once we saw stasis we now see flux and uncertainty.

So far so good, but can the new methodological approaches give us a better key to comprehending Stalinism *as a whole* than we had before? Why do contemporary writers so often find it necessary to advertise their scorn for the term 'totalitarian'? If the dreaded 'T-word' still has adherents outside academia, this may be because there is something to be said after all for using it, provided that it can be freed from politically prejudiced associations. It still seems to many a valid way of describing both the aspirations of the Stalinist leadership and the institutional set-up through which it governed, although it is less useful when applied to the society that the *apparat* sought to control and reshape, characterised as this society was by the usual human vices: self-interest, particularism, indifference and so forth. This means that the original all-encompassing concept, dating from the 1950s, needs to be refined in favour of a narrower one that takes due account of the informal limitations imposed on the Party's ability to get its way.

Having said this, we surely have to recognise that Stalin's regime in the 1930s (and still more so after 1945) did manage to achieve a greater degree of social mobilisation and control than anyone had thought possible hitherto. It is this massive concentration of power, and its abuse, that has chief claim to our attention as historians, as indeed it did to contemporaries. It is good to know more about the *de facto* restrictions on this power, so long as we do not go overboard and overlook what matters most.

The quest for higher standards of objectivity, coupled with a worthy desire to avoid explicit condemnation of what was inhuman or evil, may lead to misperceptions as serious as those resulting from excessive moralism. One example must suffice: Cynthia Ruder has given us an in some ways admirable study of the construction by forced labour in 1931–33 of the celebrated Belomor canal and its representation in literature. The officially sponsored account of the project, a collective endeavour that involved dozens of writers, praised the OGPU's concern for the workers but omitted to state that they included a number of political prisoners:

> Does this mean that it avoids the truth ...? No, because *The History of Construction* presents one kind of truth about Belomor that is as valid as any other discussion of the event ... [I]ts accuracy hinges on the first-hand accounts provided to the writers by some of the engineers, workers and OGPU personnel ... For the kind of truth it sought to convey, the volume was accurate.

Here Ruder comes close to asserting, as one of the writers involved did, that the Chekists 'know what truth is, they know what socialism is', and so risks inadvertently becoming an apologist for a system of which she clearly disapproves.[46]

This error, I suggest, stems from too rigid an adherence to the PM canon, which holds that truth is always relative, dependent on the perspective of the beholder. Contemporary social theorists tell us that what we perceive and study are merely representations (images) of reality; furthermore, that they are emanations of power, and so often intentionally misleading – myths that serve the interests of their creators; accordingly it is our task to 'deconstruct' or decode these 'discourses'. There is a parallel of sorts here with the reasoning advanced by Marxists a century or so ago, to the effect that, say, decisions made by governments were but a mask for those *really* made behind the scenes by those who controlled the relations of production. Both challenge conventional (empiricist) historians' tendency to accept easy simplifications; both appeal to our instinctive suspicion that things are not what they appear to be or ought to be.

Fortunately PM-minded historians do not in practice stand aloof from the pursuit of factual evidence, in this sharing common ground with their empiricist colleagues, even if they may use other terminology or attempt more sophisticated interpretations that sometimes evoke scepticism among the traditionalists. Since PM thinking currently dominates Western historical scholarship, and intellectual life generally, it is no use complaining about it. Even so one may agree with Thomas Saunders that, though 'we are all postmodernists now', nevertheless 'postmodernist theory offers unstable ground on which to chart historical study'.[47] All that is urged here is that post-sovietologists need to be careful and not let themselves be carried away by the appeal of fashion. Or, to use Stalinist terminology, maybe there is still room for a *pravyi uklon*?

NOTES

1. We consider here only some of the writings published since c.1997 in English, French and German. This essay is based on material collected for a forthcoming study, written together with Alter L. Litvin (Kazan'), entitled *Stalinism: Russian and Western Views at the Turn of the Millennium*.

2. Referred to here for brevity's sake as 'PM'. Hans Bertens, *The Idea of the Postmodern: A History* (Cambridge, MA: Routledge, 1995), offers an introduction to the subject but has little to say on historiography; Keith Jenkins (ed.), *The Postmodern History Reader* (London and New York: Routledge, 1997), offers a useful selection of views on historical applications of the theory but says nothing of Eastern Europe; for a critique of the theory by a leading historian, see Richard J. Evans, *In Defence of History* (London: Granta, 1997).

3. This has been taken furthest by Jochen Hellbeck, 'Feeding the Stalinist Soul: The Diary of Stepan Podlubnyi, 1931–1939', *Jahrbücher für Geschichte Osteuropas* 46 (1996), pp.344–73; idem (ed. and trans.), *Tagebuch aus Moskau 1931–1939* (Munich: Deutscher Taschenbuch Verlag, 1996); idem, 'Fashioning the Stalinist Soul: the Diary of Stepan Podlubnyi, 1931–1939', in Sheila Fitzpatrick (ed.), *Stalinism: New Directions* (New York and London: Routledge, 2000), pp.77–116; Jochen Hellbeck, 'Speaking Out: Languages of Affirmation and Dissent in Stalinist Russia', *Kritika* 1 (2000), pp.71–96; idem, 'Writing the Self in the Time of Terror: Alexander Afinogenov's Diary of 1937', in Laura Engelstein and S. Sandler (eds.), *Self and Story in Russian History* (Ithaca, NY: Cornell University Press, 2000), pp.69–93; and Jochen Hellbeck, 'Stalin-Era Autobiographical Texts', *Russian Review* 60 (2001), pp.340–59; cf. Paul Bushkovitch and Andrea Graziosi (eds.), 'Assessing the New Soviet Archival Sources', *Cahiers du monde russe* 40 (1999), esp. the article by Matthew E. Lenoe, 'Letter-writing and the State: Reader Correspondence with Newspapers as a Source for Early Soviet History', pp.139–70. One by-product has been a useful discussion on the reliability of the svodki.
4. T. Geiger defines mentalité as 'the pattern of unconscious attitudes and interpretations that individuals need in order to cope with the world in which they live'; it is by definition held to be a collective phenomenon. Cited by T. Undulag in *International Review of Social History* 47 (2002), p.35.
5. 'Negotiation' is a term used in a specialised sense and does not necessarily imply that bargaining was carried on in a conscious way through organised lobbies or institutions.
6. Lynne Viola, *Peasant Rebels under Stalin: Collectivisation and the Culture of Peasant Resistance* (Oxford: Oxford University Press, 1996, 1999); idem, 'Popular Resistance in the Stalinist 1930s: Soliloquy of a Devil's Advocate', *Kritika* 1 (2000), pp.45–69; idem, 'The Peasants' Kulak: Social Identities and Moral Economy in the Soviet Countryside in the 1920s', *Canadian Slavonic Papers* 42 (2001), pp.431–60; and idem (ed.), *Contending with Stalinism: Soviet Power and Popular Resistance in the 1930s* (Ithaca, NY: Cornell University Press, 2002); Andrea Graziosi, *The Great Peasant War: Bolsheviks and Peasants, 1918–1933* (Cambridge MA: Harvard University Press, 1997).
7. D'Ann R. Penner, 'Stalin and the Ital'ianka Campaign of 1932–3 in the Don Region', *Cahiers du monde russe* 39 (1998), pp.27–68; idem, 'Ports of Access into the Mental and Social Worlds of Don Villagers in the 1920s and 1930s', *Cahiers du monde russe* 40 (1998), pp.171–98; Pauline Peretz, 'La grande Famine ukrainienne de 1932–1933: essai d'interprétation', *Revue d'études comparatives Est-Ouest* 30/1 (1999), pp.31–52; and Stephen G. Wheatcroft, 'Nutrition and Mortality in Famines, 1917–21, 1931–33', *Cahiers du monde russe* 38 (1997), pp.525–58.
8. Sheila Fitzpatrick, *Stalin's Peasants: Resistance and Survival in the Russian Village after Collectivisation* (New York and Oxford: Oxford University Press, 1994); idem, 'Readers' Letters to Krestianskaia gazeta, 1938', *Russian History – Histoire russe* 24 (1997), pp.1–2; Stefan Merl, 'Bilanz der Unterwerfung: die soziale und ökonomische Reorganisation des Dorfes'; and Gábor T. Rittersporn, 'Das kollektivierte Dorf in der bäuerlichen Gegenkultur', both in Manfred Hildermeier (ed.), *Stalinismus: Neue Wege der Forschung* (Munich: Oldenbourg, 1998), pp.119–45, 147–67 respectively; and Diana Siebert, *Bäuerliche Alltagsstrategien in der Belarussischen SSR, 1921–1941* (Stuttgart: Franz Steiner, 1998).
9. Mary Buckley, 'Krestianskaia gazeta and Rural Stakhanovism', *Europe-Asia Studies* 46 (1994), pp.1387–1407; idem, 'Why be a Shock Worker or a Stakhanovite?', in Rosalinde Marsh (ed.), *Women in Russia and Ukraine* (Cambridge: Cambridge University Press, 1996), pp.199–213; Mary Buckley, 'Categorizing Resistance to Rural Stakhanovism', in Kevin McDermott and John Morison (eds.), *Politics and Society under the Bolsheviks: Selected Papers from the Fifth World Congress of Central and*

RECENT WESTERN VIEWS OF STALIN'S RUSSIA

East European Studies, Warsaw, 1995 (Basingstoke and London: Macmillan, 1999), pp.160–88; Mary Buckley, 'Was Rural Stakhanovism a Movement?', *Europe-Asia Studies* 51 (1999), pp.299–314; and Lewis H. Siegelbaum, '"Dear Comrade, You Ask What We Need": Socialist Paternalism and Soviet Rural "Notables" in the Mid-1930s', *Slavic Review* 57 (1998), pp.107–32.

10. Lewis H. Siegelbaum and Ronald G. Suny (eds.), *Making Workers Soviet: Power, Class and Identity* (Ithaca, NY: Cornell University Press, 1994); the fruit of a conference held at Michigan State University in 1990, this volume jettisoned the once popular quasi-Marxist approach to class, now seen as constituting a 'cultural paradigm'.

11. David L. Hoffmann and Y. Kotsonis (eds.), *Russian Modernity: Politics, Knowledge, Practices* (New York: Macmillan, 2000), p.258.

12. Kenneth M. Straus, *Factory and Community in Stalin's Russia: The Making of an Industrial Working Class* (Pittsburgh, PA: University of Pittsburgh, 1997).

13. Jeffrey J. Rossman, 'A Workers' Strike in Stalin's Russia: The Vichuga Uprising of April 1932', in Viola (ed.), *Contending with Stalinsism* (note 6), pp.44–83, 81; idem, 'Weaver of Rebellion and Poet of Resistance: K. Klepikov (1860–1933) and Shopfloor Opposition to Bolshevik Rule', *Jahrbücher für Geschichte Osteuropas* 46 (1996), pp.374–408; and idem, 'The Teikovo Cotton Workers' Strike of April 1932: Class, Gender and Identity Politics in Stalin's Russia', *Russian Review* 56 (1997), pp.44–69.

14. Wendy Z. Goldman, 'Babas at the Bench: Gender Conflict in Soviet Industry in the 1930s', in Melanie Ilič (ed.), *Women in the Stalin Era* (Basingstoke and New York: Palgrave, 2002), pp.69–88. This article offers a foretaste of her forthcoming monograph, Women at the Gates.

15. Gabriele Gorzka, 'Krasnyi Perekop: Betriebsalltag und Arbeiterinteressen am Beispiel der Textilarbeiterschaft in Jaroslavl', in Stefan Plaggenborg (ed.), *Stalinismus: Neue Forschungen und Konzepte* (Berlin: Arno Spitz, 1998), pp.209–42; and Gabriele Gorzka, 'Work and Leisure among Textile-workers in Soviet Russia: Yaroslavl in the 1930s', in McDermott and Morison (note 9), pp.140–59.

16. Laura L. Phillips, *Bolsheviks and the Bottle: Drink and Worker Culture in St. Petersburg, 1900–1929* (DeKalb, IL: Northern Illinois University Press, 2000).

17. Melanie Ilič, *Women Workers in the Soviet Interwar Economy: From 'Protection' to 'Equality'* (London and New York: Macmillan, 1999).

18. Claudia Kraft, 'Wo steht die Frauen- und Geschlechtergeschichte in der Osteuropa-Forschung?', *Jahrbücher für Geschichte Osteuropas* 50 (2002), pp.102–7.

19. Frances L. Bernstein, '"The Dictatorship of Sex": Science, Glands, and the Medical Construction of Gender Difference in Revolutionary Russia', in Hoffmann and Kotsonis (note 11), pp.138–60; Frances L. Bernstein, 'Prostitutes and Proletarians', in William G. Husband (ed.), *The Human Tradition in Modern Russia* (Wilmington, DE: Scholarly Resources, 2000), pp.113–28; and article in Christine Kiaer and Eric Naiman (eds), Everyday Subjects (forthcoming).

20. Greta Bucher, '"Free and Worth Every Kopeck": Soviet Medicine and Women in Postwar Russia', in Husband (note 19), pp.175–86; Greta Bucher, 'Struggling to Survive: Soviet Women in the Postwar Years', *Journal of Women's History* 12 (2000), pp.137–59; and Chris Burton, 'Minzdrav, Soviet Doctors and the Policing of Reproduction in the Late Stalinist Years', *Russian History – Histoire russe* 27 (2000), pp.197–221.

21. Carmen Scheide, *Kinder, Küche, Kommunismus: das Wechselverhältnis zwischen sowjetischen Frauenalltag und Frauenpolitik von 1921 bis 1930 am Beispiel Moskauer Arbeiterinnen* (Zürich: Pano, 2002); an earlier treatment was Wendy Z. Goldman, *Women, the State and Revolution: Soviet Family Policy and Social Life, 1917–1936* (Cambridge and NY: Cambridge University Press, 1993, 1995).

22. Barbara Engel and Alexandra Posadskaya-Vanderbeck, *A Revolution of Their Own: Voices of Women in Soviet History* (Boulder, CO: Westview, 1998); and Sheila Fitzpatrick and Yury Slezkine (eds.), *In the Shadow of the Revolution: Life Stories of*

Russian Women from 1917 to the Second World War (Princeton, NJ: Princeton University Press, 2000). To these should be added, on women in the Gulag, Semen Vilensky (ed.), *Till My Tale is Told: Women's Memoirs of the Gulag*, trans. John Crowfoot, prepared J. Crowfoot and Z. Vesyolaya (Russian edn. 1989; Bloomington and Indianapolis, IN: Indiana University Press, 1999); and Meinhard Stark, *'Ich muss sagen, wie es war.' Deutsche Frauen des Gulags* (Berlin: Metropol, 1999), based on 17 interviews with survivors.

23. Engel and Posadskaya-Vanderbeck (note 22), pp.219–21.
24. Helen Goscilo and Beth Holmgren (eds.), *Russia – Women – Culture* (Bloomington, IN: Indiana University Press, 1996).
25. Catriona Kelly and David Shepherd (eds.), *Constructing Russian Culture in the Age of Revolution, 1881–1940* (Oxford: Oxford University Press, 1998); Catriona Kelly and David Shepherd (eds.), *Russian Cultural Studies: An Introduction* (Oxford: Oxford University Press, 1998); Catriona Kelly, *Refining Russia: Advice Literature, Polite Culture and Gender from Catherine to Yeltsin* (Oxford: Oxford University Press, 2001); Lynne Attwood, *Creating the New Soviet Woman: Women's Magazines as Engineers of Female Identity, 1922–1953* (London: Macmillan, 1999); idem, 'Women Workers at Play: The Portrayal of Leisure in the Magazine Rabotnitsa in the First Two Decades of Soviet Power', in Ilič (note 14), pp.29–48; Rebecca B. Neary, 'Mothering Socialist Society: The Wife-Activists' Movement in the Soviet Culture of Everyday Life, 1934–1941', *Russian Review* 58 (1999), pp.396–412; Thomas Schrand, 'Soviet Civic-minded Women in the 1930s: Gender, Class and Industrialisation in a Socialist Society', *Journal of Women's History* 11 (1999), pp.126–50; and J. Hessler, 'Cultured Trade: The Stalinist Turn toward Consumerism', in Fitzpatrick (note 3), pp.182–209.
26. Sheila Fitzpatrick, *Everyday Stalinism: Ordinary Life in Extraordinary Times: Soviet Russia in the 1930s* (New York and London: Oxford University Press, 1999), pp.156–61.
27. Karen Petrone, *'Life Has Become More Joyous, Comrades': Celebrations in the Time of Stalin* (Bloomington, IN: Indiana University Press, 2000); Mate Rolf, 'Feste des "roten Kalenders": der grosse Umbruch und die sowjetische Ordnung der Zeit', *Zeitschrift für Geschichtswissenschaft* 2 (2001), pp.101–18; and idem, 'Feste der Einheit und Schauspiele der Partizipation: die Inszenierung von Oeffentlichkeit in der Sowjetunion um 1930', *Jahrbücher für Geschichte Osteuropas* 50 (2002), pp.163–71.
28. Ronald Stites (ed.), *Culture and Entertainment in War-time Russia* (Bloomington, IN: Indiana University Press, 1995).
29. Glennys Young, *Power and the Sacred in Revolutionary Russia: Religious Activists in the Village* (University Park, PA: Pennsylvania State University Press, 1997); for more on the parish, see Gregory L. Freeze, 'The Stalinist Assault on the Parish, 1929–1941', in Hildermeier (note 8), pp.209–32.
30. Daniel Peris, 'Commissars in Red Cassocks: Former Priests in the League of Militant Godless', *Slavic Review* 54 (1995), pp.340–64; and idem, *Storming the Heavens: The Soviet League of the Militant Godless* (Ithaca, NY: Cornell University Press, 1998).
31. Sandra Dahlke, *An der antireligiösen Front: Der Verband der Gottlosen in der Sowjetunion der 20er Jahre* (Hamburg: Dr Kovač, 1998); and idem, 'Kampagnen für Gottlosigkeit: zum Zusammenhang zwischen Legitimation, Mobilisierung und Partizipation in der Sowjetunion der 20er Jahre', *Jahrbücher für Geschichte Osteuropas* 50 (2002), pp.172–85.
32. William G. Husband, *'Godless Communists': Atheism and Society in Soviet Russia, 1917–1932* (DeKalb, IL: Northern Illinois University Press, 2000), pp.xiii, 100.
33. Arto Luukkanen, *The Religious Policy of the Stalinist State: The Central Standing Commission on Religious Questions, 1929–1938* (Helsinki: Societas Historica Finlandiae, 1997), p.57.
34. Dmitri Pospielovsky, '"The Best Years" of Stalin's Church Policy (1942–1948) in the Light of Archival Documents', *Religion, State and Society* 25 (1997), pp.139–62;

idem, *The Orthodox Church in the History of Russia* (Russian edn., Moscow: Bibleisko-bogoslovskii institut, 1995; Crestwood, NY: St Vladimir's Seminary Press, 1998); Felix Corley, 'The Armenian Church under the Soviet and Independent Regimes', *Religion, State and Society* 24 (1996), pp.9–53; 26 (1998), pp.291–356; Anna Dickinson, 'A Marriage of Convenience? Domestic and Foreign Policy Reasons for the 1943 Church-State "Concordat"', *Religion, State and Society* 28 (2000), pp.337–46; and Bohdan R. Bociurkiw, *The Ukrainian Greek Catholic Church and the Soviet State, 1939–1950* (Edmonton: Canadian Institute of Ukrainian Studies, 1996).

35. Michael David-Fox, *Revolution of the Mind: Learning among the Bolsheviks, 1918–1929* (Ithaca, NY: Cornell University Press, 1997), p.22; cf. idem, 'Symbiosis to Synthesis: The Communist Academy and the Bolshevisation of the Imperial/Soviet Academy of Sciences, 1918–1929', *Jahrbücher für Geschichte Osteuropas* 46 (1998), pp.219–43; and idem, 'The Assault on the Universities and the Dynamic of Stalin's "Great Break", 1928–1932', in M. David-Fox and G. Péteri (eds.), *Academia in Upheaval: Origins, Transfers and Transformations of the Communist Academic Regime in Russia and East Central Europe* (Westport, CT: Bergin and Garvey, 2000), pp.73–103.

36. Vera Tolz, *Russian Academicians and the Revolution: Combining Professionalism and Politics* (Basingstoke: Macmillan, and New York: St Martin's Press, 1997).

37. Dietrich Beyrau (ed.), *Im Dschungel der Macht: Intellektuelle Professionen unter Hitler und Stalin* (Göttingen: Vandenhoeck and Ruprecht, 1999), pp.9–42; the volume contains important contributions by Russian scholars.

38. Nikolai L. Krementsov, *Stalinist Science* (Princeton NJ: Princeton University Press, 1997), p.3.

39. Ibid., p.6. The 'game-playing' argument is also advanced by Alexander Kojevnikov, 'Rituals of Stalinist Culture at Work: Science and the Games of Interparty Democracy circa 1948', *Russian Review* 57 (1998), pp.25–52.

40. Krementsov (note 39), pp.275–9; Peter Kneen, 'Physics, Genetics and the Zhdanovshchina', *Europe-Asia Studies* 50 (1998), pp.1183–1202; idem, 'De-Stalinisation under Stalin? The Case of Science', *Journal of Communist Studies and Transition Politics* 16 (2000), pp.107–26; and Paul R. Josephson, *Red Atom: Russia's Nuclear Power Program from Stalin to Today* (New York: W.H. Freeman, 2000); Holloway's classic study of the Soviet 'Manhattan project' dates from 1994, David Holloway, *Stalin and the Bomb: The Soviet Union and Atomic Energy* (New Haven, CT: Yale University Press, 1994).

41. Christoph Mick, 'Wissenschaft und Wissenschaftler im Stalinismus', in Plaggenborg (note 15), pp.321–61; Susanne Schattenberg, 'Die Sowjetunion als technische Utopie: die alten Ingenieure und das neue Regime', *Forum für osteuropäische Ideen- und Zeitgeschichte* (Cologne, Weimar, Vienna) 5 (2001), pp.241–69; idem, *Stalins Ingenieure: Lebenswelten zwischen Technik und Terror in der 1930er Jahren* (Munich: Oldenbourg, 2002); Wim Van Meurs, 'Soviet Ethnography: Hunters or Gatherers?', *Ab imperio* (Kazan, March 2001), pp.8–42; and Kenneth M. Pinnow, 'Cutting and Counting: Forensic Medicine as a Science of Society in Bolshevik Russia, 1920–1929', in Hoffmann and Kotsonis (note 11), pp.115–37.

42. Joachim Hösler, *Die sowjetische Geschichtswissenschaft 1953–1991: Studien zur Methodologie- und Organisationsgeschichte* (Munich: Otto Sagner, 1995); and Roger D. Markwick, *Rewriting History in Soviet Russia: The Politics of Revisionist Historiography, 1956–1974* (Basingstoke and New York: Palgrave, 2001).

43. Maureen Perrie, *The Cult of Ivan the Terrible in Stalin's Russia* (Basingstoke and New York: Palgrave, 2001), p.89; cf. Kevin M.F. Platt and David L. Brandenberger, 'Terribly Romantic, Terribly Progressive, or Terribly Tragic: Rehabilitating Ivan IV under Stalin', *Russian Review* 58 (1999), pp.635–54.

44. Rainer Lindner, *Historiker und Herrschaft: Nationsbildung und Geschichtspolitik in Weissrussland im 19. und 20. Jahrhundert* (Munich: Oldenbourg, 1999), p.330; idem,

'Nationalhistoriker im Stalinismus. Zum Profil der akademischen Intelligenz in Weissrussland 1921–1946', *Jahrbücher für Geschichte Osteuropas* 47 (1999), pp.187–209; Serhy Yekelchyk, 'How the "Iron Minister" Kaganovich Failed to Discipline Ukrainian Historians: A Stalinist Ideological Campaign Reconsidered', *Nationalities Papers* 27 (1999), pp.579–604; and idem, 'Stalinist Patriotism as Imperial Discourse: Reconciling the Ukrainian and Russian "Heroic Pasts", 1939–1945', *Kritika* 3 (2002), pp.51–80.

45. For example, Petrone (note 27), p.97, seems to read more into the sources than is there when she discusses a New Year elka fete for children of top-flight officials (1937) at which toy telephones were displayed and the children were said to have carried on business-like conversations across the hall. 'The use of the adjective delovoi by the fir-tree organisers underlined the fact that real telephones were important tools used by the cadres who ruled the Soviet Union ... The implication was that these children would become devoted Party and government officials.' But might not the implication have just been parental pride at their tots' seemingly adult behaviour?

46. Cynthia A. Ruder, *Making History for Stalin: The Story of the Belomor Canal* (Gainesville, FL: University Press of Florida, 1998), pp.92, 145.

47. Thomas J. Saunders, 'The Postmodern Twenties?', *Neue Politische Literatur* 46 (2001), pp.205–15; Bertens (note 2), p.11 sees 'a massive but exhilarating confusion'.

Abstracts

Stalinism and the Soviet State Order

ROBERT SERVICE

Stalin's rule was so violent and so distinctive in ideas, policies and practices that it is conventional to consider it in its own terms with little reference to the periods preceding and following it. This chapter considers Stalin and Stalinism in the framework of the entire Soviet period and emphasises that the state order which Stalin dominated had been invented largely by others. That order had inherent defects from the viewpoint of its Communist rulers and a pattern of pressurisation and accommodation was in place already in Lenin's time; and it survived through to the late 1980s under Gorbachev. The modalities of Communist leadership were indeed conditioned by time, place and individual leader; but the basic requirements to maintain and enhance the Soviet state order were constant in important ways. The murderousness of Stalin has to be traced not only to the historical contingency of each period but also to the entire duration of the USSR.

Stalinism, Totalitarian Society and the Politics of 'Perfect Control'

FELIX PATRIKEEFF

Conceptualising Stalinism remains a difficult task, even 50 years after the death of the dictator. This essay explores the early attempts to do so, distorted as they were by the then-pervasive school of totalitarianism, which, in an excessively convenient way, drew together the man, the system and practical exercise of power, and imparted upon this nexus the notion of politics of 'perfect control'. The discussion then turns to later perspectives and debate, in which efforts were made to disentangle these strands of analysis, but with the distinction between the uniqueness of Stalinism and ordinary dictatorship remaining opaque. I have attempted to offer a fresh way of seeing Stalinism, revising the manner in which the pinnacle (Stalin) and the base (the population at large) have been approached in the past. Central to this revised view is the need to re-assess the role of 'the People' in generating what Jean Elleinstein aptly described as the 'Stalin Phenomenon'.

Stalin's Politics of Obligation

JEFFREY BROOKS

Under Stalinist political culture, Soviet citizens were indebted to the leader and the Party-State for their well-being as well as for ordinary goods and services. Soviet publicists used the slogan 'Thank You Comrade Stalin for a Happy Childhood' to express society's obligation. This cultural construct reflected and reinforced aspects of Soviet life, including Stalin's cult, patronage, relations with the intelligentsia, and Russian predominance in the Empire. After the Second World War, the Soviet government used the politics of obligation to shape Moscow's ties with the new communist countries and the wider world. This feature of Stalin's cult served to concentrate agency in the leader and subsequently to absolve others of responsibility. Its holding power may help explain the absence today of a full accounting for past atrocities and misdeeds.

Stalin and Foreign Intelligence

CHRISTOPHER ANDREW and JULIE ELKNER

This article analyses the key priorities of Soviet foreign intelligence operations under Stalin. It argues that the operational advantages enjoyed by the Soviet intelligence services vis-à-vis their Western counterparts were ultimately outweighed by deep flaws in Soviet intelligence tasking and analysis. The nature of Soviet authoritarianism and ideology, as well as Stalin's own penchant for conspiracy theory and close personal involvement with the work of the intelligence agencies, led to serious – and at times absurd – distortions in the identification of targets and threats, and in the interpretation of information. The article also examines less conventional aspects of foreign intelligence operations under Stalin. In particular, it looks at the relentless pursuit and attempted 'liquidation' of 'enemies of the people' abroad – chief among them leaders of the White émigré community, Trotsky and his followers, and Marshal Tito. These operations, which could be accomplished only by the OGPU and its successors, need to be seen as crucial elements of Stalin's foreign policy.

Stalin's Martyrs:
The Tragic Romance of the Russian Revolution

MICHAEL G. SMITH

This essay offers an interpretive reading of the culture of violence and martyrdom in the life of the Bolshevik Party and in the career of I.V. Stalin. It does not mean to characterise that career once and for all; but only to explore a rather neglected dimension of his self-representation: that of living martyr and martyr survivor. This was a public mantle that Stalin drew from the 'passion' (*pafos*) of other Bolsheviks; that he found reflected in the poetry of Walt Whitman; and that he and others expressed in the words and images of Soviet literature, propaganda and history. With Party members, he discovered profound meaning in violent struggle and individual suffering, experiences that represented their common birth through tragedy.

From Stalinism to Post-Stalinism:
De-Mythologising Stalin, 1953–56

POLLY JONES

This article examines the early transition from Stalinism to post-Stalinism, to expose the hesitations and difficulties that attended the Soviet leadership's initial attempts to deal with the Stalinist past. 'De-Stalinisation' began almost immediately after Stalin's death, as the post-Stalinist regime attempted to reduce Stalin's charismatic power and to increase its own legitimacy, through undermining Stalinist thinking (which had dominated every policy domain) and through

reducing the influence of the Stalin cult on Soviet public life.
However, efforts to dismantle the mythologies surrounding Stalin did
not begin in earnest until 1956. The initial attempts at radical de-
Stalinisation (Khrushchev's 'Secret Speech') are shown as
unsuccessful, since they generated significant resistance and
provoked an unprecedented diversity of public response. To achieve
greater consensus and control over the 'Stalin question', the Soviet
authorities instead had to propagate a more moderate and ambiguous
image of Stalin and Stalinism, which necessitated a hesitant approach
to the symbols of the cult. The paradoxes of Stalin's public image
during de-Stalinisation in 1956 are exemplified through case studies
of Soviet education and political symbolism. This article is based on
doctoral research carried out in a number of state and Party archives
at the central (Moscow) and local (Volgograd, Moscow) levels, using
materials declassified as late as the latter half of the 1990s.

Recent Western Views of Stalin's Russia:
Social and Cultural Aspects

JOHN KEEP

This survey of recent (post-1997) Western writing on the Stalin era
focuses on the treatment of social and cultural issues by
conventionally minded (empiricist) scholars, as well as those who
employ postmodernist methodologies. Both schools are found to
have major successes to their credit. The traditionalists were
challenged first by revisionist social historians ('history from below')
and later by protagonists of the 'cultural turn' who directed attention
to identity formation, everyday life and symbolic communication.
The innovators sometimes go beyond the limits of their evidence or
confuse style with substance, but they have convinced most of their
rivals that there was more disarray in government and popular
disaffection than had previously been thought. Even so, the term
'totalitarianism', if suitably redefined, can still be part of a serviceable
analytical explanation, above all of political and juridical phenomena.
Topics covered here include peasant revolts, gender relations, mass
festivals, religious observance, academic life, science and
historiography.

About the Contributors

Christopher Andrew is Professor of Contemporary History at the University of Cambridge, official historian of the Security Service (MI5), and co-editor of *Intelligence and National Security*. His most recent book, with Vasili Mitrokhin, is *The Mitrokhin Archive* (1999).

Jeffrey Brooks is Professor of European History at the Johns Hopkins University. He is the author of *Thank You, Comrade Stalin! Soviet Public Culture from Revolution to Cold War* (2000), *When Russia Learned to Read: Literacy and Popular Literature, 1861–1917* (2003, 1985), and many articles on Russian politics and culture.

Julie Elkner is a Ph.D. student at King's College, University of Cambridge. Her current research examines the figure of the chekist in Soviet and post-Soviet culture. She has also worked on the Soldiers' Mothers Committees; Soviet military culture and human rights violations in the Russian military; and patriotic historical narratives of Russia's engagement with Chechnya.

Polly Jones is the Max Hayward Fellow in Russian Literature and Culture at St Antony's College, Oxford. She has just completed her doctorate at St Antony's on 'Strategies of De-Mythologisation in Post-Stalinism and Post-Communism: A Comparison of De-Stalinisation and De-Leninisation'. She is currently working on an article about changes to Soviet military and civil decorations for a forthcoming special edition of *Geneses*, and on editing a collection of essays on the cultural and social history of the Khrushchev era.

John Keep was from 1970 to 1988 Professor of Russian History at the University of Toronto. His works include *Last of the Empires: A History of the USSR* (1995, reissued 2002), and ed. and trans., Alter L. Litvin, *Writing History in 20th-Century Russia* (2001).

Felix Patrikeeff is currently Lecturer in International and Comparative Politics at the University of Adelaide, before which he taught at the universities of Warwick, Oxford and Sydney. He has researched and published widely on Russian and Asian themes. His most recent book is *Russian Politics in Exile: The Northeast Asian Balance of Power, 1924–1931* (2002).

Robert Service is Professor of Russian History at Oxford University. He writes on both historical and contemporary themes and his latest book is *Russia: Experiment with a People, from 1991 to the Present* (2002).

Harold Shukman is retired University Lecturer in Modern Russian History at Oxford and an Emeritus Fellow of St Antony's College, where he was Director of the Russian and East European Centre. His books include studies of the Russian Revolution, biographies of Lenin, Stalin and Rasputin, and (with Geoffrey Elliott) *Secret Classrooms*, an account of the National Service Russian Course. He recently edited *The Winter War (1939–40)*.

Michael G. Smith teaches History at Purdue University. He is the author of *Language and Power in the Creation of the USSR, 1917–1953* (1998) and recent articles in *Jahrbücher für Geschichte Osteuropas* and *Journal of Contemporary History* (2001). His current work explores Russian approaches to rocketry, space travel and cosmism.

Index

Abakumov, Viktor, 82–3
Abwehr, 79, 80
administrative system, corrupt and
  untrustworthy, 13
administrators, sectional interests, 15
Afghanistan, 18
agency, theft of, 47–8, 64, 65
agriculture, collectivisation, 10
Akhmatova, Anna, 65
Aladzhalov, 127, 128
Alliluyeva, Svetlana, 71
Andreev, A.A., 55
Andrew, Christopher, 69
Andropov, Yuri, 17
Armenia, 59
Armenian Orthodox Church, 157
Aron, Raymond, 27–9, 30
Arsenidze, R., 101
artists, 58–61
asceticism, 51–2, 99
atheism, state-sponsored, 156–7
atomic bomb, Soviet, 84, 89 n3
Austria, 77
Azerbaijan, 71, 102

Babel, Isaac, 58, 60
Baku, 101–2
Baku Commune, 104–5
Bakunin, Mikhail, 113
Batum, 100
Bazhanov, Boris, 84
Beck, Jozef, 74
Belarus, 159
Beneš, Eduard, 73
Beria, L.P., 71, 80, 82, 84, 128
Bernstein, Frances, 154
biology, Soviet, 158
blat, 52–3
Bloody Sunday (1905), 103
Blunt, Anthony, 81–2, 89 n3
Bolshevik Party, 35
Bolsheviks, 97, 116–17

legitimisation, 49
  martyrdom and ritual, 98–103
bomb plot 1944, 82–3
Borodin, Mikhail, 29
Bourdieu, Pierre, 49–50
Brezhnev, L.I., 4, 11, 14, 15, 16–17, 20
bribery, 50
Britain, 4
  intelligence operations, 71, 72, 81–3, 90
    n20, 90 n21
  intelligence target, 73–4, 75–7, 81–2
Brodskii, Isaak, 109
Brooks, Jeffrey, 47
Brüning, Heinrich, 81
Brzezinski, Z., 23, 30, 31
Bukharin, N.I., 18, 21, 114
Bulgakov, Mikhail, 58
Bulganin, N.A., 140
Burgess, Guy, 73, 81, 89 n3

Cairncross, John, 73, 81, 89 n3
Cambridge Five, 73, 81–2, 89 n3
Carlyle, Thomas, 35–6
Caucasus, 41
censorship, 8, 9
Cheka, 9, 69, 70
Chen, Percy, 29–30
Chernenko, K.U., 17
Chilston, Viscount, 72
China, 36–7, 78, 83
Chkalov, V.P., 57
Chubar, V., 55
Chukovsky, Kornei, 60
Churchill, W.S., 77, 79, 80, 81, 83, 88
CIA, 72, 87
Ciliga, Ante, 40–2
citizens
  input into social and political process,
    150–1
  subjectivities, 150
Civil War, 3, 9, 10, 15, 16, 51, 53, 60, 79,
    103–6